Gender in an Era of Post-truth Populism

Bloomsbury Gender and Education

Series Editors:
Marie-Pierre Moreau (Anglia Ruskin University, UK)
Penny Jane Burke (University of Newcastle, Australia)
Nancy S. Niemi (University of Maryland, Eastern Shore, USA)

The **Bloomsbury Gender and Education** series publishes rigorous, critical and original research exploring the relationship between gender and education in a range of institutional, local, national and transnational contexts. Books in the series will cover a range of issues, themes and debates of key interest in contemporary societies and will be relevant to an international and diverse readership. The series will contribute work that speaks to key contemporary themes, debates and issues and to theoretical, methodological and empirical concerns in the field.

Themes explored across the series will include attention to gender in relation to schooling, tertiary education and lifelong learning, digital and social media, educational policies and practice, gendered and sexual violence, and gender identities and sexual orientation. As such, the series is an essential resource for academics and researchers working in fields including gender and education, sociology and gender studies, as well as those interested in gender issues and social justice more broadly.

Advisory Board:
Anita Kit Wa Chan (Education University of Hong Kong, Hong Kong), Marilia Carvalho (Universidade de Sao Paulo, Brazil), Claudia Cervantes-Soon (Arizona State University, USA), Julia Coffey (University of Newcastle, Australia), Debbie Epstein (University of Roehampton, UK), Helen Fisher (University of Roehampton, UK), Jessica Gagnon (University of Portsmouth, UK), Akane Kanai (Monash University, Australia), Elina Lahelma (University of Helsinki, Finland), Nicky Le Feuvre (University of Lausanne, Switzerland), Uvanney Maylor (University of Bedfordshire, UK), Julie McLeod (University of Melbourne, Australia), Heidi Mirza (Independent Researcher, UK), Lauren Misiaszek (Beijing Normal University, China), Barbara Read (Glasgow University, UK), Jessica Ringrose (UCL Institute of Education, University College London, UK), Vanita Sundaram (York University, UK), Carol Taylor (University of Bath, UK)

Forthcoming in the series:
Academic Women: Voicing Narratives of Gendered Experiences,
edited by Michelle Ronksley-Pavia, Michelle Neumann, Jane Manakil and
Kelly Pickard-Smith
Teaching to Support Science and Success: Stories of British South Asian Women,
by Saima Salehjee and Mike Watts

Gender in an Era of Post-truth Populism

Pedagogies, Challenges and Strategies

Edited by
Penny Jane Burke, Julia Coffey, Rosalind Gill
and Akane Kanai

BLOOMSBURY ACADEMIC
LONDON • NEW YORK • OXFORD • NEW DELHI • SYDNEY

BLOOMSBURY ACADEMIC
Bloomsbury Publishing Plc
50 Bedford Square, London, WC1B 3DP, UK
1385 Broadway, New York, NY 10018, USA
29 Earlsfort Terrace, Dublin 2, Ireland

BLOOMSBURY, BLOOMSBURY ACADEMIC and the Diana logo are trademarks
of Bloomsbury Publishing Plc

First published in Great Britain 2022
This paperback edition published 2023

Copyright © Penny Jane Burke, Julia Coffey, Rosalind Gill and
Akane Kanai and contributors, 2022

Penny Jane Burke, Julia Coffey, Rosalind Gill and Akane Kanai and contributors have
asserted their right under the Copyright, Designs and Patents Act, 1988,
to be identified as Author of this work.

For legal purposes the Acknowledgements on p. xviii constitute
an extension of this copyright page.

Cover design: Charlotte James
Cover image © Vince Cavataio/Getty Images

All rights reserved. No part of this publication may be reproduced or transmitted
in any form or by any means, electronic or mechanical, including photocopying,
recording, or any information storage or retrieval system, without
prior permission in writing from the publishers.

Bloomsbury Publishing Plc does not have any control over, or responsibility for, any
third-party websites referred to or in this book. All internet addresses given in this book
were correct at the time of going to press. The author and publisher regret
any inconvenience caused if addresses have changed or sites have ceased
to exist, but can accept no responsibility for any such changes.

A catalogue record for this book is available from the British Library.

A catalog record for this book is available from the Library of Congress.

ISBN: HB: 978-1-3501-9459-5
PB: 978-1-3501-9482-3
ePDF: 978-1-3501-9460-1
eBook: 978-1-3501-9461-8

Series: Bloomsbury Gender and Education

Typeset by Integra Software Services Pvt. Ltd.

To find out more about our authors and books visit www.bloomsbury.com
and sign up for our newsletters.

Contents

List of Figures	ix
List of Contributors	x
Series Editors' Foreword	xvi
Acknowledgements	xviii

Troubling Post-truth Populism: Feminist Interventions
Penny Jane Burke, Julia Coffey, Rosalind Gill and Akane Kanai   1

Part 1   Truth

1. Truth Parasites, Right-Wing Fury and the Predicaments of Feminist Expertise   *Jane Kenway*   21
2. The Weaponization of 'Gender' beyond Gender: The Entrenchment of 'Coloniality of Power' and 'Pedagogies of Cruelty'   *Isis Giraldo*   43
3. Truth, Power, Pedagogy: Feminist Knowledge and Education in a 'Post-truth' Time   *Raewyn Connell*   65
4. Something Resembling 'Truth': Reflections on Critical Pedagogy in the New 'Post-truth' Landscape   *Sondra Hale*   79

Part 2   Feminism and Education

5. Situating the Feminist Classroom: Between Free Speech and Media Myth   *Nicola Rivers*   99
6. Persistence, Patience and Persuasion: Critical Reflections on Creating Space for Indigenous Content in Australian University Curricula   *Susan Page*   113
7. Anti-feminist Misogynist Shitposting: The Challenges of Feminist Academics Navigating Toxic Twitter   *Xumeng Xie, Idil Cambazoglu, Bárbara Berger-Correa and Jessica Ringrose*   131
8. Embodied Wilfulness: #MeToo Girls' Activism, Affects and 'Complaint as Feminist Pedagogy'   *Ileana Jiménez*   157

Part 3 Gender Politics beyond the Classroom

9   Populist Politics in a Market-Leninist State: (Re)Thinking Gender in Vietnam *Thanh-Nhã Nguyễn and Matthew McDonald* 173
10 Embracing Feral Pedagogies: Queer Feminist Education through Queer Performance *Alyson Campbell, Meta Cohen, Stephen Farrier and Hannah McCann* 193
11 Fight the Patriarchy: Digital Feminist Public Pedagogy and Post-feminist Media Culture in Indonesia *Annisa R. Beta* 211

Conclusion: Beyond True and False: Reflecting and Rebuilding towards Feminist Pedagogies of Care *Akane Kanai, Julia Coffey, Penny Jane Burke and Rosalind Gill* 229

Index 237

Figures

7.1	Andrew Old responding to Prof. Ringrose's first Tweet	136
7.2	Screenshot of Prof. Ringrose's two Tweets	137
7.3	Peter Lloyd's first Tweet (parody account)	138
7.4	Peter Lloyd's second Tweet (responding to student's comment)	139
7.5	Snowman meme	144
7.6	Anti-feminist meme 'THE SHOOMER'	146

Contributors

Bárbara Berger-Correa is a PhD student at the UCL Institute of Education, University College London, UK. She works in the intra-action of psychoanalytical, post-human and new materialist concepts to study how flirting works among teens in Chile within discursive-material-affective assemblages. She is interested in youth sexuality and inclusive, sex-positive sexuality education.

Annisa Beta is Lecturer in Cultural Studies at the School of Culture and Communication, the University of Melbourne, Australia. Her research is broadly concerned with youth, new media and political subjectivity in Southeast Asia. She has published her work in *New Media & Society*, *Feminist Media Studies*, *International Communication Gazette*, *Asiascape: Digital Asia*, *Inter-Asia Cultural Studies* and *Media and Communication*. She has also had her writings published in *South China Morning Post*, *The Jakarta Post* and anotasi.com.

Penny Jane Burke is Global Innovation Chair of Equity and Director of the Centre of Excellence in Equity in Higher Education at the University of Newcastle, Australia. Passionately dedicated to developing methodological, theoretical and pedagogical frameworks that enable critical and feminist praxis, generating time-space for the reframing of equity in higher education, she has published widely across gender and social justice in higher education and lifelong learning. Penny is co-editor of the Bloomsbury Gender and Education book series, Global Chair of Social Innovation at University of Bath, Honorary Professor at University of Exeter and has held the posts of Professor at the University of Roehampton and the University of Sussex, and Reader at the Institute of Education, University of London.

Idil Cambazoglu is a PhD candidate at the UCL Institute of Education, University College London, UK. She works in the intersection of sociology of gender, education and youth, with a particular focus on masculinities. For her doctoral thesis, Idil examines elite-school boys' performances of masculinities in Turkey through interviews and visual digital methods and methodologies. Her research interests are masculinities, online and offline youth culture(s), elite-schooling and network(s).

Alyson Campbell is an award-winning theatre director whose work spans a broad range of companies and venues in Australia, the UK and the US. Most recently, Alyson directed *Cake Daddy*, a hybrid cabaret/theatre/cake event on queerness and fatness co-created with Lachlan Philpott and Ross Anderson-Doherty. She is an Associate Professor in Theatre at the Victorian College of the Arts, University of Melbourne. Alyson is the co-editor of the collections *Queer Dramaturgies: International Perspectives on Where Performance Leads Queer* (with Stephen Farrier, Palgrave, 2015) and *Viral Dramaturgies: HIV and AIDS in Performance in the Twenty-first Century* (with Dirk Gindt, Palgrave, 2018) and has published widely in performance journals and edited collections.

Julia Coffey is Senior Lecturer in Sociology at the University of Newcastle, Australia. Her feminist sociological research focuses on gender, affect and the body with particular interests in gendered body work practices. She has authored a number of books, most recently *Everyday Embodiment: Rethinking Youth Body Image* (Palgrave Macmillan, 2021). Her other books include *Body Work: Youth, Gender and Health* (Routledge 2016), the co-edited collection *Learning Bodies: The Body in Youth and Childhood Studies* (Springer, 2016) and *Youth Sociology* (co-author, Red Globe Press, 2020).

Meta Cohen is a queer composer, dramaturg, sound designer and emerging researcher. Her work spans music, theatre and interdisciplinary art. Meta's music has been commissioned by ensembles such as the Sydney Children's Choir and Mosaic Voices, and performed in diverse venues ranging from London Synagogues to the Sydney Opera House. In her theatre work, she specialises in sonic dramaturgies and musical thinking in theatre-making, and her research currently explores 'queer musicality' in theatre. Meta is an associate artist at Alyson Campbell and Lachlan Philpott's queer performance collective, wreckedAllprods. In 2019 she completed a Master of Dramaturgy at the Victorian College of the Arts, University of Melbourne.

Raewyn Connell is Professor Emerita, University of Sydney, Australia, and Life Member of the National Tertiary Education Union. She has taught in several countries and is a widely-cited sociological researcher, the author of *Gender & Power*, *Masculinities* and *Southern Theory*. Her recent books include *The Good*

University and *Gênero em termos reais*. Her work has been translated into twenty languages. Raewyn has been active in the labour movement, and in work for gender equality and peace. Details at www.raewynconnell.net and Twitter @raewynconnell.

Stephen Farrier is Reader in Theatre and Performance at the Royal Central School of Speech and Drama, University of London, UK, where his work focuses on queer theory, performance, gender and the relations of theatre and performance to community. He co-edited *Queer Dramaturgies: International Perspectives on Where Performance Leads Queer* (with Alyson Campbell, Palgrave, 2015), *Contemporary Drag Practices and Performers: Drag in A Changing Scene Volume One* and *Drag Histories, Herstories and Hairstories: Drag in a Changing Scene Volume Two* (both with Mark Edward, Bloomsbury, 2020/2021). He sits on the editorial board of *Studies in Theatre and Performance* and on the advisory board of *Contemporary Theatre Review*.

Rosalind Gill is Professor of Social and Cultural Analysis at City, University of London, UK. She is interested in questions of power, culture and subjectivity and is author of several books including *Gender and the Media* (Polity, 2007), *Mediated Intimacy: Sex Advice in Media Culture* (with Meg-John Barker and Laura Harvey, Polity, 2018) and *Confidence Culture* (with Shani Orgad, Duke University Press, 2022).

Isis Giraldo is a researcher and an educator. Her work belongs within the fields of cultural and media studies from critical approaches that recentre power and social justice. Empirically, her work mostly focuses on Colombia and aims at showing how cultural hegemony has helped maintain stark imbalances of power along the axes of gender, race and social class, and justify regimes of rule by a privileged few. Theoretically, it aims at connecting Northern feminist theories and postcolonial studies with critical thought on gender, race and coloniality as developed from within Latin America. Giraldo's work has been published in journals such as Feminist Media Studies, Feminist Theory and Postcolonial Studies, Cultural Studies, among others.

Sondra Hale is Research Professor and Professor Emerita, Anthropology and Gender Studies Departments, University of California, Los Angeles (UCLA), USA. In addition to chairing Gender Studies, she co-directed UCLA's Center for Near Eastern Studies and co-edited The Journal of Middle East Women's

Studies (JMEWS). Among her research interests are social movements, women's organizing, knowledge production, critical pedagogy, feminist and Sudanese art and conflict areas. She has published dozens of articles and co-edited three books – one on feminist art, another on Sudan's Killing Fields and two with with Gada Kadoda. In 2017 they published *Networks of Knowledge Production in Sudan: Identities, Mobilities, and Technologies*. Hale's monograph is *Gender Politics in Sudan: Socialism, Islamism and the State*. She has received numerous awards for teaching, activism, service and life-time achievement awards: such as Sudanese Studies Association and Association for Middle East Women's Studies, plus special awards from Sudan: Sudanese Knowledge Society, Salmmah Women's Research Center and an honorary PhD from Ahfad University for Women.

Ileana Jiménez is the creator of Feminist Teacher (feministteacher.com), @feministteacher and the hashtags #HSfeminism and #K12feminism. A teacher-activist for twenty-five years, she teaches Black and Latina feminisms, pedagogies,and curricula to high school and graduate students. Her doctoral research in English Education at Teachers College, Columbia University focuses on critical feminist pedagogies in schools and feminist digital and school-based activisms. In 2011, Jiménez received a Distinguished Fulbright Award to work with queer youth in Mexico City. Globally, she has presented in Argentina, Australia, Greece, India, Mexico and the UK. Jiménez has published in Youth Sexualities: Public Feelings and Contemporary Cultural Politics, Meridians: feminism, race, transnationalism, Radical Teacher; and One Teacher in Ten in the New Millennium: LGBT Educators Speak Out. She received her BA in English Literature at Smith College and an MA in English Literature at Middlebury College.

Akane Kanai is Lecturer in the School of Media, Film and Journalism, Monash University, Australia. Her research areas include gender, race and the politics of affect and identity online and in popular culture. In 2021, she was awarded an Australian Research Council Discovery Early Career Researcher Fellowship to explore the everyday uses of online feminism by young women.

Jane Kenway is an elected Fellow of the Academy of Social Sciences in Australia, Emeritus Professor (Monash University, Australia) and Professorial Fellow (University of Melbourne, Australia). Prior to this she was a Professorial Fellow with the Australian Research Council and Professor of Global Education Studies in the Education Faculty at Monash University. Her research expertise is in educational sociology. Broadly, she studies education and education policy in the context of wider social and cultural change, focusing particularly on power, politics and inequality.

Hannah McCann is Senior Lecturer in Cultural Studies at the University of Melbourne, Australia. Her research in critical femininity studies explores feminist discourse on femininity, queer femme LGBTIQ communities, beauty culture and queer fangirls. She has published in various journals including *European Journal of Women's Studies*, *Women's Studies Quarterly* and *Australian Feminist Studies*. Her monograph, *Queering Femininity: Sexuality, Feminism and the Politics of Presentation,* was published by Routledge in 2018 and her co-authored textbook *Queer Theory Now: From Foundations to Futures* was published by Red Globe Press in 2019.

Matthew McDonald is Professor of Critical Social Psychology on the Psychology Program, Fulbright University, Ho Chi Minh City, Vietnam. His research interests include the application of Continental philosophy (existentialism, critical theory) to social psychology and gender relations in Vietnam. Matthew has published numerous books including *Critical Social Psychology: An Introduction* (Second Edition) (with Brendan Gough and Marjella McFadden, Red Globe Press, 2013) and *Social Psychology and Theories of Consumer Culture: A Political Economy Perspective* (with Stephen Wearing, Taylor & Francis, 2013). He has published in range of journals including *Gender, Technology and Development*, *Journal for the Theory of Social Behaviour*, *Journal of Humanistic Psychology* and *Social and Personality Psychology Compass*.

Thanh-Nhã Nguyễn is a graduate student in the Department of Gender Studies at the Central European Unviersity, Vienna, Austria. Her previous research has focused on several topics including media consumption, gender, sexuality and identity in Vietnam. Her current dissertation project explores the sexual subjectivities of young women in urban Vietnam through narratives of intimacy, family and morality in the nexus of postsocialism, postcoloniality and neoliberalism.

Susan Page is an Aboriginal academic and is currently Associate Dean (Indigenous) and Director of the Centre for the Advancement of Indigenous Knowledges in the Faculty of Arts and Social Sciences at the University of Technology Sydney, Australia. Previously, Susan led a university-wide Indigenous graduate attribute project and was Head of the Department of Indigenous Studies at Macquarie University (2008–2012). Her research focuses on Aboriginal and Torres Strait Islander peoples' experience of learning and academic work in higher education and student learning in Indigenous studies. Susan has been awarded a number of competitive grants, has received a national award for Excellence in Teaching and is well published in the area of Indigenous higher education. From 2015–2018, Susan was an elected Director of the National Aboriginal and Torres Strait Islander Higher Education Consortium and she is currently an appointed Indigenous representative for the Universities Australia Deputy Vice-Chancellors (Academic) committee.

Jessica Ringrose is Professor of Sociology of Gender and Education at the UCL Institute of Education, University College London, UK. She is an internationally recognised expert on gender equity in education, digital sexual cultures and feminist participatory research methodologies, and has collaborated on funded research on these topics with colleagues in UK, Canada, USA, Australia, New Zealand and Europe. She is the 2020 Recipient of the Distinguished Contributions to Gender Equity in Education Research Award, from the American Educational Research Association, which recognises her commitment to societal impact and making research matter beyond academic audiences.

Nicola Rivers is Lecturer in Social Sciences, Arts and Humanities at SOAS, University of London, UK. She is also the author of *Postfeminisms and the Arrival of the Fourth Wave* (Springer International Publishing AG, 2017). Her research interests span across contemporary feminism, post-feminism and popular culture, as well as feminist pedagogy and attitudes towards students and higher education.

Xumeng Xie is a PhD candidate at the UCL Institute of Education, University College London, UK. Her doctoral research project draws on digital ethnographic methods and feminist social theory to explore how Chinese young women understand, experience and learn about feminism and gender across offline and online spaces. Xumeng is particularly interested in the affective-discursive aspects of youth digital feminist practices and how social media has enabled new forms of connections, networks and activism.

Series Editors' Foreword

Marie-Pierre Moreau, Penny Jane Burke and Nancy Niemi

Contemporary debates concerned with the global urgencies of addressing inequalities point to the topicality and social significance of the field of gender and education. The intersection of gender and education is a buoyant site of scholarly and political mobilisation occupied by a multitude of ontological and epistemological positions, theories and methodologies. Key themes shaping the field range from schooling, tertiary education and lifelong learning, digital and social media, educational policies and practice, gendered and sexual violence, gender identities and sexual orientation, the politics of representation and 'truth', the relationship of gender equity to environmental justice, embodiment and difference, and knowledge production. However, this is not an exhaustive list, and gender and education as a field relates to multiple historical, contemporary and intersectional issues of our times.

This research series is concerned with publishing rigorous and original research which critically engages with contemporary debates about gender and education as they unfold in a range of institutional, local, national and transnational contexts, in, across and between the spaces that are often hidden from view through complex geopolitical and inequitable global relations. Indeed, these debates include critical attention to the problematic of spatial and geopolitical relations, which are attached to categorisations in their many troubling forms. Intersectional and international perspectives are a central tenet of the series to broaden, provide depth and extend the field of gender and education in all of its complexities. Engaging with insights from across gender and education studies – including theories of intersectionality that provide a critical lens on gender and its relationship to other identity markers, positionalities and systemic inequalities – the series engages societal debates and theoretical developments within the field. It invites a growing understanding of the intersections between and across different structural and political forces that shed light on gender inequalities.

Linked to its feminist ethos, the series is a home for monographs and edited volumes authored by emerging and established scholars concerned with gender inequalities and social justice as they pertain to intersectional aspects of gender and education in a broad range of social and institutional contexts. This intersectional and international outlook is also a strong feature of the editorial team. The editors are based in the UK, the US and Australia, with a strong commitment to generating knowledge from positions of inter/national, institutional and/or positional marginalisation and/or difference, and the series benefits from the insights of our outstanding editorial board including researchers from across the world.

The series is intended for a readership composed of academics and postgraduate research students, as well as feminist practitioners and activists from across the world with an interest in gender and education and, more broadly, social justice. In particular, we hope that it will appeal to academics whose work is broadly located in the field of gender and education and with a subject background in education, sociology, gender studies or in other social science or humanity subjects; to students enrolled on these programmes; and to practitioners based in schools, higher education and non-governmental organisations.

Considering the influential role of feminist networks in the development of the field of gender and education, it is perhaps fitting that the opening volume is edited by the team who hosted the *2018 Gender and Education Association Conference* at the University of Newcastle, New South Wales, Australia. This volume brings together scholars from across the world who, through a feminist lens, engage with maybe one of the timeliest and most controversial issues: gender in times of post-truth populism. The book takes us on a journey which spans several continents. It engages with issues which are challenging and even staggering for those concerned with gender equity. Perhaps most crucially, by engaging with feminist pedagogies, practices and activisms in a socio-political context characterised by deliberate attempts to weaken gender and other interconnected equity issues, it sets the ground for a feminist response to the misogynistic political frameworks which have appropriated truth over the recent years.

Acknowledgements

This book collection has its roots in a number of collaborative projects that we would like to acknowledge. It originated with a special issue of *Teaching in Higher Education*, co-edited by Penny Jane Burke and Ronelle Carolissen. The special issue benefited from feedback and discussion amongst the *Teaching in Higher Education* executive editorial team, including Sian Bayne, Lesley Gourlay, Neil Harrison, Peter Khan and the late Suellen Shay. We want to acknowledge the highly professional contribution of the journal manager, Alison Stanton. The special issue then provided the impetus for the 2018 Gender and Education Association (GEA) conference, supported by an advisory group chaired by Penny Jane Burke with Julia Coffey, Akane Kanai, Ros Smith, Ros Gill, Belinda Munn and the team at GEA, Jessica Ringrose, Jessica Gagnon and Vanita Sundaram. We would like to acknowledge the many stimulating and thought-provoking papers for both the special issue and the conference that provided the foundation for this book collection.

Most importantly is the high-quality, professional support and insight provided for the special issue, conference and finally this book. This includes acknowledgement of the entire team at the Centre of Excellence for Equity in Higher Education, with special thanks to Julia Shaw, Emily Fuller, Felicity Cocuzzoli and Belinda Munn amongst many others who supported the conference. Special thanks also to Alison Carter, Julia Shaw and Micky Pinkerton for their support in preparing the manuscript for this collection. Thank you to the reviewers of this proposal who provided such important feedback, and to the Bloomsbury team, including Alison Baker and Evangeline Stanford. And, finally to Marie-Pierre Moreau and Nancy Niemi, co-editors of the Bloomsbury Gender and Education series, for all their support.

Troubling Post-truth Populism: Feminist Interventions

Penny Jane Burke, Julia Coffey, Rosalind Gill and Akane Kanai

A troubling rise of post-truth populism in recent years has raised pressing concerns related to the undermining of gender equity and a range of interconnected social justice issues. Populism is a historically varied and much-contested phenomenon, characterized recently as 'parasitical, unstable, excessive, corrupt, inexact, threatening' (Fidotta, Neves and Serpe 2020). Ernesto Laclau famously observed that 'few terms have been so widely used in contemporary political analysis', and 'few have been used defined with less precision' (1977: 143). We use it here to signify 'a political strategy used to form a hegemonic alliance unified by the cultural symbolism of 'the people" (Zeglen and Ewen 2020: 271) that is mobilized to serve authoritarian and exclusionary purposes. In Europe over the past decade, such populism has been connected to discourses of crisis over multiculturalism (Lentin and Titley 2011), a crisis of masculinity (Mishra 2018) and the institutional strengthening of neoliberal austerity policies, creating affective-discursive resources for right-wing politicians to mobilize (Zeglen and Ewen 2020). More recently, in the United States, the nation's leader from 2016 to 2021 was a high-profile exemplar of the radical dismissal of the rights and dignity of women and people of colour. We observe that for some time now, this populist politics of denial and *ressentiment* has been located at the heart of contemporary Western politics. However, we recognize that populism is not singular or monolithic in its contemporary global articulations and aim to interrogate Northern-centric analyses by engaging critiques emerging from the Global South. We do so by analysing the inter-relationship of post-truth populism, gender and education across complex geopolitical relations. We understand post-truth populism as unevenly impacting people and regions, requiring attention to the ways that gendered, racialized and classed inequalities are deepening across and within specific sociocultural and geopolitical relations, identities and contexts. We want to understand the theoretical perspectives that emerge from transnational political subjectivities, experiences and analyses to consider the possibilities for feminist pedagogical interventions as a form of resistance against harmful populisms.

As the onslaught of racist and misogynist populism continues to be foregrounded on a daily basis on the world stage, social commitments to sharing knowledges from different perspectives have come under attack as collectively settled agreements on truth, however tenuous and contingent, are seen as restraints on the power and authority of political leaders. We have seen stark refusals of accountability for the authoritarian decisions made by political leaders across borders: Bolsonaro in Brazil; Erdogan in Turkey; Orbàn in Hungary; Modi in India; among the high-profile engineers of Brexit in the UK and nativist politics in the United States. The term 'post-truth' became the Oxford Dictionary's word of the year in 2016, sealing its discursive place in the contemporary imagination, and in the same year the Trump administration coined the notion of 'alternative facts' as a response to mainstream news media reporting the relatively small number of people who attended the President's inauguration ceremony. Put together, these contemporary moments have amounted to explicit challenges to the fundamental principles of democratic systems, leading some commentators to argue that disorder has itself become a novel form of populist governance in which right-wing 'delinquents' lie with impunity and even readily admit to breaking international law (Harris 2020; Malik 2020; Rawnsley 2020). Populist politics has wreaked havoc on the hard-won gains of decades of feminist struggle for the rights of women, LGBTQI+ communities, people of colour, those with disabilities, immigrants and refugees.

This book has emerged from such concerns and sits alongside a wider commitment among feminists internationally to collectively engage the specific challenges posed by such politics. Described by some as a 'thin-centred ideology', post-truth populism purposefully manufactures divisions that rest on notions of a struggle of 'the people' against a supposed corrupt elite, including feminists and other social justice activists, intellectuals, and mainstream political parties and the media (Harsin 2018: 36; Rinaldi and Bekker 2020: 141). Lacking a clear policy agenda, post-truth populism largely functions through 'narrative antagonism' and relies on appeals to conservative ideologies of individualism and personal belief, manipulating feelings of 'political vertigo' and causing 'retreats into tribal epistemologies' (Harsin 2018: 36). Through such post-truth populist manoeuvres, entrenched resentments against an imagined Other are mobilized with powerful and dangerous effects.

This collection provides a feminist response to the many challenges posed by post-truth populism, in exploring the potentials and possibilities for feminist pedagogies, practices and activisms in educational and social contexts. Offering the first detailed feminist intervention in this space, the collection explores the significance of this moment for feminist pedagogies and practices in relation to gender and education. This collection addresses broader and urgent questions of our times regarding knowledge, authority, truth, power and harm: what does it mean to be pedagogical in a post-truth landscape? How might feminist thought and action work to intervene in this environment? And how might we negotiate the challenges posed to a feminist ethics of pedagogical care? Coming from several years of engagement with feminist scholars and activists across the globe to consider the implications of post-truth populism for feminist pedagogical praxis, it started from the development of a special issue for *Teaching in Higher Education* (Burke and Carolissen 2018). This special issue then prompted the organization of the 2018 International Gender and Education Association conference hosted by the Centre of Excellence for Equity in Higher Education at the University of Newcastle, Australia. The book draws from the outstanding contributions made to both the 2017 special issue and the 2018 conference and broadens this to include further voices from feminist scholar activists in different contexts across the world. In our work together, as editors and authors of this collection, our aim is to bring to light the misrepresentative, oppressive and harmful politics of post-truth populism, the significance of diverse feminist perspectives across a range of contexts and to open up debate. As part of this, we hope to offer rich material to strongly reassert the importance and power of collective feminist scholarly activism and feminist pedagogical interventions. This collection brings together diverse voices to examine and counter post-truth populist attacks on critical race and queer theories, feminisms, Indigenous and First Nations knowledges and truths, and those associated with intellectual labour and expertise.

The 2017 *Teaching in Higher Education* special issue was initially provoked by the Brexit referendum and the Trump election, both of which were connected to a form of 'post-truth populism' related to stark and confronting expressions of anti-feminism, racism, anti-immigration, misogyny, homophobia, anti-environmentalism and a relentless string of blatant lies. This included the increasing use of social media as a vehicle to mobilize these stark expressions and to communicate misinformation. During this period there was growing attention into the undermining of democratic processes, including the high-profile Mueller investigation of potential Russian interference in the 2016 US election and the uncovering of the Facebook-Cambridge Analytica data scandal, which was suggested to have influenced the Brexit referendum and US election (e.g. Cadwalladr 2017a, 2017b; Osborne 2018; Rosenberg et al. 2018).

However, post-truth populism is certainly not limited to the United States and the UK. There are examples across the globe, and this collection includes contributions that examine post-truth populism in Asia, Latin America, Europe, Britain, the United States and Australia, highlighting a range of concerns, perspectives and contestations. Although it is important to recognize differences across countries and geographical regions (Rinaldi and Bekker 2020), there are key characteristics that are important to note for this collection in contestations over truth and the implications of this for ongoing and deepening social injustices. These include an attack on experts and expert knowledge, the rapid rise of misinformation and disinformation (Baker 2020), often spread virally via social media platforms. These also include attacks on institutions including the civil service, the media and universities, through the erasure of accountability. Post-truth populism is characterized by opposition to experts and expertise, which is often misrepresented as a form of elitism. This has very significant consequences, for example with a forceful anti-vaccination discourse circulating across and beyond social media sites in the context of the COVID-19 global pandemic, despite medical experts urging the importance of vaccination. Indeed, Twitter has become a primary mechanism to circulate unverified content. This has happened alongside high-profile instances in which powerful male world leaders have explicitly threatened journalists, undermining their capacity to raise important questions, with many journalists across the world arrested and jailed for doing their work.

The ongoing attack of post-truth populism on those associated with intellectual labour has discursively constructed 'intellectualism' as a form of elitism rather than as a tool for analysing and dismantling social inequalities, divisions and conflicts. As such, this anti-intellectual discourse has raised direct challenges to feminist, Indigenous, Black, critical race and other critical epistemologies and ontologies, as well as to the overall capacity to mobilize resistance to the anti-intellectualist discourses being expressed at the highest levels of government as well as in social media. Relatedly, feminist efforts to examine and reveal the processes by which knowledge is produced, embodied, institutionalized and legitimated have become increasingly threatened. Indeed, post-truth populism has arguably intensified a broader tendency to undermine feminist considerations of the relationship between knowledge and power, to intersectional differences and inequalities, to affective politics, to the relationship between lived, embodied experience and to analysis of institutionalized, structural and systemic forms of oppression. Some of the gains struggled for over many decades, such as women's reproductive rights and the urgent need to tackle gendered and racialized violence, harassment and abuse, whether physical, verbal, sexual or symbolic have been eroded. Indeed, it often appears that such feminist commitments to social justice are being deliberately unravelled via the strategically mobilized resurgent discourse that the 'the real losers' of globalized neoliberalism are white and male. In the United States and the UK this is seen also in the contemporary attacks on 'critical race theory' (Trilling 2020). Such discourse is not genuinely interested in understanding the experiences of marginalization of (white) working-class communities, but rather centres on silencing or outlawing notions of 'white privilege' – as seen in the declaration by UK Conservative Equalities Minister, during a Parliamentary debate to mark Black History Month, that teaching such critical concepts 'is breaking the law'. Yet the articulation of this concern distinctively erases and devalues the classed experiences of non-white and non-Western populations transnationally and within Western nations, reinforcing 'the boundaries around whiteness, while rejecting attempts at more encompassing and representative visions of who works and who is exploited' (Lentin 2017). It appears too clear that existing forms of gendered, classed and racialized senses of entitlement have been deliberately mobilized to increase the power of the so-called alt-right in connection with post-truth populism and perhaps this was most visibly demonstrated on Western media with the storming of the US Capitol on 6 January 2021, which led to five deaths.

However, while there appears to be a tidal wave of post-truth populist attacks to the long-term struggles against discrimination, oppression and marginalization, the use of social media as an immediate tool to communicate across the world has also offered the fuel for re-emerging social and feminist movements. The emergence of digital feminist activism, including the #MeToo movement, has signalled a strong, collective effort to challenge sexism and gendered violence (e.g. Banet-Weiser 2018; Fileborn and Loney-Howes 2019; Mendes, Ringrose and Keller 2019; Mendes and Ringrose 2019). Indeed, as we have engaged in the process of preparing this collection, there have been important demonstrations of activism in response to systemic discrimination, violence and oppression, including widespread reference to the #BlackLivesMatter movement[1] during a series of large-scale and world wide protests provoked by the murder of George

Floyd by a Minneapolis police officer in 2020. The #MeToo movement has been reinvigorated most recently in Australia with thousands of people across the country marching against gendered violence and inequality after the exposure of sexual assault linked directly to Parliament, as well as ongoing outrage at the shocking numbers of women being killed through the 'shadow pandemic' (Mlambo-Ngcuka 2020) of domestic violence, which has only worsened through the impacts of COVID-19. However, digital feminist activism has renewed collective action and signals high levels of resistance to ongoing misogynistic and racist violence. Notions of identity and belonging have become weaponized to drive increasing polarization across ideological and political party lines. Increasing polarization and division seems to benefit populist political aims, with a particular form of entrenched relativism that simultaneously works to further marginalize feminist epistemologies. The feminist problematization of positivist claims to truth, and the feminist understanding of knowledge as situated, partial and contextualized, arguably intensifies the struggle to contest 'post-truth' discourses that enable an 'anything goes' (or, perhaps better, 'anything with power goes') ontological position to 'truth'.

Truth

The challenge to feminist epistemologies has become increasingly apparent as wide-scale untruths, normally expected to be challenged through systems established in the name of democracy, are being left in place to circulate and create forms of division, hostility and violence that have profound gendered implications and effects. This collection is concerned with exploring what this means for feminist pedagogies. What does this mean for how feminists engage students with questions of truth, knowledge and power? If feminism has argued for knowledge that recognizes subjectivity, emotion and positionality, how might feminists grapple with a form of populism that on the surface makes a call to the affective and personal dimensions of knowledge, but refuses its relational and deliberative elements? Identity politics is and has been a complex terrain for feminists to negotiate and articulate, as differences across and between feminisms have also generated exclusion, marginalization and othering. We suggest commitment to recognizing difference and an ethics of care is needed to confront the fuelling of violence and polarization normalized by populist politics. A key question for this book then is how might feminist pedagogical strategies encourage consideration of the complex relationship across materiality, emotionality, objectivity, subjectivity and contextualization in the age of post-truth populism? How do we locate the emergence of post-truth populism in the twenty-first century with historical contestations over knowledge and truth, over which feminists have been actively engaged for decades? This volume provides a feminist response to the challenges provided by post-truth populism, in exploring the potentials and possibilities for feminist pedagogies, practices and activisms in educational and social contexts.

The volume opens with a searing polemic by Jane Kenway, which asks why 'post-truth' has travelled so rapidly and extensively, and demonstrates how intimately entangled it is with attacks on women and feminism and also on universities. She argues that contemporary post-truth populisms have emerged from 'right-wing fury' centred around multiple themes and mobilizations. This fury is centred on identity and identification – particularly gender, race and religion; it is organized through notions of threat and loss; it is reactionary – in seeking to restore a previous social order; and it is both defensive and offensive, characterized by symbolic and physical violence. Kenway contends that we are living in a time of 'truth parasites' who 'deliberately, and cynically, manipulate the truth'. She explains, 'Truth parasites have a corrosive relationship to truth. They eat away at it, drain it of meaning and of moral integrity. They deplete the broad notion of truth and gain strength from doing so.' Exploring examples from Milo Yiannopoulos to Bettina Arndt, Kenway dissects the different strategies used in post-truth attacks on feminism, their cruel and misogynistic tenor and the diverse ways in which they seek to destroy feminist gains – through ultra nationalist and white supremacist ideas to spurious constructions of 'crisis' (e.g. 'free speech crisis') to de-funding the arts, humanities and social sciences.

Concluding this dazzling intervention, Kenway asks 'what about us?' – what role have feminists played in this state of affairs and how can we 'create healthier living conditions that might deprive the truth parasites of nutrition'? Our best hopes, she suggests, lie in adopting the radical ideas of the 'feminism of the 99%' (Arruzza, Bhattacharya and Fraser 2019), opening up and shifting understandings of feminism so that they are built on more inclusive notions of expertise and truth, and address 'activism, the steep decline of the social wage, racism and imperialism, gendered violence, the regulation of sexuality, environmental destruction and democracy and peace'.

Isis Giraldo's chapter, 'The Weaponisation of "Gender" Beyond Gender: The Entrenchment of "Coloniality of Power" and "Pedagogies of Cruelty"', follows this intervention. Giraldo takes a decolonial lens to explore the socio-historical location where gender has become a core theme of 'ideological struggle'. Giraldo situates these struggles in Latin American and Colombian contexts as indicative of the ways current ideological conflicts emerge from broader dynamics and harms of coloniality and capitalism. Giraldo argues that the current debates playing out about 'gender ideology' are an extension of a broader process of weaponization of social justice concerns that has been occurring over several decades. Giraldo situates these ideological debates as having a much longer history than recent 'populist' articulations. Drawing on Rita Segato's work, Giraldo argues this ideological work is concerned with entrenching coloniality through 'pedagogies of cruelty'. Giraldo provides a piercing critique of the current ideological landscape in which the inequalities stemming from postcolonial injustices are justified as inevitable, shoring up the colonial–capitalist system of exploitation to continue. It is this system and the 'pedagogies of cruelty' by which it operates which have incorporated gender as part of a larger attempt to dismantle social justice efforts. Giraldo's analysis decisively recentres 'the coloniality of power' and contextualizes the broader projects of social justice, including feminist projects relating to gender and sexuality justice efforts, which are under attack. Her chapter provides a rich and powerful analysis of the wider colonial and capitalist forces at play and the challenges these pose to feminist ethics of pedagogical care.

This theme is also taken up in Raewyn Connell's chapter, which argues that struggles for gender justice and struggles for truth are fundamentally connected. Connell's chapter historicizes the issues differently, asking what is new about post-truth populism. Tracing a genealogy that includes colonial conquest, Stalinism, Nazism and McCarthyism, Connell suggests that against 'this vast landscape of self-interested untruth' what is perhaps most distinctive about the current iteration is that twenty-first-century authoritarians are less clear than previous generations that they are lying. 'What has changed', she contends, 'is not the scale of the lying but its discursive presupposition. Perhaps we are seeing a weakening of the tension between truth and falsehood that underpins the concept of a "lie"'.

Connell's chapter also brings to the fore the role of economic institutions, fossil fuel industries and scientific expertise in undergirding the post-truth context – highlighting that it is not only about politicians but also about social media platforms. Climate change denial, for example, is a potent case of 'post-truth' funded by the super-rich Koch brothers and other powerful interests who have sought – with some success – to refute, undermine or buy off scientific endeavour about the devastating impacts on the planet of human activity. The fact that the economy has become incomprehensible even to those who work in it has further aided the extent to which the forces that shape our world are increasingly outside the control of elected governments. Nevertheless, Connell also reminds us of feminists' *successes* – in educational participation for girls and in literacy rates, as well as in transforming the academy. She urges us to more collective work and imagines a future in which socially relevant, open and democratic research becomes the norm. It is in 'feminist-knowledge-*making*' as a social process that we have the best opportunity to contest the 'Big Lies' of our time.

Sondra Hale's chapter offers nuanced reflections on what critical pedagogy might look like in a 'post-truth' landscape in which – to quote Hannah Arendt - the 'distinction between fact and fiction, true and false, no longer exists'. Hale starts from a personal experience, sixty years ago while teaching in Sudan, in which she was shaken and unmoored when a student insisted that the world was flat. What tools do critical feminist educators have, she asks, to engage with such assertions but in a way that is ethical and respectful and not part of a practice of power in which universalist truths produced by colonial powers in the Global North are simply imposed on others? This question haunted her and preoccupied her long before the current waves of post-truth populisms.

To address possible responses Hale takes us on a journey that is both personal and, at the same time, a story of feminist, LGBTQ, Freirean, critical race and decolonial pedagogy over several decades. Hale's chapter highlights beautifully some of the tensions within and between these projects: from deconstructing absolutes such as reason, logic, positivism and universality versus wanting to speak truth to power; from celebrations of consciousness raising to rejections of the idea that an 'unknowing, perhaps ignorant subject' needs to be 'brought into the light'; from a desire to 'validate' the experiences of all learners to dealing with hostility and pain and incommensurable ideas. Drawing on the work of numerous scholars from Paulo Freire to Gloria Anzaldúa to Patricia Hill Collins, Hale sets out her own thoughts as a 'recovering anthropologist' animated by political solidarity and liberatory agendas, and a restless drive to self-interrogation. Care is needed, she concludes, that in responding to the 'post-truth' era that 'we' do not unwittingly impede decolonizing and democratizing processes in the process; critical pedagogical strategies are more important than ever.

Feminism and Education

The discourses associated with post-truth populism have profound implications for feminist pedagogies across educational contexts, including universities. Across varying global contexts, feminist successes have been demonstrated through gains in education, such as the high level of female participation in higher education in many countries worldwide. Policies of access and equity have contributed to growing diversity in higher education, and female students have increasingly outnumbered male students in many contexts. Conservative political voices seeking to dismantle anti-sexist policies and practices have been gaining ground in educational institutions in many national contexts. The increased level of backlash discourses and the apparent legitimation of this in some high-profile instances at the level of institutional politics point to the ongoing need for feminist critique.

Related to contestations over knowledge and truth, as discussed above, the editors and authors of this collection are concerned with the re/positioning and re/articulation of feminist interventions in and through education, including via particular feminist pedagogical principles and aims. This is within a shared understanding that there is no one feminist pedagogy, whilst also recognizing that there are similarities across feminist pedagogical commitments, as Sondra Hale's chapter elegantly explores. This includes a commitment to interrogating truth claims that have the potential to do harm to those misrecognized and/or misrepresented by those truth claims. Although a contested field of praxis across different contexts and concerns, feminist pedagogues have grappled with complex questions of power, identity, embodiment, difference and the emotional, temporal and spatial inequalities that are entangled in key sites of knowledge-formation, including universities. A key question for this section of the volume is: what feminist pedagogical tools are available across difference and how might these be re/imagined, re/shaped and re/framed in the context of contemporary struggles over knowledge, knowing and truth?

Nicola Rivers contributes a powerful articulation of how the politics of knowledge plays out in relation to attacks on gender studies via the misrepresentation of feminist and critical race theories, pedagogies and practices. She skilfully examines this in relation to debates about free speech in the UK, which construct feminist concerns to challenge racist and misogynist perspectives as censorious. The discursive construction of students as 'oppositional' is another form of misrepresentation that undermines the key issues that are of concern to (often feminist) students. Illuminating how gender studies has been attacked via populist discourses, Rivers identifies the important forms of misrepresentation at play; that courses such as gender studies are constructed as dangerous sites of subversion, outdated, connected to grievance or victimhood and are generally lacking in rigour. This maps onto the wider turn against expert knowledge, shifts towards marketized higher education, the valuing of the sciences and the international trend towards closing down humanities and social sciences courses and departments. Connected to these attacks on feminism and gender studies, is the general misrepresentation of university commitments to diversity and inclusion, fuelling narratives about the radicalization of university campuses. The circulation of these debates within mainstream political and popular discourse then produces an overall misrepresentation of higher education, creating a populist myth of the contemporary university as out of touch with ordinary people or a hotbed of left-wing activism.

The silencing of the historical and ongoing oppression of Indigenous Australians is foregrounded powerfully in the opening of Susan Page's chapter, to bring to view the context in which she explores questions of higher education curriculum and cultural capability in relation to (the silencing of) Indigenous Knowledge. She connects this to concerns about the potential reproduction of inequities that occurs when graduates enter positions of influence in the workforce without engaging with Indigenous histories, knowledge and perspectives. This ignorance is deeply threatening to the pursuit of equity and social justice in and through higher education. Indeed, in the wider context of post-truth populism, she points out that the challenges of articulating Indigenous truth is further exacerbated. The entrenched inequities that circulate around contestations of truth are wedged in a history of curricula absences in which many Australians are unaware of both the violent oppressions waged against Indigenous people and the rich cultural knowledge that is held by Aboriginal and Torres Strait Islander people that have profoundly shaped Australia. Page provides highly relatable personal reflections as an Aboriginal academic on these significant challenges, focusing on three key themes underpinning her experiences of contributing to collective anti-racist actions: persistence, persuasion and patience. Persuasion requires the development of approaches that address wider staff and student resistances to embedding Indigenous Knowledge in curriculum and in preparing students to become responsible and culturally capable graduates. Forms of resistance include anger, hostility and disengagement or a belief that Indigenous knowledge in a particular disciplinary context is irrelevant or unnecessary. She suggests it might also occur in relation to not knowing how to embed Indigenous Knowledge in the curriculum. Patience recognizes the temporalities of creating change and that this takes time. Page points out that patience is not a highly valued disposition in the academy, which is important to consider in the wider accelerated pace of the expectations of academic performance in universities. Persistence is central to acting in the face of long-standing adversity and has been key to opening up spaces for Indigenous people to fully participate in higher education. In her compelling chapter, Page strongly demonstrates how persuasion, patience and persistence are critical for reframing approaches to knowledge and truth in higher education.

Xumeng Xie, Idil Cambazoglu, Bárbara Berger-Correa and Jessica Ringrose, in their chapter 'Anti-feminist Misogynist Shitposting: The Challenges of Feminist Academics Navigating Toxic Twitter', describe their experience being trolled by men's rights activists on Twitter. Whilst teaching a Masters online module about 'sex positive sex education', which involved an activity using Play-Doh to mould vulvas with a focus on the clitoris, a tweet depicting this activity was seized upon and shared by a men's rights activist with his populist, nationalist, misogynist followers who trolled the researchers. The chapter provides a comprehensive analysis of the discourses which were mobilized in this trolling: first, academia and education in a legitimacy crisis in need of correction; second, Professor Ringrose's account and feminist academia as a parody; third, about masculinist projections of penile superiority debasing women's sexual pleasure and empowerment; and fourth, moral panics about childhood innocence and protectionist discourses, framing education on sexuality as harmful. Their chapter shows how the affordances of Twitter as a platform were enabled gender-trolling, which specifically aims to disrupt certain subordinated or marginalized groups (e.g. non-whites, immigrants, feminists women) through 'shitposting' (luring opponents into pointless and time-consuming discussion). They ask institutions and digital platforms to be accountable for the impacts associated with unwanted visibility associated with trolling and shitposting, where feminist academics become subjected to ongoing episodes of abuse and reputational defamation. Their chapter provides a potent example of what is at stake for teaching and sharing feminist sex education in digital space in a post-Trump, 'free speech' era of Twitter hate.

In the institutional context of a private New York high school, Ileana Jiménez invites us to think through the affective politics of complaint and the gendered vulnerabilities that are frequently silenced in such institutions. Drawing on Sara Ahmed's considerable work on feminism, affect and wilfulness, and her work as a teacher and queer feminist scholar-activist, Jiménez foregrounds the embodied resistance of one student, Gabi, in high school feminism. The chapter makes a number of temporal shifts as Jimenéz centres the importance of memory, reflecting on links between the current moment: the storming of the White House in 2021, and Jiménez's collaboration with students' feminist educational activism emerging in the middle of the Hillary Clinton/Donald Trump election campaign in 2016. As 'pussy grabbing' surfaced in the news cycle as a banal, everyday act that could be perpetrated by a candidate for the US presidency, Jiménez's students discovered the absence of a sexual harassment policy at the school. Agitating against this gaping absence, Jiménez documents the feminist activism of these students via poetry and performance attesting to their experience of sexual assault. Centring the embodied wilfulness of one student, Gabi, who was particularly vulnerable in this activism, and Gabi's reflections some years later, Jiménez's chapter reflects on survival of the Trump years as a form of abuse on a national scale.

Feminism beyond the Classroom

Feminism has long gained its power from its ability to draw on personal, rather than formal or institutionalized knowledges. Consciousness-raising as a strategy has sought to create spaces where women theorized gender oppression from their own experiences, using it to construct a sense of collective struggle. In this way, knowledge from the margins has long been intertwined in feminist political strategies.

Populist politics of course is not confined to the West only. Thanh-Nha Nguyen and Matthew McDonald analyse how the strategies and techniques of populist style politics have been used to subjugate women to state control. Tracing through the history of war, division and poverty in Vietnam up to the period from 1986 of Đổi Mới (translated as *renovation*), the authors study the emergence of post-truth populism in Vietnam through the move away from Stalinist central planning towards a socialist-oriented market economy. Populist post-truth politics became a way to counter the perceived threat of Western values and lifestyles which came with this shift towards a market economy. They argue that Vietnam's style of populist politics focuses on correct attitudes to culture, in an effort to maintain the government's one-party rule. Nguyen and McDonald illustrate that through overt manipulation and implicit seduction, the Vietnamese government mobilizes post-truth populism to promote traditional values and mobilize authoritarianism. This has not only significantly undermined scientific knowledge, debate and political compromise, but has been used to deny women's lived experience of inequality, subordination and oppression. The intentional circulation of gendered discourses to reassert the gender order has taken place with the government linking economic prosperity of the country to the conservative notions of the family and women's proper place in it. The Vietnamese government created a moral panic around the perceived poison of

Western values and lifestyles through targeting vulnerable women. The authors explain that under the conditions of Đổi Mới it is seen to be a woman's national duty to fulfil their primary roles in the family, and those who fail are seen to be rightfully punished via violence and oppression, thus exacerbating gendered violence. In order to redress gender discrimination, oppression and educational disadvantage, they argue for new forms of knowledge production related to progressive education and gender equity.

In their chapter, 'Embracing feral pedagogies: Queer feminist education through queer performance', Stephen Farrier, Alyson Campbell, Hannah McCann and Meta Cohen grapple with how to 'do' queer theory, outside of the university, drawing attention to how the university itself participates in the hierarchization of knowledge. The chapter attends to the need to break out of institutionalized modes of thinking and progression and presumptions of knowledge and ease with queer embodiment. The reflections provide a rich sense of the embodied sense of sharing space, discomfort, possibilities of expansion and retraction in thinking through 'queer'. Their chapter explores potentials for 'queer feral pedagogies' in bridging queer pedagogies beyond the confines of university structures as 'holding' and circulating queer knowledges. The reflections open towards a range of interesting questions relating to how to 'do' queer work and how to 'be' in these different spaces, and struggles over what 'counts' as legitimate knowledge in a post-truth era.

Outside of formal educational settings, we cannot ignore the use of online spaces to create and share knowledges and vernacular in relation to identity, including gender, sexuality and race. Yet this is a more complicated landscape. On the one hand, the networked capacities, immediacy and reach of digital culture have altered possibilities for consciousness raising, allowing the shaping of public conversations by individuals who may not have considered themselves activists or cultural intermediaries. Such affordances of digital culture have helped to push the continuing misogyny and abuses of power by powerful men to the forefront of public conversation. Online culture is now a crucial destination for youth, in particular, seeking to 'educate' themselves about gender, race and sexuality (Byron et al. 2019; Keller 2016). Through its participatory culture, ranging from the personal sharing of experience through to memes and infographics, digital culture offers personalized access to feminist frameworks for understanding the gender politics of everyday experiences, ranging from consent in intimate relationships, to 'microaggressions' at school and work. The ubiquity and pace of social media have catalysed transformations in identities, social practices and political affiliations for young people (Harris et al. 2010;

Vromen 2017). They have also given rise to new knowledge cultures, and new norms of learning and information-seeking.

On the other hand, men's rights groups, white supremacists and right-wing subcultures have also exploited the possibilities of online culture in shaping new 'commonsense', or 'alternative facts'. For example, Jesse Daniels discusses how American white supremacist groups use online pages to create bonds of sociality but also to simply and explicitly recentre whiteness as key to the founding of America. The trolling and abuse of women, particularly non-white women, has been well documented (Ging and Siapera 2018; Jane 2017; Lawson 2018). This oppositional culture leaves women – particularly women of colour – particularly vulnerable to personal attacks when seeking to participate in online discussion and knowledge exchange around feminism. Notably, the term 'post-truth' is often used to observe cultural changes around adherence to accepted, institutional norms of knowledge catalysed through the transformations of digital culture. Practically, it is used to describe the reckless abandon of institutional knowledge by those in power, manifested through the circulation of blatant untruths on social media. Yet such a framework has also been weaponized by right-wing populists to denounce women's accounts of sexual assault and other critiques as 'fake news'.

Further, the spread of feminism online belies the challenges for learning and making truth claims even within formally feminist circles. Social media amplifies the visibility of controversy, conflict and 'clickbait', normalizing antagonism in online culture (Elerding 2018). Further, the popular incitation to use one's 'voice' online in the interests of democracy is not met with the same injunctions to listen, or to converse. This raises new and critical questions of what young people, who often use digital culture as a primary form of learning around the world, are learning and mobilizing through their online feminist education. How are feminists actually able to use digital culture and continue to break new ground in transformative notions of justice?

In her chapter, 'Fight the Patriarchy: Digital Feminist Public Pedagogy and Post-feminist Media Culture in Indonesia', Annisa Beta explores how young feminists in Indonesia strategically use Instagram as a platform of digital feminist public pedagogy. She shows the importance of addressing the historical and political settings within which a digital feminist public pedagogy platform is located to understand the contours and practices informing how feminism is enacted, looking beyond Western-centric narratives of 'post-feminism'. The chapter situates debates about digital feminist public pedagogies in a transnational context and focuses on a popular young feminist Instagram account called Lawan Patriarki (@lawanpatriarki) to demonstrate the emergence of online feminist groups led by young Indonesian women. The chapter explores the particular feminist histories of protest and activism in Indonesia which have led to the current 'moment', and argues for the need to investigate feminist social media activist practices as deploying ambivalent and multi-referential narratives of feminism which emerge from specific socio-historical contexts.

These chapters represent myriad accounts and readings of the operation of power and resistance in feminist scholarship, pedagogies and activisms. They offer different ways of reflecting on what we have witnessed and are witnessing, and how we can build alternative political relationalities. They take seriously questions of care and collectivity and the role that knowledge and education has to play in building and repairing the social fabric, whilst attending to questions of difference through an ethics of care. This collection provides, we hope, a space to take stock and build and re-surface feminist frameworks in attending to power relations governing truth, harm, believability and authority in the current moment.

Note

1. The Black Lives Matter Movement was created in 2013 by Alicia Garza, Patrisse Cullors and Opal Tometi after George Zimmerman was acquitted of the murder of seventeen-year-old Trayvon Martin.

References

Arruzza, Cinzia, Tithi Bhattacharya and Nancy Fraser (2019), *Feminism for the 99%. A Manifesto*, London: Verso.

Baker, Stephanie Alice (2020), *Tackling Misinformation and Disinformation in the Context of Covid-19*, UK Government Cabinet Office, C-19 Seminar Series, July 2020.

Banet-Weiser, Sarah (2018), *Empowered: Popular Feminism and Popular Misogyny*, Durham: Duke University Press.

Burke, Penny Jane and Ronelle Carolissen (2018), 'Gender, Post-truth Populism and Higher Education Pedagogies', *Teaching in Higher Education*, 23 (5): 543–47, DOI: 10.1080/13562517.2018.1467160

Byron, Paul, Brady Robards, Benjamin Hanckel, Son Vivienne and Brendan Churchill (2019), '"Hey, I'm having these experiences": Tumblr use and young people's queer (dis)connections', *International Journal of Communication*, 13: 2239–59.

Cadwalladr, Carole (2017a), 'Mark Zuckerberg says change the world, yet he sets the rules', *The Guardian*, 19 February. Available online: https://www.theguardian.com/commentisfree/2017/feb/19/mark-zuckerberg-says-change-world-he-sets-rules (accessed 18 March 2021).

Cadwalladr, Carole (2017b), 'The great British Brexit robbery: How our democracy was hijacked', *The Guardian*, 7 May. Available online: https://www.theguardian.com/technology/2017/may/07/the-great-british-brexit-robbery-hijacked-democracy (accessed 18 March 2021).

Elerding, Carolyn (2018), 'The social media agon as differencing machine', *Communication Culture & Critique*, 11: 162–78.

Fidotta, Giuseppe, Joshua Neves and Joaquin Serpe (2020), 'Editorial introduction to media populism', *Culture Machine*, 19: 1–6. Available online: https://culturemachine.net/vol-19-media-populism/editorial-introduction-media-populism/

Fileborn Bianca, Loney-Howes Rachel (eds) (2019), *#MeToo and the Politics of Social Change*, Cham: Palgrave Macmillan.

Garza, Alicia (2014), 'A herstory of the #Black Lives Matter movement', *The Feminist Wire*, 7 October.

Ging, Debbie and Eugenia Siapera (eds) (2018), *Gender Hate: Understanding the New Anti-feminism*, Cham: Palgrave Macmillan.

Harris, Anita, Johanna Wyn and Salem Younes (2010), 'Beyond apathetic or activist youth: "Ordinary" young people and contemporary forms of participation', *Young*, 18 (1): 9–32.

Harris, John (2020), 'Disruption, destruction and chaos has become the new way of governing', *The Guardian*, 13 September. Available online: https://www.theguardian.com/commentisfree/2020/sep/13/tories-new-unscrupulous-politics-misinformation

Harsin, Jayson (2018), 'Post-truth populism: The French anti-gender theory movement and cross-cultural similarities', *Communication Culture & Critique*, 11 (2018): 35–52.

Jane, Emma (2017), *Misogyny Online: A Short (and Brutish) History*, London: Sage.

Keller, Jessalynn (2016), *Girls' Feminist Blogging in a Postfeminist Age*, London: Routledge.

Laclau, Ernesto (1977), *Politics and Ideology in Marxist theory: Capitalism, Fascism, Populism*, London: New Left Books.

Lawson, Caitlin (2018), 'Platform vulnerabilities: Harassment and misogynoir in the digital attack on Leslie Jones', *Information, Communication & Society*, 21 (6): 818–33.

Lentin, Alana (2017), 'On class and identity politics', *Inference Review*, 3 (2). Available online: https://inference-review.com/letter/on-class-and-identity-politics

Lentin, Alana and Gavin Titley (2011), *The Crises of Multiculturalism: Racism in a Neoliberal Age*, London and New York: Zed Books.

Malik, Nesrine (2020), 'For the Tories, breaking the law is just a sign of strength', *The Guardian*, 14 September. Available online: https://www.theguardian.com/commentisfree/2020/sep/14/tories-breaking-law

Mendes, Kaitlynn and Jessica Ringrose (2019), 'Digital Feminist Activism: #MeToo and the Everyday Experiences of Challenging Rape Culture', in B. Filebor and R. Loney-Howes (eds), *#MeToo and the Politics of Social Change*, Cham: Palgrave Macmillan.

Mendes, Kaitlynn, Jessica Ringrose and Jessalyn Keller (2019), *Digital Feminist Activism: Girls and Women Fight Back against Rape Culture*, Oxford: Oxford University Press.

Mishra, Pankaj (2018), *Age of Anger: A History of the Present*, London: Penguin Press.

Mlambo-Ngcuka, Phumzile (2020), 'Violence against women and girls: The shadow pandemic: Statement by the Executive Director of UN Women', UN Women, 6 April. Available online: https://www.unwomen.org/en/news/stories/2020/4/statement-ed-phumzile-violence-against-women-during-pandemic

Osborne, Hilary (2018), 'Tory donors among investors in Cambridge Analytica parent firm', *The Guardian*, 21 March. Available online: https://www.theguardian.com/politics/2018/mar/21/tory-donors-among-investors-in-cambridge-analytica-parent-firm-scl-group (accessed 19 March 2021).

Rawnsley, Andrew (2020), 'The escalating delinquency of Boris Johnson and his gang of blue anarchists', *The Guardian*, 15 September. Available online: https://www.theguardian.com/commentisfree/2020/sep/13/the-escalating-delinquency-of-boris-johnson-and-his-gang-of-blue-anarchists

Reuters Staff (2019), 'More than 120 journalists still jailed in Turkey: International Press Institute', *Reuters*, 20 November. Available online: https://www.reuters.com/article/us-turkey-security-media-idUSKBN1XT26T (accessed 19 March 2021).

Rinaldi, Chiara and Marlene Bekker (2020), 'A scoping review of populist radical right parties' influence on welfare policy and its implications for population health in Europe', *International Journal of Health Policy Management* 10 (3): 141–51.

Rosenberg, Matthew, Nicholas Confessore and Carole Cadwalladr (2018), 'How Trump consultants exploited the Facebook data of millions', *The New York Times*, 17 March. Available online: https://www.nytimes.com/2018/03/17/us/politics/cambridge-analytica-trump-campaign.html (accessed 18 March 2021).

Trilling, Daniel (2020), 'Why is the UK government suddenly targeting "critical race theory"', *The Guardian*, 23 October. Available online: https://www.theguardian.com/commentisfree/2020/oct/23/uk-critical-race-theory-trump-conservatives-structural-inequality

Vromen, Ariadne (2017), *Digital Citizenship and Political Engagement*, London: Palgrave Macmillan.

Zeglen, David and Neil Ewen (2020), 'National populists: Right-wing celebrity politicians in contemporary Europe', *Celebrity Studies*, 11 (3): 271–86.

Part One

Truth

1

Truth Parasites, Right-Wing Fury and the Predicaments of Feminist Expertise

Jane Kenway

Introduction

Truth is always contested. This chapter is concerned with some contemporary contestations, their links to right-wing fury and the ways in which gender and feminism are implicated. In discussing these I identify some of the issues confronted by those who research and teach about gender, sexuality and feminism. I begin with a discussion of the elusive notion of truth, the recent concept of 'post-truth' and suggest some reasons why the latter has emerged. I coin the term 'truth parasites' to help explain the practices involved in the current diminishment of truth. This diminishment is evident in the ways that the truth parasites of the alt-right and the conservative right invoke gender and feminism. It is also evident in right-wing attacks on the contemporary university. Those I address are right-wing claims that universities are facing a free speech crisis and attempts to undermine the humanities and social sciences. I conclude by speculating about how we might diminish the truth parasites while recognizing the predicaments they pose for us.

I use the broad term 'the right' to refer to parties, groups, movements and currents which subscribe to particular politics, policies and ideas. While they range across a spectrum from conservative to extreme and, while they include populists and the alt-right, they tend to share some common ideologies. First, they are usually about *identity and identification* – about defining one's own kind and asserting, and trying to affirm, its unity. Race, religion, gender, national identity, even civilization are regular unifying factors. Second, they habitually mobilize around notions of *threat and loss*. Threats are seen to be posed by other, dangerous, beings and by certain ways of thinking, and loss is associated with the demise of their social position. Thirdly, then, they are usually (not always) *reactionary*. They seek to restore a previous order in which their identities were secure and unchallenged. This previous order did not necessarily exist and may be an imagined past. Fourthly, the posture of right-wing movements is both *defensive and offensive*. It is defensive in the sense that it is about defending one's own kind. Their own kind are identified as the people who are under siege and who need to be defended, reclaimed and redeemed by the movement. They also adopt an offensive posture. Symbolic violence is normal and physical violence is always imminent and often real.

Truth and Post-truth

Truth is elusive. The more one interrogates it, as a concept, the more difficult it is to pin down. Nonetheless, it is usually ascribed a moral value. Commonplace notions associate it with fact, accuracy and reality. Truth-telling is associated with candour, sincerity and integrity. Truth tellers are seen as honest, authentic and trustworthy. Truth's opposite involves fiction, falsehood and fraudulence. Tellers of untruths are seen as deceivers, fabricators, cheats and imposters. Clear lines are drawn between truth and deceit. No matter how much we complicate the notion, its links to virtue and trust tend to remain. But not in straightforward ways – once one moves beyond common-sense notions of truth.

A dilemma for such common-sense notions is that truth is a battlefield. It involves struggles over meaning and materiality, over constituencies and consent. The story of the battle over truth is long and convoluted as Sophia Rosenfeld (2019) astutely explains. It is often associated with science specifically, or knowledge more broadly, with expertise and authority, with credibility. But, as many histories and philosophies of science demonstrate, truths are constantly challenged and changed as are the methods adopted to reach them. Further, as sociologies and philosophies of knowledge show, knowledge and power are inseparable. From these perspectives, dominant truths are linked to the dominant – to the most powerful. As are authority and expertise. Their core questions are 'Whose truths are these, who do they serve, how can others' truths be heard and make claims?' From such perspectives, truth is a matter of standpoint and positionality. Speaking 'truth to power' has become a catch-cry in support of subordinate and insubordinate truths. But, overall, no matter what the specific skirmish, and its resolution, truth has long been regarded as a virtue that is worth striving for, defending and extending.

The recent notion of post-truth is yet another skirmish in the battle over truth. The term seems to have begun with Donald Trump during his campaign for the Presidency of the United States in 2016. It quickly ricocheted around the world. The truth, that we are all post-truth, went viral. Now, the truth that there is no truth is a ubiquitous truth. The accompanying term 'fake news' is even more ubiquitous. Everything has become deniable, or claimable, on any grounds or on no grounds at all. And, conspiracies abound (Muirhead and Rosenblum 2019).

Why has the notion of post-truth travelled so rapidly? The many reasons include the following. The notion of post-truth seems to speak to vast reservoirs of uncertainty, discontent and anger across the economic and political spectrum. It also seems to speak to loss – a widespread loss of material and ontological security. These shifts have been accompanied by such questions as 'What bad truths got us into this mess?' and 'What authorities can we blame for such bad truths?'

There has been a loss of epistemological certainty. The truth about post-truth speaks to a loss of trust in authority per se. It speaks to a loss of trust in authoritative sources, in experts and expertise, in short, a loss of trust in those conventionally understood as expert truth tellers. Gil Eyal (2019) unravels the complexities of this 'crisis of expertise' showing it is not at all straightforward.

Those who have been credentialed as truth tellers include many professionals and specialists. Amongst them are academics including those who research and teach about gender, sexuality and feminism – us. In the post-truth era such truth tellers are portrayed as a problem. And, in some ways, they/we are, as I will show shortly. But, I suggest, the problems mainly arise from those I call truth parasites.

Truth Parasites

Truth parasites deliberately, and cynically, manipulate the truth for unedifying purposes. Academics cannot be regarded as truth parasites as different notions of truth inform their work. For instance, some subscribe to quite straightforward notions – perhaps drawing on positivist sensibilities. Others problematize singular notions of truth – perhaps offering multiple or subaltern truths. Whatever the case we seek truths that 'open forward' and are 'constantly revisable' (Eyal 2019: 2). We usually strive to achieve credible truths that, in one way or another, extend knowledge and understanding. Of course there are some academics who are exceptions but these are rare.

In contrast, truth is a host for various sorts of truth parasites. Parasites are organisms that live in, or on, a host. They get their nourishment, their energy, from the host and at the host's expense. They deplete their host, cause it harm and may alter the host's behaviour. Truth parasites, then, have a corrosive relationship to truth. They eat away at it, drain it of meaning and of moral integrity. They deplete the broad notion of truth and gain strength from doing so.

I identify two broad groups of truth parasites. First, those who belong to certain occupations. Their job is specifically to manipulate and massage the truth. I call them the *professional truth parasites*. Second, those who lodge themselves inside particular truth territories and then multiply. This contaminates the territory itself. I call them the *territorial truth parasites*.

Both groups belong to a range of *parasitic ecologies of truth*. These are the breeding grounds that nourish truth parasites and within which they proliferate. Within such ecologies parasites of truth feed off each other. In effect they become hyper-parasites. In the 'natural world' these are a type of parasite that uses other parasites as a host. As Engberg (2013) says their parasitic behaviour involves 'elaborate, nested relationships' and leads 'to what might appear to be an endless progression of interspecies abuse'.

There are many professional truth parasites and many parasitic ecologies that enable them to flourish and that flourish through them. First are the political and corporate 'communications' people, better known as public relations (PR) or spin-doctors. They usually produce highly partial and slanted truths on behalf of their employers and with a view to persuasion. Second, and increasingly similarly, are those who work in advertising and marketing. Here the truth about a product or service is embellished in order to profit from it. The embellishment is the lure, veracity is not. Most 'influencers' belong in this category. They claim to undermine traditional authorities and to offer authentic 'renegade knowledges' instead. But as Rojek and Baker (2019) reveal they usually manufacture their 'authenticity' for sale. Third are those professional truth parasites who work in the news media. All such media are perspectival and are therefore slanted. Historically, a guiding ethic, lived up to or otherwise, has been accurate, balanced, responsible, independent reporting based on authoritative sources. And, undoubtedly, some journalists continue to live by this ethic. However, this ethic, along with investigative journalism, is seriously on the wane – hence the necessary rise of fact checkers. The perspectival has morphed into the highly partisan particularly in certain news outlets, for example those that are part of Murdoch's News Corp. Indeed, according to

Rudd (2020: para. 3), 'News Corp is no longer interested in reporting facts. It operates like a mafia syndicate with a well-funded protection racket for politicians who back its commercial interests and espouse its hard-right ideology on issues like climate change.' Overall, there is an increasing elision between news, corporate and government spin, and advertising. Click-bait has helped spawn a further elision – one between news, entertainment and voyeurism.

Arguably, such professional truth parasites have helped to usher in the post-truth era. They are its historical antecedents and its fellow travellers. They have paved the way for such notions as post-truth and fake news and have undermined the notion of authoritative sources and expertise. Further, these professional truth parasites have helped to undermine the notion of truth as a virtue that is worth pursuing and defending. They diminish the value of truth.

No parasitic ecology of truth is more significant than the digital world with its giant platforms (Google, Facebook, Twitter), complex algorithms, big data, bots, trolls and 'dark web' (O'Neill 2016). This ecology allows the rapid and extensive circulation of misinformation, untruths, propaganda and conspiracy (Kakutanai 2018). It is underpinned by, what Srnicek (2017) calls, 'platform capitalism'.

In proclaiming the end of truth, the notion of post-truth undermines attempts to tell the truth – any truth, no matter what. In proclaiming the end of the expert, it undermines experts – all experts, no matter who. No matter what their field. All bodies of knowledge potentially become hosts for truth parasites including the self-proclaimed producers of 'renegade knowledges'.

Of course, there are many truths that matter a great deal to our everyday lives and our futures. Examples include, say, the truths associated with the built environment. In order for bridges and buildings to be reliable and safe we rely on the unambiguous truths associated with the specialist expertise of architects, engineers and construction workers. We rely on medical expertise to help address our health problems. We rely on historical honesty so that we can know about the fullness of our past and thus can properly consider its implication for current and future times. We rely on the truths of climate scientists to help us save the planet from extinction. In general, we rely on the tellers and seekers of truth.

Denials of such veracity mean that the post-truth discourse, truth parasites and parasitic ecologies of truth are dangerous. For example, climate change denialists are dangerous. Anti-vaxers are dangerous. Such denialism places our research and teaching in jeopardy especially when the university itself becomes a target.

Right-Wing Fury and the Diminishment of Truth

Now to consider the territorial truth parasites, right-wing fury and their direct and indirect diminishment of truth.

In Australia, in 2017, Milo Yiannopoulos conducted his Troll Academy tour (Kenway 2017b). Yiannopoulos used to be a favourite of the far right in the United States (Kenway 2017c). Now he is pretty much forgotten. But in 2017, he was treated as a celebrity by his fan base, certain right-wing politicians and the tabloid and social media. Together, they formed a parasitic truth ecology that amplified his hyper-sexist and hyper-racist messages.

Yiannopoulos is an obvious example of a territorial truth parasite who also thrives on stoking disgust and hate. In Australia he gorged on feminism and feminists, Indigenous Australians and women of 'othered' migrant groups, particularly Muslim women. The following widely circulated remarks are typical: 'Feminism Is Cancer', 'Birth Control Makes Women Unattractive and Crazy', 'Islam Is the Real Rape Culture' and 'Aboriginal Art Is Shit'.

Yiannopoulos appealed to certain young men, 'Young Liberals from the campuses, frat boys, overgrown gamers from their lounge rooms and aging Trump lovers – they came to the shows in their hundreds' (Kenway 2017c: np). They loved his style and his cultivated urbane, delinquent and 'dangerous faggot' persona. During his Australian visit, many stated, online, that they wanted him to come to their school and their campus on his next Australian visit. He was seen as excitingly *Dangerous* (2017) as the title of his self-published book tells us.

In his day, Yiannopoulos resonated with elements of the online alt-right. Angela Nagle (2017) documents the culture wars in internet cultures and subcultures. She distinguishes between those who identify as the alt-right, those who are in its orbit and those, she calls, the 'alt light'. The latter are alt-right figureheads who became high-profile celebrity figures in mainstream and social media. They include Milo Yiannopoulos, Gavin McInnes and Richard Spenser. Nagle describes the alt-right thus:

> The alt right is to varying degrees preoccupied with IQ, European demographic and civilizational decline, cultural decadence, cultural Marxism, anti-egalitarianism and Islamification but most importantly, as the name suggests, with creating an alternative to the right-wing conservative establishment, who they dismiss as "cuckservatives" for their soft Christian activity and of metaphorically cuckholding their womenfolk/nation/race to the non-white foreign invader.
>
> (Nagle 2017: 16–17)

This alt-right repertoire, then, includes 'extreme nativist, ultra-nationalist and white supremacist ideas' (Kenway 2017a: np). The alt-right includes men's rights activists and members of the 'mano-sphere'. In its many crossover sites anti-feminism and misogyny meet. Here are the many varieties of misogyny, and its links to entitlement and disgust, that Kate Manne documents so compellingly (2018).

Some common features of these online sites are as follows. First, they are virulently and viciously anti-feminist. Feminism is regarded as poison. It has led to the decline of Western masculinity and is a threat to Western civilization. Secondly, they are extremely misogynistic and celebrate their misogyny. Women, they claim, are biologically impulsive, sluts, stupid, fat, lazy, shallow, hysterical, narcissistic and untrustworthy. These sites are usually exceptionally vulgar and cruel and filled with hate and resentment. They claim that women need to be punished and they often try to incite violent retribution against them. Their trolling of women is highly threatening – often chillingly and terrifyingly so. This is clearly illustrated by the terrorist attacks on women conducted by incels (involuntary celibates). These include 'a yoga studio in Florida, where Scott Beierle shot seven women, killing two. Beierle had posted videos, titled *The Rebirth of my Misogynism* and *The American Whore*, and called for the crucifixion of promiscuous women' (Roose 2018).

A third feature is unreconstructed hyper-masculinity. This is promoted and celebrated. Most sites stress masculinist and neo-masculinist ('rebel' masculinity) themes. Many subscribe to a form of male social Darwinism – only strong men should/will survive. They demand heightened male assertiveness that, for example, challenges 'false accusations' against men including lies about domestic violence and rape. This involves a sort of masculinist vigilantism. Some stress the need for male separatism, 'Men Going Their Own Way', so they won't be weakened/poisoned by, what they see as, the monstrous feminine. Some see themselves as 'brothers in arms' in league with neo-Nazis, Fascists and other fanatical right-wing groups. While those who subscribe to these particular modes of masculinity are reactionary in the extreme, they nonetheless like to constitute themselves as heroic and anti-heroic.

According to Nagle, young males are a major demographic and a key hunting grounds in these online right-wing sites. And some commentators infer, from certain content, that young men at universities are highly involved. One can certainly infer, from Phipps' (2017) work about universities in the UK, that this is so. Those who are part of certain currents like to think of themselves as edgy, ironical, witty, technologically ultra-sophisticated and super-smart.

They talk about history, film, philosophy (libertarianism) and they claim certain philosophers as their inspiration – Nietzsche or the Stoics. They also like to, ironically, draw inspiration from the counter-cultural left – from the situationists or from Bakhtin's notions of the carnivalesque and the grotesque. Their key filmic reference points are *Fight Club* and *The Matrix*. Engaged in a highly affective politics of 'nonconformity', and 'transgression' (Nagle 2017: 31) they see themselves as iconoclastic, taboo busting and take pride in being 'politically incorrect'. Further, they glory in their outsider status and mobilize any slurs directed towards them as badges of honour.

These territorial truth parasites and hyper-parasites, then, engage in feeding frenzies in this online, alt-right, parasitic ecology. This ecology intersects with offline parasitic ecologies of truth – those in the wider media and in formal and informal political circles where the right-wing conservative establishment swarm. In these circles the professional truth parasites and the territorial truth parasites feed together and off each other. And they both feed into the broader politics of right-wing leaders, political parties and activist groups in various countries in Europe, Brazil, India and the United States. In many national and subnational elections right-wing parties are achieving success and translating it into hard-right policies and political practices. According to Faulkner et al. (2017), we are witnessing 'creeping fascism'.

In assorted ways, gender, sexuality and feminism are implicated in this dramatic lurch to the far right. Feminist achievements are being attacked across Europe as Eszter Kováts explains:

> certain women's rights (e.g. reproductive rights in Spain), certain LGBT issues (e.g. same-sex marriage in Croatia, France and Slovenia; human rights strategy of the government in Slovakia), government gender policies (e.g. ratifying the Istanbul Convention in Poland, gender-sensitive education in schools in France), gender mainstreaming as an administrative policy tool (e.g. in Austria, Germany, Poland), progressive sexual education programmes (in Croatia, Germany and Poland), or gender studies departments and their financing (in Germany and Poland).
>
> (2017: 175)

In most of these circles, feminists are portrayed as purveyors of the bad truths that have led to the decline of the traditional gender order. This, in turn, is blamed for the structural changes that have had such damaging material consequences for everyday people. Feminist truths are presented as dangerous. They promote 'radical gender theory', 'gender ideology', 'gender fluidity' and 'genderism'. Feminists are blamed for spreading their gender propaganda in policy circles, schools, universities, the culture industries and elsewhere. They are seen to hate men and want women to lead the world. To this end they have succeeded in winning reforms (childcare, maternity leave, quotas) in various systems. These have allowed women to take over high-level jobs and positions of leadership that, rightly, belong to men. They have 'pushed' their way through various institutions and 'taken them over'.

As such feminists have been constructed as integral members of certain cultural and political 'elites'. They are seen as out of touch, narrowly focused and condescending. Thus, their feminist truths do not speak to the needs and issues of ordinary women, let alone to ordinary people's most pressing concerns. They have deployed their misplaced truths to wage gender/culture wars against everyday people.

Feminists are also seen to have silenced ordinary people through their language of political correctness. Because of this such people can no longer speak freely on questions of gender and sexuality or indeed, on race or religion. And they have particularly silenced men, undermined their identities and rights, and made their lives difficult and miserable. In sum, feminists are seen to have weaponized truth and waged war against the traditional gender order, carelessly overturning the lives of ordinary people.

Clearly, feminism and gender relations have become highly strategic rich pickings for these territorial truth parasites. They circulate misleading and false information about the purposes and successes of feminism as well as conspiracies about it, and they do much of this under the sign of free speech. Free speech has become a host in the war over truth. It has its own professional and territorial truth parasites and *hyper-parasites* and its own parasitic ecology within which they thrive and multiply.

The free speech hyper-parasites indulge in a particular reading of the notion of free speech. There are two types of free speech parasites, conservative and libertarian, but they sup together. According to the libertarians, all truths are created equal, everyone should be free to circulate their particular truth, no matter how ill-informed or harmful. Ignorance, opinion, prejudice and bigotry, for example, must be as free to circulate as any other truths. All are entitled to a podium. Attempts to curtail bigoted and hate speech are portrayed as authoritarian and are derided via such titles as 'virtue signalling', 'cancel culture' and 'political correctness gone mad'.

On the other hand, the conservatives condemn those whose views they oppose. A single tweet, by a public figure, on a sensitive or controversial topic, can ignite fire-storms of right-wing fury. Apparently only some should be free to speak and, even then, only on certain topics and from particular perspectives. But this is not seen as akin to the despised 'cancel culture'.

Devouring the University

Such free speech parasitic behaviours and ecologies, fuelled by right-wing fury, are having damaging effects on universities. Our universities are already under siege financially and ideologically. Indeed, they employ their own professional truth parasites to massage the market, especially when wanting to hide image-damaging truths (Phipps 2017).

In 2017 *The Weekend Australian* published an article by Bettina Arndt – a long-term public figure in Australia. As a social commentator and sex therapist, she has published widely and has a high public profile. She has been an advisor to conservative governments on family and reproduction matters. In the 1990s she became an outspoken men's rights and anti-feminist campaigner and joined the ranks of the truth parasites. Arndt holds denialist views about domestic violence, sexual assault, sexual harassment, rape within marriage and paedophilia. No amount of research-based truth will convince her that these are major issues. Nonetheless, men's groups and right-wingers in politics and the media regard her as a credible source. Indeed in 2020, she was awarded an Australia Day Honour 'for significant service to the community as a social commentator, and to gender equity through advocacy for men' (Zhou 2020).

Her article in *The Weekend Australian* laments the rise of young left-wing female activists and insists that the conservative side of politics must address this threat. It draws on an 'audit of history teaching' conducted by the Institute of Public Affairs – an influential right wing think tank. According to Arndt this study argues that:

> history is being taught from a narrow ideological perspective, that focuses almost exclusively on class, race and gender with hardly a word on democracy, liberalism and capitalism, the essential tenants of Western Civilization.
>
> (9 December 2017)

Arndt generalizes from this alleged crisis in history teaching and explains that in 'the humanities and teaching faculties' students are being indoctrinated by postmodernism, feminism and neo-Marxism. And further, according to Arndt, universities per se have policies that are 'hostile to free speech'.

In 2018 and 2019 Arndt sought to demonstrate this. She toured university campuses speaking about the 'Fake Rape Crisis'. At that time an Australian Human Rights Commission report (2017), along with many other reports (e.g. Funnell and Hush 2018) pointed to the high rates of sexual harassment and assault on university campuses and in university colleges. She claimed, on the basis of no evidence, that the rates were exaggerated and that the research arose from anti-male standpoints – hence her slogan #MenToo. Her ill-informed and harmful views were condemned by many women's groups and anti-violence activists. Students protested against her on campus at the University of Sydney. She then formally complained to the University of Sydney about this threat to her free speech and called for the students to be disciplined. She also used the students' protest to lobby for a government inquiry into free speech in universities.

Arndt's antics attracted gleefully furious media coverage, particularly in Murdoch's *The Australian* newspaper. This fed into the insistent campaigning of right-wing think tanks, including the Centre for Independent Studies and the Institute of Public Affairs (IPA). The IPA published 'audits' in 2016, 2017 and 2018 documenting the 'free speech crisis' in Australian universities and insisting on regulation and sanctions. Lesh's (2018) audit updated the earlier ones.

In response to this and other pressure, in 2018 the Commonwealth government commissioned an Independent Review of Freedom of Speech in Australian Higher Education Providers. It was led by former Chief Justice of the High Court, Robert French, who rejected the claim that Australian universities are experiencing a free speech crisis. Nonetheless, French suggested that universities adopt the code of practice that he developed or a variation thereof. Many did.

However, none of this satisfied the free speech crisis campaigners. They continued their indignant laments even in the face of serious and scholarly revelations that their evidence base was unconvincing. For example, Davis (2018) said the following:

> it is sobering to read carefully the evidence offered in support of a free speech crisis. This turns out to be a small number of anecdotes repeatedly retold, warnings about trends in the US, implausible readings of university policies, and unsourced claims that staff and student feel oppressed. We are offered scraps of unrelated incidents. Tenuous and sometimes tendentious claims. Occasional concerning incidents. Some poorly framed policies. As though these sum to a higher mark… But to date those asserting a crisis have provided no systematic evidence of a meaningful, sustained and growing threat to free speech on campus.

Others pointed out that many of these claims about a free speech crisis in Australian universities are unselectively transplanted from similar claims, and similar groups, in the UK and United States. As Evan Smith, who has written a comprehensive history of no-platforming in the UK (2020b), says:

> "No platforming", "safe spaces" and "trigger warnings" have been held up by conservatives, libertarians and "classic liberals" as the holy trinity of campus censorship methods – supposed threats to free speech and academic freedom.
>
> (Smith 2020a)

Similar points have been made about the situation in the United States with regard to the ways in which political correctness, woke-ness, critical race studies, identity politics, liberal bias, leftist orthodoxies and conservative-speech-suppression are closing down free speech on campus. But as Gelber (2020) explains these claims are overblown on many counts. For example, with regard to de-platforming, she says:

> The "de-platforming" of speakers (rescinding their invitation to speak) is also not very common. The Foundation for Individual Rights in Education (FIRE) in the United States maintains a database of disinvitation attempts. According to their own database, in 2016 there were 42 disinvitations. Eleven of these were of one speaker – Milo Yiannopoulos.

Despite all such critical observations (Forsyth 2020), in August 2020 the Commonwealth government 'established an independent review to evaluate the progress that universities have made implementing the Robert French Model Code on university free speech' (2020).

This sumptuous buffet attended by free speech hyper-parasites is associated with another lavish dining experience in which the humanities and social sciences are the host. Here the territorial truth parasites engage in furious feasting involving three forms of *depletion*.

First, the territorial truth parasites feast in order to *discredit* contemporary directions in the humanities and social sciences. These fields are seen to have deviated from fundamental truths and from fundamentalist notions of truth. History has long been a particular target hence the ongoing 'history wars' in Australia (Macintyre and Clark 2004). To be critical of Australia's colonial past is to adopt a 'black armband' perspective involving too much mourning about the horrific effects of occupation on Indigenous Australians (Clark 2002).

Second, these truth parasites' feasting activities are directed towards *reclaiming* these knowledge fields and *returning* them to acceptable truths. A prominent example in Australia is the establishment of the philanthropically funded Ramsay Centre. Its vision statement says, 'Our aim is to advance education by promoting the study of the "great conversations" of Western Civilisation'. In partnership with three universities it offers 'great books programs, undergraduate and post graduate scholarships, summer schools, public lectures, seminars and symposia'. Ex-Prime Ministers John Howard (Chair) and Tony Abbott are on its board. Both are Liberal party conservatives. Abbott was instrumental in shaping its agenda which is, largely, to uncritically respect and celebrate Western Civilization. Abbott made this clear in *Quadrant* (2018).

> The key to understanding the Ramsay Centre for Western Civilisation is that it's not merely about Western civilization but in favour of it. The fact that it is "for" the cultural inheritance of countries such as ours, rather than just interested in it, makes it distinctive. The fact that respect for our heritage has largely been absent for at least a generation in our premier teaching and academic institutions makes the Ramsay Centre not just timely but necessary.

He also said, 'A management committee including the Ramsay CEO and also its academic director will make staffing and curriculum decisions'.

The establishment of the Centre became controversial, attracting considerable media and interest-group agitation. Despite the fact that the proposed Centre brought considerable funds it faced protracted difficulty in finding university partners. Academic staff concerns were largely over appointments and the curriculum – over who controlled them and how Western Civilization was to be represented. There was also concern that, if universities were to partner with Ramsay, this would legitimize a programme that is unashamedly involved in 'white washing the West' (Reimer 2019) and in 'the promotion and endorsement of "Western civilisation" as a superior form of human existence' (Reimer 2018).

Such views are especially distressing for Australia's First Nations people for they reiterate:

> the notion that Australia was *terra nullius* before the arrival of Europeans. It is, therefore, a worldview that relegates First Nations Australians to a backwater of history. It is also the invention of a 'West' that is free of criminality. It is an attempt to rehabilitate a colonial past that white Australia can celebrate, a denial of the history that has harmed Indigenous Australia in significant and continuing ways. In a very clear way then, it is an issue for the elevation and rehabilitation of First Nations Australia, but also all groups that do not fit into the narrow space reserved for those the Ramsay Centre feels are its own.
>
> (Jack23 2019)

This is shockingly insensitive to Australia's Indigenous people. The *Uluru Statement from the Heart* is a landmark document produced by a national convention of Indigenous people in 2017. It specifically calls for a Makarrata Commission that 'Would also oversee a process of truth-telling about Australia's history and colonisation' (2017).

The third feature of the territorial truth parasites involves attempts by the Commonwealth government to seriously *diminish, if not destroy*, these fields by starving them of students and thereby marking them as undesirable. In June 2020 it announced changes to the ways it will fund universities to teach domestic students. As a result, from 1 January 2021, the cost of degrees in humanities and communications subjects will dramatically increase, while many other fields will have fees decreased. Fees for humanities and communications subjects will rise by 113 per cent putting them into the same fee band as commerce and law. As Visentin (2020) explains:

> to study a full year of an arts degree (eight subjects) in 2020 students were charged $6684 in fees while the government picked up the rest of the tab ($6116). In 2021, students will be charged $14,500 for a full year of an arts degree, while the government has lowered its contribution to $1100.

'Job readiness' is the justification. The provision of cheaper degrees in science, technology, engineering, mathematics, teaching and nursing is designed to encourage students to enter these fields and then to move into the labour market where apparently jobs will be plentiful. This intimates that humanities and communications are bad employment investments. But as many have explained, the facts do not bear this out (e.g. Hurley 2020). Ironically, though, as Patrick Stokes points out, the minister 'has effectively just told the market that a BA is as valuable as a law degree'. The high price may turn these fields into Veblen knowledge goods wherein, because of exclusivity and status, the demand increases as the price increases. But either way the price hike is likely to

> split students into two camps: those paying less for a credential that will get them into jobs like teaching and nursing, and those who can pay more for the 'indulgence' of a non-vocational degree… It would turn the humanities into a gated community for people whose parents can buy them the time to study *Beowulf* or learn formal logic.
>
> (Stokes 2020)

These three acts of depletion are an indirect assault on studies of gender, sexuality and feminism. To attack the humanities and social sciences is to attack those fields where studies of gender, sexuality and feminism have had the most influence and where race, social class and other axes of inequality are taken seriously – where intersectional and interdisciplinary approaches thrive. To restrict access to the wealthy and white is to deprive other students of the galvanizing benefits of these fields. To try to return these fields to studies of Western civilization is to try to return them to studies of great men and of great men's great books. But more than that, it links these fields into Eurocentric and white supremacist ideas and to the fears of Western civilizational decline that are so popular among the alt-right and the right more broadly.

What about Us?

There is no easy way to get rid of parasites. Sometimes they go away of their own accord, especially if the body's immune system is healthy. Sometimes creating healthier living conditions will deprive them of nutrition. But usually one needs to take some sort of medication. Whatever the case they must not be ignored. If ignored they can cause serious illness.

Those of us who research and teach about gender, sexuality and feminism have certainly not ignored the truth parasites of the right. Our anti-parasitic medication includes knowing our critics intimately. Feminist literature that critiques the right is expanding rapidly. It seeks to unpack the right's links to gender, sexuality and feminism and the ways in which these are put in the service of their national, racial, religious or class-based political agendas. The right's explicit and implicit policies, their party membership and support bases (electoral or otherwise), their ideologies, cultures and political practices are all identified. Also scrutinized are mainstream media and social (digital) media representations of the right including the manner in which it represents itself. Various right-wing textual and musical artefacts and symbolic registers are examined.

There are several common foci in such literature. One is on women and womanhood on the right ranging from those who vote for right-wing parties, to women leaders in right-wing mainstream politics (national, municipal and regional) through to members of clandestine and violent groups. Another focus is on the ideological functions women perform for right-wing groups and parties which include assisting them to broaden their appeal. Various invocations and inflections of masculinity and sexuality in right wing politics, groupings and thought are the focus of a fourth body of work. Then there is the focus on the right's responses to the progressive projects associated with gender equality, LGBTQI+ rights and multiculturalism. And finally, a core concern is how to challenge and defeat the right's anti-women and anti-feminism as well as its nationalistic racism. Locating and developing examples of successful interventions is an urgent quest.

Valuable examples of this anti-parasitic medication include *Gender and Far Right Politics in Europe* (Köttig, Bitzan and Pető 2017) and *Gender Hate Online: Understanding the New Anti-Feminism* (Ging and Siapera 2019) and Spierings, Zaslove, Mügge and De Lange's special issue of *Patterns of Prejudice* (2015) on gender and populist radical right politics. Such texts are excellent resources for feminist pedagogies in and beyond the classroom. It is crucial that our students develop the critical tools that will help them recognize, and medicate against, truth parasites.

How healthy is our immune system, our resistance, when it comes to truth and post-truth parasitic politics? Our broad epistemic community has long had a varied and uncomfortable relationship to truth, reason, knowledge, authority and expertise. Some of us have deployed positivist methods in many disciplines and in the body politic to address some of the many absences in positivist truths about gender and sexuality. Some have challenged and disrupted truths across the disciplinary spectrum and the body politic. We have thus produced many counter contentions, many mutinous truths. Our research and pedagogies are strongly associated with uncomfortable truths. They offend some and defend others, promote some and demote others. Because our truths reconfigure virtue and trust they are sometimes hard for others to accept.

Also, over time, as in many fields, we have challenged much of our own earlier assurance. As our field has grown and diversified, we have produced multiple truths. Sometimes these enrich us (e.g. Banet-Weiser, Gill and Rottenberg 2020). Sometimes these divide us. Constituencies fragment. Truth splinters. Tensions around truths become toxic. These tensions have occasionally resulted in splintered solidarities within our epistemic community. Such tensions have tended to draw our attention away from right-wing assaults on our disciplines and our universities.

Ironically, our epistemic uncertainty and multiplicity make our truths vulnerable to territorial truth parasites. Feminist expertise is easily discredited. We just have our opinions which are regarded as no better than anyone else's. And, to the free speech advocates, our dangerous ideologies mean we are deep throat activists in the leftist hotbed university.

How might we create healthier living conditions that might deprive the truth parasites of nutrition? Answering this question involves some introspective discomfort which includes assessing the extent to which any of the right's critiques of feminism ring true. There are, I think, some kernels of truth in its critiques of feminist elitism.

Feminist studies of, and opinion pieces about, conservative right-wing populism tend to read the people involved in a somewhat condescending and scornful manner. They imply that they are uneducated, unenlightened and stuck in the past – ignorant, bigoted and coarse. For example, Hillary Clinton's widely reported comment that Donald Trump supporters were a 'basket of deplorables' was greeted with smug approval by the feminist establishment in the United States. In effect, the people involved were shamed and blamed for responding 'badly' to economic crises not of their own making and which disproportionally affect them. Shame-shifting and blaming 'down' are time-honoured strategies of all elites.

Such feminist commentary is often informed by the logics of liberal and/or neoliberal feminism. And, importantly, it can be inferred that it is these strains of feminism that provoke the greatest negativity from the right. Why?

Together these tend to be the most longstanding, visible and mainstream feminist projects. In many ways, and despite their differences, liberal and neoliberal feminism have come to be seen as feminism per se. Liberal feminism's critique of the gendered inequalities of liberalism led it to push for greater numbers of women in positions of power and authority in the public and corporate spheres. Sometimes summarized as 'glass ceiling' feminism, it is now frequently associated with the ascent of 'top' women into the 'top' of current power structures. Neoliberal feminism is some-times called 'lean in' or 'having it all' feminism and uncritically adopts neoliberal rationality. Catherine Rottenburg's *The rise of neoliberal feminism* (2018) offers a powerful critique.

Even despite their discourses of empowerment for all women, these feminisms tend to offer an 'individualised', 'responsible-ised', 'atomised' and 'depoliticised' feminist agenda (Rottenburg 2018: 128). They primarily speak to women who are privileged in class, race and sexuality terms. Their feminism does not necessarily 'trickle down'. They demonstrate little sense of the everyday difficulties, or sensibilities, of the many. They thus don't necessarily speak to, with or for women beyond their privileged enclosures – even despite their progressive gloss.

'Progressive neoliberalism' is the term Nancy Fraser coined to describe the current mobilization of notions of diversity, empowerment, non-discrimination and meritocracy (2016: 17). She argues that this involves a 'cosy alliance between progressives and high-end symbolic and service-based business sectors (Wall St, Silicon Valley, Hollywood)' (2016: 11). Liberal and neoliberal feminism are part of this 'cosy alliance'. So too are post-feminism and, what Sarah Banet-Weiser (2018) calls 'popular feminism', the genre spread by consumer and popular culture.

When such discourses are co-opted and amplified by the privileged and powerful for the privileged and powerful and/or when they are largely about individualized self-sufficiency, self-help and choice, or about commodified confidence-building and self-branding, it is not surprising that they are seen as unhelpful and alienating and as having little credibility.

We could start to deprive the truth parasites of nutrition if we steer away from such feminisms. Alternative directions are suggested in *Feminism for the 99% A Manifesto* (Arruzza, Bhattacharya and Fraser 2019). It juxtaposes feminism for the one per cent against feminism for the ninety-nine per cent. This

> champions the needs and rights of the many – of poor and working-class women, of racialized and migrant women, of queer, trans and disabled women, of women encouraged to see themselves as middle class even as capitalism exploits them. (13–14)

It seeks to shift understandings of feminism in the popular/populist imagination and thus to widen feminist constituencies and alliances. It addresses militant feminist activism, the steep decline of the social wage, racism and imperialism, gendered violence, the regulation of sexuality, environmental destruction, and democracy and peace.

This Manifesto implicitly raises questions about our expertise and our capacity to hear the truths of people beyond the academy. Do we pay sufficient attention to their 'practical, tacit, embodied and situational knowledge'? (Eyal 2019: 25). Sometimes our levels of abstraction are alienating. This apparent lack of epistemic modesty certainly feeds the truth parasites. In turn, this alerts us to the need for more inclusive notions of expertise and, indeed, truth.

References

Abbott, Tony (2018), 'Paul Ramsay's vision for Australia', *Quadrant*, 24 May.
Arndt, Bettina (2017), 'Women take sharp turn to the left in expressing political opinion', *The Weekend Australian Newspaper*, 9 December.
Arruzza, Cinzia, Tithi Bhattacharya and Nancy Fraser (2019), *Feminism for the 99%. A Manifesto*, London: Verso.
Australian Government (2019), *Report of the Independent Review of Freedom of Speech in Australian Higher Education Providers*. Available online: https://docs.education.

gov.au/documents/report-independent-review-freedom-speech-australian-higher-education-providers-march-2019

Australian Human Rights Commission (2017), 'University sexual assault and sexual harassment project'. Available online: https://humanrights.gov.au/our-work/sex-discrimination/projects/university-sexual-assault-and-sexual-harassment-project

Banet-Weiser, Sarah (2018), *Empowered: Popular Feminism and Popular Misogyny*, Duke University Press.

Banet-Weiser, Sarah, Rosalind Gill, Catherine Rottenberg (2020), 'Postfeminism, popular feminism and neoliberal feminism? Sarah Banet-Weiser, Rosalind Gill and Catherine Rottenberg in conversation', *Feminist Theory*, 21 (1): 3–24.

Clark, Anna (2002), 'History in black and white: A critical analysis of the black armband debate', *Journal of Australian Studies*, 26 (75): 173–93.

Davis, Glyn (2018), 'Special pleading: Free speech and Australian universities', *The Conversation*, 4 December. Available online: https://theconversation.com/special-pleading-free-speech-and-australian-universities-108170

Engber, Daniel (2013), 'Do parasites get parasites?', *Popular Science*, 20 May.

Eyal, Gil (2019), *The Crisis of Expertise*, Cambridge: Polity.

Forsyth, Hannah (2020), 'How a fake "free speech crisis" could imperil academic freedom', *The Conversation*, 26 August. Available online: https://theconversation.com/how-a-fake-free-speech-crisis-could-imperil-academic-freedom-144272

Fraser, Nancy (2016), 'Progressive neoliberalism versus reactionary populism: A choice that feminists should refuse', *Nordic Journal of Feminist and Gender Research*, 24 (4): 281–4.

Faulkner, N with Samir Dathi, Phil Hearse and Seema Sayeda (2017), *Creeping Fascism: Brexit, Trump, and the Rise of the Far Right*, London: Public Reading Rooms.

Funnell, Nina and Anna Hush (2018), *The Red Zone Report: An Investigation into Sexual Violence and Hazing in Australian University Residential Colleges*, EROC Australia. Available online: https://apo.org.au/node/134766

Gelber, Katharine (2020), 'Is there a "free speech crisis" in Australian universities?', *ABC Religion and Ethics*, 15 July. Available online: https://www.abc.net.au/religion/katharine-gelber-free-speech-crisis-in-australian-universities/12459718

Ging, Debbie and Eugenia Siapera (eds) (2019), *Gender Hate Online: Understanding the New Anti-Feminism*, Springer.

Hurley, Peter (2020), 'Humanities graduates earn more than those who study science and maths', *SBS News*, SBS Television. Available online: https://www.sbs.com.au/news/humanities-graduates-earn-more-than-those-who-study-science-and-maths

Jack23 (2019), 'The Ramsay Centre is infiltrating tertiary education and that is a problem for first nations Australia', *WhyNot?*, 12 August. Available online: https://www.whynot.org.au/identity-diversity-and-inclusion/theramsaycentreisinfiltratingtertiaryeducation/

Kakutanai, Michiko (2018), *The Death of Truth*, London: William Collins.

Kenway, Vashti (2017a), 'The murky world of the alt-right', *Red Flag*, 6 March. Available online: https://redflag.org.au/node/5705

Kenway, Vashti (2017b), 'Monday night in Flemington', *Overland*, 6 December.

Kenway, Vashti (2017c), 'Melbourne tells Milo: Get out!', *Socialist Worker*, 7 December. Available online: https://socialistworker.org/2017/12/07/melbourne-tells-milo-get-out

Köttig, Michaela, Renate Bitzan and Andrea Pető (eds) (2017), *Gender and Far Right Politics in Europe*, London and New York: MacMillan.

Kováts, Eszter (2017), 'The emergence of powerful anti-gender movements in Europe and the crisis of liberal democracy', in M. Köttig, R. Bitzan and A. Pető (eds), *Gender and Far Right Politics in Europe*, 175–89, London and New York: Palgrave Macmillan.

Lesh, Matthew (2018), *Free Speech on Campus: Audit 2018*, Institute of Public Affairs.

Macintyre, Stuart and Anna Clark (2004), *The History Wars*, Melbourne University Press.

Manne, Kate (2018), *Down Girl: The Logic of Misogyny*, New York: Oxford University Press.

Muirhead, Russell and Nancy L. Rosenblum (2019), *A Lot of People are Saying: The New Conspiricism and the Assault on Democracy*, Princeton: Princeton University Press.

Nagle, Andrea (2017), *Kill All Normies: Online Culture Wars from 4chan and Tumblr to Trump and the Alt-Right*, Washington: Zero Books.

O'Neill, Cathy (2016), *Weapons of Math Destruction: How Big Data Increases Inequality and Threatens Democracy*, USA: Crown Penguin.

Phipps, Alison (2017), 'Speaking up for what's right: Politics, markets and violence in higher education', *Feminist Theory*, 18 (3): 357–61.

Phipps, Alison (2019), '"Lad culture" and sexual violence against students', in S. Anitha, and B. R. Lewis (eds), *Gender Based Violence in University Communities: Policy, Prevention and Educational Initiatives*, 41–60, Bristol: Policy Press.

Riemer, Nick (2018), 'Ramsay course offers stark choice to Australian universities', *Sydney Morning Herald*, 6 September. Available online: https://www.smh.com.au/politics/federal/ramsay-course-offers-stark-choice-to-australian-universities-20180905-p501yt.html

Reimer, Nick (2019), 'The Ramsay Centre and the reality of ideology', *Overland*, 28 March.

Rojek Chris and Stephanie A. Baker (2019), *Lifestyle Gurus: Constructing Authority and Influence*, UK: Polity.

Roose, Joshua (2018), 'Are men's movements a new form of terrorism?' *ABC News*, ABC Television, November 25. Available online: https://www.abc.net.au/news/2018-11-25/incel-alt-right-mens-movement-masculanism-proudboys-milo/10482032

Rosenfeld, Sophia (2019), *Democracy and Truth: A Short History*, Philadelphia: University of Pennsylvania Press.

Rottenburg, Catherine (2018), *The Rise of Neoliberal Feminism*, New York: Oxford University Press.

Rudd, Kevin (2020), 'Why News Corp is a cancer on our democracy only a royal commission can excise', *Crikey*, 21 October. Available online: https://www.crikey.com.au/2020/10/21/kevin-rudd-news-corp-royal-commission-petition/

Smith, Evan (2020a), 'The university "Free Speech Crisis" has been a right-wing myth for 50 years', *The Guardian*, 22 February. Available online: https://www.theguardian.com/commentisfree/2020/feb/22/university-free-speech-crisis-censorship-enoch-powell

Smith, Evan (2020b), *No Platform: A History of Anti-Fascism, Universities and the Limits of Free Speech*, London: Routledge.

Spierings, Neils, Andrej Zaslove, Lisa M. Mügge, Sarah L. De Lange (eds) (2015), 'Special issue: Gender and populist radical right politics', *Patterns of Prejudice*, 49 (1–2).

Srnicek, Nick (2017), *Platform Capitalism*, UK: Polity.

Stokes, Patrick (2020), 'Higher fees for arts degrees: Why does the government have it in for the humanities?', *The New Daily*, 20 June. Available online: https://thenewdaily.com.au/news/national/2020/06/20/humanities-degrees-higher-fees/

Tehan, Dan (2020), Media release: Evaluating progress on free speech (7 August 2020). Available online: https://ministers.dese.gov.au/tehan/evaluating-progress-free-speech

Uluru Statement from the Heart (2017). Available online: https://ulurustatement.org/

Visentin, Lisa (2020), 'University fees are changing. How will it affect you?', *Sydney Morning Herald*, 17 October. Available online: https://www.smh.com.au/politics/federal/university-fees-are-changing-how-will-it-affect-you-20201009-p563ib.html

Yiannopoulos, Milo (2017), *Dangerous*. Available online: pdf-dangerous-milo-yiannopoulos-pdf-download-free-book-9b95d17.pdf

Zhou, Naaman (2020), 'Bettina Arndt awarded Australia Day honour for services "to gender equity"', *The Guardian*, 25 January. Available online: https://www.theguardian.com/australia-news/2020/jan/25/bettina-arndt-awarded-australia-day-honour-for-services-to-gender-equity

2

The Weaponization of 'Gender' beyond Gender: The Entrenchment of 'Coloniality of Power' and 'Pedagogies of Cruelty'

Isis Giraldo

Introduction

The issue of 'the challenges posed to a feminist ethics of pedagogical care' in the current 'post-truth' global era is one of the questions driving this collection. It is an important one because it is structured around notions that encapsulate what I identify as some of the core issues at stake in contemporary global 'ideological struggles': the ethics of justice and pedagogies of care. I start from the assumption that the most visible aspect of these struggles has been the weaponization of gender from within broad Catholic/Christian coalitions on both sides of the Atlantic and via attacks articulated around the 'gender theory' and 'gender ideology' tropes. I advance two interconnected arguments. First, that although 'gender' is the entry point for the articulation of these attacks, what is at stake goes well beyond so as to encompass social justice. Second, that these attacks do not exemplify nor emerge from a so-called 'populist' present but have a longer and broader history.

The overarching argument in this chapter is that in order to address the challenges posed by these ideological struggles in which gender has worked as a prima facie, it is necessary to carry out certain geographical, epistemological and temporal displacements and take a longer, larger, non-liberal and non-Eurocentric analytical framework. Thus, I posit Latin America as a key location (geopolitical displacement) and the emergence of the theology of liberation in the 1970s (temporal displacement), and its reverberations, as a turning point. Accordingly, I take a decolonial analytical framework (epistemological displacement). These displacements shed light into what I argue are the broader issues at stake. Hence, I claim that the current attacks – as those staged against the theology of liberation in the 1970s and 1980s – have as their main goal to make a strong case for oppression, social injustice and the exploitation of people and earth. Put otherwise: they seek to counter the pedagogies of empathy, justice, and care that have been advanced by feminist, anti-racist and anti-colonial activists and scholars for decades and thanks to which certain, though limited, gains have been made. As such, they entrench the 'coloniality of power' (Quijano 2000) and constitute 'pedagogies of cruelty' (Giraldo 2021; Segato 2018). In other words, what is sought by those weaponizing gender in the public sphere is to quell any challenge to the modernity-coloniality project (understood as the only possible future for humanity) which both depends upon and entrenches the utter exploitation of everything that is alive.

The chapter is organized as follows. In Section two, I position myself, briefly present the decolonial approach and define some of the key terms deployed. Section three points to the theoretical, political and empirical flaws of liberal readings of the weaponization of gender that isolate 'gender' in detriment of other aspects. I take the rejection, in 2016, of a peace agreement between the then Colombian government and the guerrillas of the Fuerzas Armadas Revolucionarias de Colombia (FARC; or Revolutionary Armed Forces of Colombia – People's Army) to end the world's longest conflict partly because of 'the ideology of gender' as an empirical example revealing this. While the Colombian case does not constitute the first instance of the weaponization of gender in the public sphere, its local specificities – notably, the country's six decades of experience in the effective deployment of 'red-baiting' strategies for propaganda purposes, i.e. using communism and socialism to scare voters – shed light on the issues currently at stake at a more global scale. In Section four, I further show that the late weaponization of gender goes indeed well beyond gender to include broader struggles over justice and the social order. I show that these struggles were orchestrated from above in reaction to the organized challenge from within Latin America to the Catholic orthodoxy and its justification of widespread suffering, misery, exploitation and injustice as natural phenomena that are God's will. Hence, designating them as 'populist' is theoretically flawed and politically counter-productive. I first briefly present the theology of liberation, which emerged with the purpose of contesting capitalism, inequalities, colonialism and US imperialism from within a Catholic framework. Second, I show how Catholic orthodoxy – whose main figure at the time was Joseph Ratzinger as prefect of the Congregation of the Doctrine of Faith (CDF) – read the theology of liberation and its inherent demands for social justice. I do this by focusing on *The Ratzinger Report* (Ratzinger and Messori 1985), a paramount text that provides crucial keys to support my argument. Section five aligns the twenty-first-century activism of Catholics and Christian coalitions against social justice with that of high-profile secular academic figures who are currently operating in the public sphere as global educators. I claim that the persecution they have been carrying out against fields of research that study structural inequalities and advocate for social justice constitutes a perfect instantiation of pedagogies of cruelty. The chapter concludes by briefly advancing that in order to counter the effective implementation of pedagogies of cruelty, it is necessary to devise pedagogies of care. Which pedagogies of care to devise is left for future work.

Setting the Analytical Framework

I am writing this piece from a specific locus of enunciation: as an atheist, left-wing, non-liberal, and non-white Latin American feminist whose scholarly universe has been informed by twenty-one years of life and study in Europe as a member of the Colombian diaspora. Born and raised in the Medellín of the 1970s and 1980s, I am a survivor of the multi-faceted violence that has consistently kept Colombia in the list of most violent countries on earth. Ravaged by a succession of governments pushing for the utter liberalization and exploitation of resources and the implementation of genocidal policies aimed at exterminating dissent and maintaining social hierarchies unchanged (see Giraldo 2021; Hristov 2014) and a long-lasting low-intensity armed conflict, Colombia has been the most enduring right-wing bastion of Latin America for decades on end. This is despite the fact that it boasts one of the oldest nominal democracies of the region.

Apart from being Colombian by birth, I also have spent the last ten years of my life studying Colombian mass media, politics and history. Because of my first-hand experience of researching Colombia from within an Anglo–American tradition (that I aim to open up to Latin American critical thought) while being fully integrated in a Western-European society (French-speaking Switzerland, of which I am also a citizen), I am located at an analytical vantage point. From this point I have been observing that – as I have written elsewhere (Giraldo 2021: 13) – 'dystopian Colombian reality might correspond to the utopia envisioned by the economically ultra-liberal and socially ultra-conservative governments that are now being comfortably elected across the world'. Indeed, in 2015, US army

General John F. Kelly stated that Colombia had proved to the world 'that the battle for the narrative is perhaps the most important fight of all' (Kelly 2015), while in 2020, the Trump presidential campaign in Florida (United States) used 'disinformation and red-baiting tactics exported from Colombia' in an attempt to 'to sway Florida's Latinx vote' (Salazar 2020). Moreover, 'Colombian violent tactics to enforce the modernity–coloniality project that further ensures successful upwards redistribution are now being imported by other countries in Latin America and beyond' (Giraldo 2021: 13), to the extent that some authors have asked themselves whether Colombia's present will become their country's future (Hristov 2014: 11). Even though this piece is not specifically about Colombia, it emerged and draws from an event of the weaponization of gender that took place there in 2016 and which offers keys that pinpoint what is at stake. Recentring Colombia and Latin America can help expand our analytical vision field to understand current global trends and organize accordingly.

Some key concepts I deploy in this piece require definition: 'decolonial approaches', 'modernity–coloniality', 'the coloniality of power', 'pedagogies of cruelty', 'populism' and 'the ideology of gender'. The term 'decolonial' has become ubiquitous of late in dominant (Anglo–American) academia. In the process, it has begun to be opportunistically deployed and is then becoming useless as an analytical concept and being stripped of its critical potential. I contend that, as a concept, 'decolonial' is intrinsically connected to the intellectual context from which it emerged: the critical engagement with the fifteenth-century colonial experience as enunciated from within Latin America. My drawing from 'decolonial approaches' – which I denote so for lack of a better term and which include the theology of liberation – derives not (only) from an impulse that seeks to disrupt the 'geopolitics of knowledge' (Mignolo 2002: 59), but from the fact that they offer keys to address what is currently at stake. A pivotal point in these approaches is the question of modernity, 'considered as a global phenomenon originating on 12 October 1492' with the arrival of European conquerors in Amerindia (Giraldo 2016: 160). Such a displacement has a major corollary: that 'Europe's centrality within the world-system is not the result of an internal superiority accumulated during the European Middle Ages about and against other cultures [but...] is instead a basic effect of the discovery, conquest, colonization and integration (submission) of Amerindia' (Dussel, cited in Castro-Gómez 2008: 21). Thus, from this perspective, there is no 'modernity' without 'coloniality' therefore the notion of 'modernity–coloniality' (Giraldo 2016: 160). From this derives 'the coloniality of power' (Quijano 2000: 342), which invokes the structures of power established with the colonization of Amerindia, while 'coloniality', on its own, can be defined as 'the invisible threads of power that emerge in colonial situations but extend well beyond a strictly colonial setting and period' (Giraldo 2016: 161).

Working from within a decolonial framework, Rita Segato is one of the least known scholars in Anglo–American academia. Yet her work is rich and has explanatory potential. One of her conceptual tools is that of the 'pedagogies of cruelty': acts and practices that teach, accustom and programme people to capture life in order to replace it for 'the sterility of inanimate things that are measurable, saleable, purchasable in ways that are very convenient to the current apocalyptic phase of capitalism' (Segato, cited in translation in Giraldo 2021: 9). Otherwise put, they are strategies that work towards the training of people in justifying capitalist exploitation and, as such, they entrench coloniality. I understand these pedagogies as key components of the propaganda apparatus of 'states, capitalism and the global modern-colonial project [...] which train people to accept that the predation on life and territories to transform them into tools and/or spaces for exploitation – and the extermination of anyone who hinders or threatens this exploitation or the comfort of the urban middle classes – is not only inevitable but necessary to attain or maintain *progress*' (Giraldo 2021: 11–12; emphasis added).

Contributing to disentangle the 'populist' conundrum – itself a 'conceptual minefield' (Stavrakakis and Jäger 2018) – is beyond the aim of this piece. What is central, however, is emphasizing that addressing the weaponization of gender from the perspective of mainstream populist studies obscures the issues at stake. According to Anton Jäger (2018), a systematic 'lack of historical analysis has allowed the term populism to retain a plasticity rivalled by few other concepts'. In the European context, the term has become a common epithet to designate 'everything politically odious' (Jäger 2018). Yet, as Stavrakakis and Jäger argue, what is encapsulated in populism points to the syntagma 'the people can rule' at the heart of democracy. This works as a discursive construct with the power to function as 'a crucial political call and a constitutional principle precisely because it incarnates a future-oriented emancipatory desire' (Stavrakakis and Jäger 2018: 555). Considered from such a perspective, which is the one I take here and which is heavily inspired by Laclau (2005), populism aims at 'fostering the mobilisation of excluded sectors of society with the aim of changing the status quo' (Mudde and Rovira Kaltwasser 2017: 3).

Finally, there is 'ideology', which is still widely understood in its Marxist sense of 'false consciousness'. I am aligned with approaches that have moved past this definition and take ideologies to be 'frameworks of thinking and calculation about the world – the "ideas" with which people figure out how the social world works, what their place is in it, and what they ought to do' (Hall 2016: 131). Thus, the 'ideology of gender' is indeed a concept (and a useful one for that matter), that refers to a set of ideas about gender and sexuality that are central in the current ideological struggles over the social order.

The 'Ideology of Gender' beyond Gender

Responses to the various cases of weaponization of gender in the public sphere that have taken place since the late 2000s, have succeeded one another in a variety of platforms so that a great wealth of takes on the issue have been in circulation for a while (Bracke and Paternotte 2016; Careaga-Pérez 2016; Fassin 2011; Fillod 2014; Kuhar and Paternotte 2017; Robcis 2015). Yet the vast majority of these responses (if not all) have been articulated from within liberal frameworks of critique and have roughly read it from within a 'moral panic'/backlash narrative. Most have focused on 'gender' in isolation as the main category of analysis and many have advanced the same two-fold quasi tautological argument: first, that the 'theory of gender' and the 'ideology of gender' are rhetorical strategies that reframe gender and sexuality in the realm of nature. Second, that they have been mobilized by (lay and non-lay) Catholic activists and intellectuals in order to counter the political gains obtained in the West with regard to reproductive rights for women and to the extension of marriage and adoption rights for homosexual men and lesbians (Garbagnoli 2016; Robcis 2015).

Two responses deserve a closer look because they warn against simplistic readings that take gender at first degree, thereby ignoring hidden issues, and/ or proceed from within a 'backlash narrative'. In the first one, it is argued that despite 'gender' being the explicit prima facie of the debate, these attacks reveal another malaise. In order to break the deadlock, goes the argument, it is crucial to recognize that 'the criticism of the new populist Right [...] uncover pertinent issues which resonate with the public', namely the 'undelivered promises of equality and representation' of the current realizations of liberal democracy (Grzebalska, Kováts and Pető 2017). In other words – and as the article's title makes explicit – the weaponization of the 'gender ideology', the authors claim, derives from a 'rejection of the (neo)liberal order' (Grzebalska, Kováts and Pető 2017).

In the second response, Paternotte (2019a) summarizes the theoretical, empirical and political weaknesses of the backlash narrative, first proposed by Susan Faludi in 1991 and which has already been widely critically addressed (Browne 2013; Leach 2020). The important point that emerges from his take is how a narrow focus on gender and sexuality has drawbacks because 'anti-gender' campaigns cannot be dissociated from other political and cultural articulations such as race, nation and the idea of the future of the 'European civilisation' (Fassin 2019), on the one hand, and wider attacks on academic freedom and democracy, on the other (Paternotte 2019b).

Paternotte identifies the dots, yet he fails to connect them. This derives from the fact that his critique remains securely anchored within a liberal (Western) framework of analysis (as do virtually all other responses, for that matter). The drawbacks of the liberal framework include that it is very tepid in its critique of capitalism, is stubbornly Western-centred, is obtusely obsessed with an ill-defined 'populism' – in turn perceived as the most immediate danger to democracy itself understood solely through a liberal lens – and starts from the premise that all critique addressed to the liberal world-order is by default anti-intellectual and anti-progressive (itself a problematic term). With respect to Grzebalska, Kováts and Petö (2017), it is safe to say that while the authors are correct in going beyond 'gender', their recentring of social class to the detriment of race is theoretically flawed and politically extremely questionable: it sidesteps intersectionality thus presenting a skewed analysis and offering compassion to elite-driven movements that instrumentalize the 'people' and openly peddle racial hatred. Additionally, it does not stand empirical scrutiny, as the results of the 2019 British general election – which pitted an elite-run, pro-austerity and pro-neoliberal party against an overtly anti-austerity and anti-neoliberal project led by someone virtually all mainstream media branded as a 'populist' – unmistakably showed.

Against this, my argument is that focusing on gender and remaining within a liberal framework of critique elides what is really at stake which is a quest for maintaining hegemony over a vision of the world that is cross-cut by coloniality. Otherwise put, although the Catholic organizations carrying out these attacks explicitly weaponize 'gender' – both as a category of analysis and as a field of study – their target is much wider and includes social movements aiming at a transformation of power differentials along several axes and of the social field. By the same token, what these organizations seek to defend is a world order that is anthropocentric, patriarchal and capitalist, that is, one that is traversed by coloniality. Moreover, such a world order is shared at the secular end of the ideological spectrum, the difference being its key principle: God, for the former, Science (in the traditional sense), for the latter. From within a decolonial perspective one could say that traditional Catholics look back at the first phase of modernity in which Europe was the centre of the world and the Christianism religion was omnipotent and the source from which all power emanated (as in the fifteenth century); the latter at the second phase of modernity, that is, the age of the Enlightenment, humanism, the conception of a disembodied subject of knowledge and the West as 'the point zero' (Castro-Gómez 2010: 25) of knowledge production.

The dominant liberal critique of the weaponization of the 'gender ideology' shares with the Catholic/Christian coalitions weaponizing it an understanding of the term 'ideology' in its Marxist sense. From this, three conclusions entail: first, that the second term in 'gender ideology' does rhetorical work that conjures up a world in which 'gender' would belong to the sphere of beliefs and ideas rather than to that of reality (Bracke and Paternotte 2016: 144). Second, that 'gender ideology' is an 'invention' of the Vatican and the Catholic right and that, as such, it does not correspond to a concept of analysis. Third, that 'gender ideology' is inexorably rhetorical and therefore has no real political potency. Yet it is the syntagma 'ideology' which allows us to see that what is at stake in the weaponization of gender goes beyond gender and sexuality. As a rhetorical strategy it seeks to induce fear of anything aimed at challenging the neoliberal capitalist status quo. This is why the Colombian case is enlightening: as I argue elsewhere (Giraldo n.d.) it provides an empirical example of a successful weaponization of gender orchestrated by Catholic and Evangelical organizations which entailed dreadful larger political effects (Giraldo 2017). Firstly, it mobilized the Colombian electorate to reject the 2016 referendum on the peace agreement between the Colombian state and the FARC, which aimed at putting an end to a seven-decade-long conflict. Secondly, it forced the recalling of the school manuals specifically designed by the Department of Education, to promote the respect of sexual differences in scholar environments, at the origin of the campaign successfully orchestrated by the Catholic right against the referendum.

Because of a complex array of historical reasons – including the very longevity of the FARC – the rhetoric of the cold war has never really abated in Colombia and, as the rejection of the referendum showed, it is still operative. In fact, the term 'ideology' has a lot of sway in Colombia because it conjures up a deeply ingrained hatred of anything left-wing shared widely within the social body. This has been maintained thanks to the more than seven-decade-long US-backed counter-insurgency war (Lindsay-Poland 2018), which has been thoroughly accompanied by intense anti-communist (Kirk 2003) and pro-neoliberal propaganda (Bailey 1965) up to the present (Giraldo 2021). Hence, in Colombia, the weaponization of 'gender ideology' in the months prior to the referendum managed to organize historic despise for left-wing policies (which have been amalgamated in the national imaginary as being equivalent to communism and/or guerrillas), homophobia, anti-feminism and resistance to gender-equality in effective combination. As summarized in one Facebook message widely circulated at the time: 'Colombia is in danger! Of falling under the control of a communist dictatorship and the imminent passage of a gender ideology' (Giraldo 2017).

An Elitist Defence of Widespread Misery

On the surface this might appear as a peculiarity of a local context, but the global scope of Catholicism, on the one hand, and the growing resistance to capitalism and neoliberalism across the globe, on the other, have started to shift the rhetorical ground in the West so that concepts and ideas that have been declared dead for a while – such as ideology and populism – have been dominating the debate floor of late. Moreover, and because of being home to 500 years of non-stop Indigenous and popular anti-colonial resistance, Colombia and Latin America have been pivotal locations for both the Catholic counter-reformation (Lernoux 1989), on the one hand, and the violent implementation of neoliberalism (Giraldo 2021; Hristov 2014), on the other. And these are at the heart of the ideological struggles of which the various cases of the weaponization of gender (during the previous decade) and the outlawing of critical theory (currently starting to gain steam) are instances.

The decade of the 1960s saw a number of events on both sides of the Atlantic that set into motion a chain of orchestrated actions from the hierarchy of the Catholic Church against democratic expansion and social change:

1. The emergence of critical theory and the Frankfurt School, which in turn provided intellectual force to the 1960s student movements in Europe (Bronner 2017: 90).
2. The Second Vatican Council (1962–1965).
3. The emergence of the theology of liberation.
4. Its subsequent official adoption by the Latin American episcopate in 1968.

In Latin America, the period was one of political turmoil but, as Eduardo Mendieta eloquently puts it, this was, above all, a period 'of cultural renewal and utopian yearning' (Mendieta 2020). And it was this spirit that the Catholic hierarchy (as well as Latin American dominant classes and the United States) sought to uproot. In the historical genealogy I am tracing here, I identify as the key points and figures in the quelling of any possibility of social change from within the Catholic Church John Paul II's staunch anti-communist views, Joseph Ratzinger's elitism and orthodoxy, and Colombian (first Archbishop then Cardinal) Alfonso López Trujillo's extreme pro-capitalist, anti-communist, misogynistic and homophobic views.

The Second Vatican Council (Vatican II) introduced changes on liturgy, practice and doctrine that had effects in the very understanding of the social function of the Catholic Church.[1] In Latin America, this translated into the embracing of the theology of liberation – a radical overhauling of the church, doctrine and faith (see Ellacuría and Sobrino 1990) – by the continent's ecclesiastic hierarchy. This happened at the second conference of the Consejo Episcopal Latinoamericano (CELAM) (Episcopal Conference of Latin America) which took place in 1968 in Medellín, Colombia. Because of its occurrence in the aftermath of Vatican II, the conference, as Eduardo Mendieta puts it, 'created the church context for the consolidation of what was in effect a social movement': the emergence of grassroots communities (*comunidades de base*) that allowed for a greater participation of common people in their church and society (Mendieta 2020). In a complete reversal of orthodox theology, it was the actual life experiences of those belonging to these communities which became the main point of departure for the theological exercises of the theology of liberation (Lernoux 1989: 91).

Having emerged in a continent where Catholicism had historically been so important, the theology of liberation and its bold adoption by the Latin American episcopate in 1968 had concrete and all-encompassing revolutionary potential. Firstly, it challenged the binary opposition centre/periphery (Europe/rest of the world) with regard to theology (theory making within the Church) so central in Catholicism. This was a thoroughly anti-colonial move that facilitated the development of critical currents of thought in which the notion of 'liberation' from different forms of oppression – particularly colonialism and capitalism – was key. Secondly, it approached faith through the prism of historical realities and of a serious 'commitment to work for social justice' (Lernoux 1989: 94). This, in turn, 'led to the emergence of a new, more militant faith' (Lernoux 1989: 91). Thirdly, it reversed the teachings of the Catholic Church that the accumulation of wealth in a few hands while the vast majority was impoverished was God's will (Lernoux 1989: 99).

In epistemological terms, and as Mendieta (2020) signals, it introduced a 'whole new language' and a new conceptual toolbox that influenced several currents of thought whose common thread was opposition to colonialism, imperialism and neo-imperialism. Some of the notions/approaches in this conceptual toolbox included the expression 'a preferential option for the poor', thus effectively breaking the historical allegiance – despite the widespread poverty and extreme inequalities across the continent – of the Catholic Church to the dominant classes; the 'underside of history', which points to the recentring of the periphery as a productive locus of enunciation; 'the church of the people', which highlights its pro-democratic and anti-hierarchical approach; the idea that 'orthopraxis is prior to orthodoxy', which emphasizes the precedence of acting over theoretical elucubrations (Mendieta 2020).

Unequivocally, the theology of liberation was extraordinarily radical. It entailed a turn towards a historical material framework that took reality not as a God-given, immutable design but as the result of human-made politics. From within this revised paradigm, injustice and inequality were no longer conceived as being part of a natural order that people had to accept with resignation but the product of the plans and actions of people of power on the basis of their own particular interests. Thus, it was taken by some as 'the herald of a larger movement "of the excluded – women, non-whites, the poor – onto the stage of history"' (Berryman, cited in Lernoux 1989: 96).

Not surprisingly, the theology of liberation was perceived as being 'highly subversive' (Lernoux 1989: 79), not only by the Roman Catholic hierarchy, but also by the Latin American dominant classes and the United States.[2] Its official adoption by the Latin American episcopate in the Medellín CELAM marked the onset of a ruthless counter-reaction – whose socio-political effects have been long lasting – from three ranks: the Roman Catholic hierarchy spearheaded by Cardinal Joseph Ratzinger, the reactionary wing of the Latin American church – from then on led by the late Colombian Cardinal Alfonso López Trujillo – and the United States.

Three texts published in the 1980s (Ratzinger 1984, 1986; Ratzinger and Messori 1985) advance the theological justification for the persecution of the theology of liberation and the counter-reformation. They are paramount to support my argument because they provide the keys to understand that rather than simply gender/sexuality, the struggle is over social order. However, *The Ratzinger Report* (Ratzinger and Messori 1985) is longer, broader in scope (therefore richer) and, most importantly, was addressed to a wider audience.[3] It summarizes Ratzinger's position at that point in time as prefect of the CDF – a position he was appointed to in 1981 – which derives from Vatican II and its giving birth to the theology of liberation, on the one hand, and the broader intellectual influence of critical theory and the Frankfurt School, on the other. A progressive theologian up to the 1960s, Ratzinger was profoundly affected by the student protests – intellectually inspired by the critical theory that came to be associated with the Frankfurt School (Bronner 2017) – that had swept Europe in that decade (Lernoux 1989). This moved him to the right so that by Karol Wojtyla's election, in 1978, his orthodoxy was already well known within Catholicism. As an academic himself, he was familiar with the larger European intellectual context and read the theology of liberation as being the offspring of the 'neo-Marxism' developed by 'Adorno, Horkheimer, Habermas, and Marcuse' (Ratzinger and Messori 1985: 178).

The interviews that were carried out twenty years after Vatican II and were compiled in *The Ratzinger Report* have the central aim of providing a definite interpretation of the Council's documents which, he claimed, were misinterpreted and abused by many (Ratzinger and Messori 1985: 27). A corollary of this was to make clear that the theology of liberation was akin to heresy. Three main points worthy of mention advanced in these interviews are: first, the idea of a transcendent and hierarchical Church (Reid 1987) whose 'mystery' is 'supranatural' and in which 'reformers, sociologists, organizers have no authority whatsoever' (Ratzinger and Messori 1985: 46). Second, that the 'battles of "liberation"' have been so extreme that they have given rise to the idea of 'escaping from the "slavery of nature", demanding the right to be male or female at one's will or pleasure, for example, through surgery' (Ratzinger and Messori 1985: 95). Third, that 'the defense of orthodoxy' is in fact 'the defense of the poor' because it saves 'them pain and illusions which contain no realistic prospect even of material liberation' (Ratzinger and Messori 1985: 170).

For Cardinal Joseph Ratzinger, it is the reading of reality from a historical framework that pushes the 'arbiters' of liberation to, first, recentre the concepts of 'people, community, experience, and history' against the 'totality of the Church', which must encompass 'laity and hierarchy' (Ratzinger and Messori 1985: 181). Second, argue for social justice, a goal that he sees as 'contrary to the true purpose of human life' (Ratzinger 1984). Indeed, Ratzinger is openly vocal against what he perceives as a sort of populism inherent in the theology of liberation which, rather than theology, he reads as a socio-political movement.

Teaching to Oppose Social-justice as a Pedagogy of Cruelty

The core of the argument I advance, then, is that rather than simply gender, what the Catholic and Christian coalitions that have been weaponizing it in the twenty-first century are concerned about is social justice (which includes gender/sexuality). I take an intellectual, historical approach that recentres Colombia (which also provides an empirical example), Latin America, the persecution of the theology of liberation by the Vatican in the 1970s and the theological orthodoxy of Joseph Ratzinger, thoroughly encapsulated in *The Ratzinger Report* (1985).

Although empirical support for my argument is drawn from the 2016 Colombian case, other contemporary contexts provide even more compelling evidence. One study carried out in the United States (Coley 2017) is paradigmatic because its findings perfectly encapsulate my argument. They show that 'the adoption [or rejection] of LGBT groups and inclusive non-discrimination policies' by Christian colleges follow the logic behind their respective theological approaches: those colleges with 'communal orientations', i.e. whose theological emphasis is on 'social justice' tend strongly to adopt policies of non-discrimination towards LGBT groups, whereas those with 'individualist orientations', i.e. whose theological emphasis is on 'personal piety', 'impede the adoption of such groups and policies' (Coley 2017: 87).

Coley's findings also show that there is not necessarily a direct mapping between religiosity and intolerance to sexual diversity and/or support for oppression, although this link is constantly thrust by those instrumentalizing liberal feminist agendas for Western expansionist projects and/or for justifying the implementation of racist policies.[4]

This point here is crucial because if the Catholic and Christian coalitions on both sides of the Atlantic have been efficient in weaponizing gender to push for broader agendas that reframe what is historical and political within the realm of nature, high-profile academics and pundits have been doing the same but from within secular frameworks. To put it bluntly, both Catholic/Christian coalitions and a certain high profile secular cohort have been organizing themselves to do political work – while disingenuously claiming that their motivations are non-ideological and apolitical but based on divine/scientific truth – in order to push for a clear political agenda whose aim is to entrench coloniality. A very telling example, among far too many, is the blog post *Why Universities Must Choose One Telos: Truth or Social Justice* (Haidt 2016) which has been shared via social networks by figures such as Steven Pinker.

Indeed, a wide range of academics, authors and pundits in the English-speaking world have been very diligent in manufacturing arguments from within informed frameworks explicitly aimed at thoroughly undermining the scholarly credibility of approaches within the social and human sciences – particularly gender studies, critical theory and postcolonial studies – that have shown how exploitation and social inequalities are the product of historical and political processes (therefore transformable) rather than natural (therefore immutable). The endgame here is to make a case for maintaining power differentials across multiple social and geographical axes and for capitalist exploitation. In decolonial terms, the endgame is to make a case for the further expansion of the modernity–coloniality project and therefore for the entrenchment of coloniality. This, in turn, presupposes the acceptance of a hierarchical model of social organization where the comfort of a minority depends on the suffering of a majority and accepting this requires a certain level of cruelty.[5] Hence, making a case for the entrenchment of coloniality is a strategy that aims at training people in cruelty, and this is what I call, following Rita Segato, 'pedagogies of cruelty' (Giraldo 2021; Segato 2018).

Some of the secular academics actively pursuing this strategy – such as Jordan Peterson and Steven Pinker – operate in the public sphere as global intellectuals and are thus assuming the role of global educators, a role magnified in the twenty-first century thanks to the expansion of global media – mainstream and alternative media, online magazines, the Web 2.0 and popular science books – which constitute crucial vehicles for the dissemination of ideas and values. Indeed, while the term 'pedagogy' usually conjures up formal educational frameworks, contemporary media texts also fulfil, as Lilie Chouliaraki has claimed, a pedagogical function that renders them 'effective form[s] of moral education' (Chouliaraki 2008: 832). This point about 'moral education' is crucial in the current struggles for hegemony over the social order. It is through contemporary media texts that – as I argue elsewhere (Giraldo 2021) – pedagogies of cruelty have become effective at training people in 'selective desensitisation', i.e. in teaching people to develop the capacity to entirely preclude empathy for those who have been marked in the hegemonic world order by otherness: certain women, LGBT+ persons, non-whites, disabled people, poor people and the elderly. And this constitutes a very particular form of moral education. It is one that fosters cruelty. Simultaneously, this moral education in cruelty – supported in equal measure though differently declined by Catholic/Christian activists and secular academics/pundits – is disingenuously carried out for the sake of children's rights to an education that is based on, the narrative goes, biological (divine/evolutionary) facts, not *ideological* ones.

As I was working on this piece, during late 2020 and early 2021, the reviling of critical theory – which includes the critical reading of race and racial relations in the postcolonial present – erupted fully in the UK's public sphere when during a Commons debate on Black History Month, the women and equalities minister – Kemi Badenoch, a Black woman herself, which adds symbolic potency to the fact – said that the British government did not want white children being taught about 'white privilege and their inherited racial guilt' (Murray 2020). The attack against critical theory – also articulated from within Catholic orthodoxy in the context of the persecution of the theology of liberation, as discussed above – is connected with the making of 'cultural Marxism' the bogeyman, a strategy that has been deployed for some time in the Americas (Busbridge, Moffitt and Thorburn 2020), but has only been recently imported into Europe.

All this, again, reveals that although the point of entry might vary – gender, sexuality, race, critical theory, cultural Marxism, wokeism – these contemporary ideological struggles are over the social order. Moreover, the debate is over social justice. The contemporary academic right (both liberal and conservative) has been diligently framing the debate/struggles so that critical analyses of the status quo, and/or those that read current injustices from within a larger framework that posits the colonial past as being constitutive of the inequalities existing in the postcolonial present, are made to appear as if detached from reality.

Objectively speaking, there should not be factual or interpretative contention about the statement that European colonial powers built their progress and prosperity on the exploitation of the nations they ransacked and the peoples they enslaved. Nor about the fact that the accumulation of capital thrives on labour exploitation and that inequalities guarantee a system of privileges that benefit a small portion of humanity. Yet it is the presenting of such objective facts and interpretation from within scholarly frameworks which is at the heart of the high-profile systematic harassment and smearing campaigns against entire academic fields and researchers.

Despite their claiming otherwise, the debate is actually not over facts (or how to interpret them) but over how to position oneself ethically with regard to those facts/interpretations. Indeed, recentring the suffering of those who have found themselves at the receiving end of systematic shaming strategies, murder, exploitation and plunder; or pointing out the fact that the prosperity of the North has been made possible thanks to the exploitation of the South is what ignites the ire of those engaged in hindering a critical assessment of the past while pushing for the entrenchment of coloniality. Further evidence of this is that, in reaction to the advances in critical readings of the past and present and of the historicization of social injustice, they have been coining, reappropriating, deploying and weaponizing a glossary curated with the specific aim of denigrating the very fact of having empathy: 'woke', 'snow-flake', 'virtue signalling', 'social justice warrior', 'the culture of victimhood', 'grievance studies' etc. This alone poignantly underscores that what is actively sought by such a cohort – in alignment with the Catholic–Christian orthodoxy – is to 'manufacture consent' (Herman and Chomsky 2008) with regard to exploitation, hierarchies and injustice. Otherwise put: the aim of such ideological work is to foster and expand the human capacity for cruelty. As such they constitute clear instantiations of 'pedagogies of cruelty'.[6]

Towards Pedagogies of Care

In this piece I proposed a reading of the various instances of the weaponization of gender that took the world by storm during the second decade of the twenty-first century. To do this, I shifted the epistemological ground from within the usual liberal framework towards a decolonial one – hence Latin American – that recentres the 'coloniality of power'. I proposed that what has been taking place are struggles that pit opposing views on how the world works and how it should work, that is, 'ideological struggles'. These are for hegemony over the social order. As such they put either pedagogies of cruelty or of care into play. The former aim at training people into accepting that the exploitation of life is inevitable in humanity's continual march towards the future which is, in turn, conceived as the ever expansion of the modernity-coloniality project and therefore thoroughly capitalist. The latter aim at teaching empathy, prioritising a sense of community, and building a better world for all. The debate is therefore ethical and calls for an overhaul in approach, theoretical frameworks, vocabulary and pragmatic engagement. To put it in Rita Segato's terms: we find ourselves living in a historical moment in which two projects guided by divergent approaches to well-being and happiness coexist. The first one is 'the historical project of things, whose satisfaction aim is functional to capital and produces individuals that, in turn, transform themselves [or others] into things'. The second one is 'the historical project of affective bonds, whose aims are to foster reciprocity, [and empathy, I would add,] and which produces community' (Segato 2018: 18).[7] It is to this latter pedagogy of care that this piece or chapter contributes.

Notes

1   Vatican II was not well received by the conservative wing of the Catholic hierarchy. Although only Marcel Lefebvre – a staunch defendant of Catholic fundamentalism and founder of the Society of Saint Pius X (SSPX) – decided to entirely reject it, the

orthodox wing of Catholicism, the Opus Dei, for instance, still resisted it stealthily (see Walsh 1989: 72–4). The pontificate of John Paul II (with the help of Cardinal Joseph Ratzinger, among others) brought about what can be unequivocally described as a Counter Reformation (see Lernoux 1989) that sought to reinterpret Vatican II so that orthodoxy and tradition were upheld. In this regard, Ratzinger was very clear: the root of the crisis generated by Vatican II is the idea of church itself (see Ratzinger and Messori 1985).

2   In 1969, Richard Nixon, then President of the United States, judged the theology of liberation to be more dangerous than communism itself (Martel 2020: 496), while Reagan's advisors wrote the document 'A New Inter-American Policy for the Eighties' which served as a charter to his administration and whose proposals, which were adopted, included attacks on the theology of liberation because it 'was held responsible for the church's criticism of "productive capitalism" in Latin America' (Lernoux 1989: 90).

3   In her historical genealogy moving back the point of origin of the attacks against gender orchestrated from within the Roman Catholic hierarchy from the 1990s to the 1980s, Mary Anne Case also takes *The Ratzinger Report* as a foundational text (Case 2019). However, she takes gender in isolation whereas, as I claim here, what is at stake is broader.

4   As I was writing these lines, a referendum against wearing the burqa in the public space – organized by the UDC, the Swiss far-right party – was voted for by a thin majority in Switzerland. The campaign, not surprisingly, put the emphasis on the ideas of *women's freedom* and *gender equality*.

5   Another good example is that infamous article titled 'The Case for Colonialism', published and then retracted in *Third World Quarterly*, and the controversy that ensued.

6   For a full exploration of this argument, focusing on a case of mass-murder perpetrated by the Colombian army between 2002 and 2010, see Giraldo (2021). See also Phelan (2019: 455) for an examination of 'how the notion of social justice has been articulated […] in "alt-right" sub-cultures […] and in the critique of social justice formulated by the neoliberal theories of Friedrich Hayek'.

7   Author's translation.

References

Bailey, Norman A. (1965), 'The Colombian "Black hand": A case study of neoliberalism in Latin America', *The Review of Politics*, 27 (4): 445–64.

Berryman, Phillip (1987), *Liberation Theology: Essential Facts about the Revolutionary Movement in Latin America and beyond*, Philadelphia: Temple University Press.

Bracke, Sarah and David Paternotte (2016), 'Unpacking the sin of gender', *Religion and Gender*, 6(2): 143–54.
Bronner, Stephen Eric (2017), *Critical Theory: A Very Short Introduction*, New York: Oxford University Press.
Browne, Victoria (2013), 'Backlash, repetition, untimeliness: The temporal dynamics of feminist politics', *Hypatia*, 28 (4): 905–20.
Busbridge, Rachel, Benjamin Moffitt and Joshua Thorburn (2020), 'Cultural Marxism: Far-right conspiracy theory in Australia's culture wars', *Social Identities*, 26 (6): 722–38.
Careaga-Pérez, Gloria (2016), 'Moral panic and gender ideology in Latin America', *Religion and Gender*, 6 (2): 251–5.
Case, Mary Anne (2019), 'Trans formations in the Vatican's war on "gender ideology"', *Signs: Journal of Women in Culture and Society*, 44 (3): 639–64.
Castro-Gómez, Santiago (2008), '(Post)coloniality for dummies: Latin American perspectives on modernity, coloniality, and the geopolitics of knowledge', in Mabel Moraña, Enrique Dussel and Carlos Jáuregui (eds), *Coloniality at Large: Latin America and the Postcolonial Debate*, 259–85, Durham and London: Duke University Press.
Castro-Gómez, Santiago (2010), *La Hybris del Punto Cero. Ciencia, raza e ilustración en la Nueva Granada (1750–1816)*, Bogotá: Editorial Pontificia Universidad Javeriana.
Chouliaraki, Lilie (2008), 'The media as moral education: Mediation and action', *Media, Culture & Society*, 30 (6): 831–52.
Coley, Jonathan S. (2017), 'Reconciling religion and LGBT rights: Christian universities, theological orientations, and LGBT inclusion', *Social Currents*, 4 (1): 87–106.
Ellacuría, Ignacio and Jon Sobrino (1990), *Mysterium liberationis: Conceptos fundamentales de la teología de la liberación*, Madrid: Editorial Trotta.
Faludi, Susan (1991), *Backlash: The Undeclared War against Women*, London: Vintage.
Fassin, Éric (2011), 'A Double-edged sword: Sexual democracy, gender norms, and racialized rhetoric', in Judith Butler and Elizabeth Weed (eds), *The Question of Gender: Joan W. Scott's Critical Feminism*, 143–58, Bloomington and Indianapolis: Indiana University Press.
Fassin, Éric (2019), 'Brésil: le laboratoire intersectionnel du néolibéralisme', *d'Analyse Opinion Critique*, 5 October. Available online: https//aoc.media/opinion/2019/10/04/bresil-le-laboratoire-intersectionnel-du-neoliberalisme/?loggedin=true (accessed 22 October 2020).
Fillod, Odile (2014), 'L'invention de la "thérorie du genre": le mariage blanc du Vatican et de la science', *Contemporary French Civilization*, 39 (3): 321–333.
Garbagnoli, Sara (2016), 'Against the heresy of immanence: Vatican's "gender" as a new rhetorical device against the denaturalization of the sexual order', *Religion & Gender*, 6 (2): 187–204.
Giraldo, Isis (2016), 'Coloniality at work: Decolonial critique and the postfeminist regime', *Feminist Theory*, 17 (2): 157–73.

Giraldo, Isis (2017), 'The "gender ideology" menace and the rejection of the peace agreement in Colombia', *Discover Society*, December. Available online: https://archive.discoversociety.org/2017/12/06/the-gender-ideology-menace-and-the-rejection-of-the-peace-agreement-in-colombia/ (accessed 15 May 2021).

Giraldo, Isis (2021), '"Pedagogies of cruelty", masculinity, and the patriarchal order of the Colombian Nation-State: The falsos positivos as a paradigmatic example', *Postcolonial Studies*, 24 (1): 63–81.

Giraldo, Isis (work in progress), *Regimes of Colombianidad: Beauty, Citizenship, and Sex*, Pittsburgh: University of Pittsburgh Press.

Grzebalska, Weronika, Eszter Kovátz and Andrea Pető (2017), 'Gender as symbolic glue: how "gender" became an umbrella term for the rejection of the (neo)liberal order', *Political Critique*, 13 January. Available online: http://politicalcritique.org/long-read/2017/gender-as-symbolic-glue-how-gender-became-an-umbrella-term-for-the-rejection-of-the-neoliberal-order/ (accessed 22 October 2020).

Haidt, Jonathan (2016), 'Why universities must choose one telos: Truth or social justice', *Heterodox Academy*, 21 October. Available online: https://heterodoxacademy.org/blog/one-telos-truth-or-social-justice-2/ (accessed 26 February 2021).

Hall, Stuart (2016), 'Ideology and ideological struggle', in Jennifer Daryl Slack and Lawrence Grossberg (eds), *Cultural Studies 1983: A Theoretical History*, 127–54, Durham and London: Duke University Press.

Herman, Edward S. and Noam Chomsky (2008), *Manufacturing Consent: The Political Economy of the Mass Media*, London: The Bodley Head.

Hristov, Jasmin. (2014), *Paramilitarism & Neoliberalism. Violent Systems of Capital Accumulation in Colombia and beyond*, London: Pluto Press.

Jäger, Anton (2018), 'The myth of populism', *Jacobin Magazine*, 1 March. Available online: https://jacobinmag.com/2018/01/populism-douglas-hofstadter-donald-trump-democracy (accessed 20 October 2020).

Kelly, General John F. (2015). 'Colombia's resolve merits support', *Miami Herald*, 3 May Available online: https://www.miamiherald.com/opinion/op-ed/article20047503.html (accessed 24 September 2019).

Kirk, Robin (2003), *More Terrible than Death: Violence, Drugs, and America's War in Colombia*, New York: PublicAffairs.

Kuhar, Roman and David Paternotte (2017), *Anti-gender Campaigns in Europe: Mobilizing against Equality*, London: Rowman & Littlefield International Limited.

Laclau, Ernesto (2005), *On Populist Reason*, London and New York: Verso.

Leach, Brittany R. (2020), 'Whose backlash, against whom? Feminism and the American pro-life movement's "mother-child strategy"', *Signs: Journal of Women in Culture and Society*, 45 (2): 319–28.

Lernoux, Penny (1989), *People of God: The Struggle of World Catholicism*, New York: Viking.

Lindsay-Poland, John (2018), *Plan Colombia: U.S. Ally Atrocities and Community Activism*, Durham and London: Duke University Press.

Martel, Frederic (2020), *Sodoma. Enquête au cœur du Vatican*, Paris: Robert Laffont.
Mendieta, Eduardo (2020), 'Philosophy of liberation', in Edward N. Zalta (ed), *The Stanford Encyclopedia of Philosophy*, Winter 2020, Metaphysics Research Lab, Stanford University. Available online: https://plato.stanford.edu/entries/liberation/ (accessed 23 November 2020).
Mignolo, Walter (2002), 'The geopolitics of knowledge and the colonial difference', *The South Atlantic Quarterly*, 101 (1): 57–96.
Mudde, Cass and Cristóbal Rovira Kaltwasser (2017), *Populism: A Very Short Introduction*, New York: Oxford University Press.
Murray, Jessica, (2020), 'Teaching white privilege as uncontested fact is illegal, minister says', *The Guardian*, 20 October. Available at: https://www.theguardian.com/world/2020/oct/20/teaching-white-privilege-is-a-fact-breaks-the-law-minister-says (accessed 1 October 2020).
Paternotte, David (2019a), 'Backlash: A misleading narrative', *Engenderings*, 13 February. Available online: https://blogs.lse.ac.uk/gender/2020/03/30/backlash-a-misleading-narrative/(accessed 22 October 2020).
Paternotte, David (2019b), 'Gender studies and the dismantling of critical knowledge in Europe', *American Association of University Professors*. Available online: https://www.aaup.org/article/gender-studies-and-dismantling-critical-knowledge-europe#.X5G-K5qxWEJ (accessed 15 May 2021).
Phelan, Sean (2019), 'Neoliberalism, the far right, and the disparaging of "social justice warriors"', *Communication, Culture & Critique*, 12 (4): 455–75.
Quijano, Aníbal (2000), 'Colonialidad del poder, eurocentrismo y América Latina', in Edgardo Lander (ed), *La colonialidad del saber: eurocentrismo y ciencias sociales. Perspectivas Latinoamericanas*, 201–46, Buenos Aires: CLACSO.
Ratzinger, Joseph Cardinal (1984), *Instruction on Certain Aspects of the 'Theology of Liberation'*. Available online: https://www.vatican.va/roman_curia/congregations/cfaith/documents/rc_con_cfaith_doc_19840806_theology-liberation_en.html (accessed 18 October 2020).
Ratzinger, Joseph Cardinal (1986), *Instruction on Christian Freedom and Liberation*. Available online: http://www.vatican.va/roman_curia/congregations/cfaith/documents/rc_con_cfaith_doc_19860322_freedom-liberation_en.html (accessed 18 October 2020).
Ratzinger, Joseph Cardinal and Vittorio Messori (1985), *The Ratzinger Report: An Exclusive Interview on the State of the Church*, San Francisco: Ignatius Press.
Reid, J. K. S. (1987), 'The Ratzinger report', *Scottish Journal of Theology*, 40 (1): 125–33.
Robcis, Camille (2015), 'Catholics, the "theory of gender," and the turn to the human in France: A new Dreyfus affair?', *The Journal of Modern History*, 87 (4): 892–923.
Salazar, Miguel (2020), 'Could Colombian politicians help Trump win Florida?', *The Nation*, 30 October. Available online: https://www.thenation.com/article/politics/trump-biden-florida-election/ (accessed 5 November 2020).
Segato, Rita (2018), *Contra-pedagogías de la crueldad*, Buenos Aires: Prometeo libros.

Stavrakakis, Yannis and Anton Jäger (2018), 'Accomplishments and limitations of the "new" mainstream in contemporary populism studies', *European Journal of Social Theory*, 21 (4): 547–65.

Walsh, M. (1989), *The Secret World of the Opus Dei*, Glasgow: Grafton Books.

3

Truth, Power, Pedagogy: Feminist Knowledge and Education in a 'Post-truth' Time

Raewyn Connell

Introduction

In the half century since the women's liberation movement launched its critique of men's dominance in school systems and universities, feminists have put great energy into developing distinctive pedagogies and distinctive approaches to knowledge. The two projects have not always worked together, but often enough they have. The results are both a rich literature, and a great deal of practical experience, in epistemology and education.

Is this literature and experience still relevant? We are vehemently told that we live in New Times. Admittedly this has been said before, by Dr Marx and Mrs Thatcher among others. But there is a new version of the New Times idea, in which knowledge and education are particularly at stake. If young people now know the world mainly through their mobile devices, if knowledge is now basically a commodity that corporations can buy and sell, if well-known truths about the world can profitably be ignored by authoritarian politicians and the mega-rich, then it seems that key assumptions made by generations of feminist researchers and educators no longer hold.

My chapter is a reflection on this problem. I consider some changes in social worlds that underlie the 'post-truth' idea; then the contemporary restructuring of gendered power; and finally some implications for feminist intellectual and educational practice. The chapter first took shape as an address to a conference held in the Australian city of Newcastle, at thirty-three degrees south, in the shadow of an abandoned steelworks.

Post-truth Times?

In 2016 the Oxford Dictionaries declared 'post-truth' to be their Word of the Year. Merriam-Webster had made 'truthiness' their Word of the Year already in 2006. The idea has been around for a couple of decades, that politics is now dominated by appeals to emotion and identity rather than fact. Politicians repeat their talking points over and over again, simply ignoring proof that they are wrong – and win campaigns by doing so.

The most visible case in the Global North was the 2016 Trump presidential campaign, with its barrage of slanders against the opposing candidate and sweeping claims to restore America's greatness. Second was the unexpectedly successful Brexit campaign in the UK, with its massive misrepresentation of the costs of European Union membership. The Trump administration is now ended, though its electoral defeat was narrow. What remains is a paranoid style of politics, spread via the Tea Party movement in the United States and the anti-immigrant and ultra-nationalist movements in both countries. In these milieux, conspiracy stories and fear memes have been spread thickly by social media, by far-right mass media (especially, though not only, the Murdoch conglomerate) and by increasingly influential racist parties and their leaders.

An important part of the story is the rejection of scientific findings about climate change, in a far-reaching campaign funded mainly by the fossil-fuel industries, including the mega-rich Koch brothers. The rhetoric represented scientists and their research as part of a conspiracy against America, against jobs and cars, against freedom, economic growth and common sense. Something similar had been managed in earlier years by the tobacco industry, against cancer research, but that deception has lost ground. The new campaigns gained much more traction. They expanded into attacks on green movements, on wind farms, on environmental protection and on scientific and professional expertise generally. The attitude to truth was perfectly captured by the Trump ambassadorial nominee who declared that she believed 'both sides of the science' (Gander 2018: np).

The United States and the UK are not the only places with these symptoms. Australia contributed a notable moment, the 'Children Overboard' fraud during the 2001 election campaign. The right-wing government's 'border protection' rhetoric was given a huge boost by ministerial claims that refugees had thrown their own children into the sea, to force Australian ships to rescue them. The claims were not challenged by the mass media at the time, though later shown by a Senate committee to be false. The demonization of President Dilma in Brazil, the Chinese government's systematic lying about the concentration camps in Xinjiang and the current Hindu-nationalist government's systematic lying about Kashmir show that the techniques of misrepresentation and denial are widespread.

But is this new? The Tea Party and Trump may epitomize 'the paranoid style in American politics', but it was in 1964 that Richard Hofstadter published the famous article of that name. Hofstadter's first example was Senator Joseph McCarthy, who in the 1950s peddled the fantasy that the American government was riddled with communist subversives. Hofstadter's main point, however, was that the political style was older and wider than McCarthyism. If we travel in time and space beyond the United States, it is not far to the era of the Big Lie as practiced by Iosif Stalin and Joseph Goebbels. The fantastic lying by Stalin's regime in the murderous show trials of the 1930s is hard to beat, though Goebbels certainly tried. Not long before those efforts came the magnificent British lies of the First World War, such as the carefully circulated tale of the corpse factory where the wicked Germans were supposed to be boiling down soldiers' corpses for their fat.

And going back before that, we come to the high tide of colonialism. European empire legitimated itself through fantasies of degraded and primitive peoples waiting to be civilized by more advanced peoples, such as those very advanced souls who gathered in November 1884 around Bismarck's table in Berlin to carve up Africa. We come to the sinister idea of *terra nullius* – a social attitude more than a legal doctrine – that defined the homelands of many millions as empty lands 'belonging to nobody'. This idea legitimated settler colonialism and genocide from Canada and the United States, to Siberia, Argentina and Australia.

Given this vast landscape of self-interested untruth, is there anything distinctive about the era of Boris Johnson, Narendra Modi, Donald Trump or Scott Morrison? Not in terms of the intensity or the reach of the distortions. If Trump made unprecedented use of social media, Goebbels in his day made unprecedented use of radio, while the 'yellow press' of late nineteenth-century New York became famous for both large circulation and fabricated news.

Yet one has the uncomfortable feeling that while Stalin, Goebbels and the British chief of army intelligence who claimed to have invented the corpse factory knew perfectly well that they were lying, that is not convincingly the case with twenty-first-century authoritarians. What has changed, we might argue, is not the scale of lying but its discursive presupposition. Perhaps we are seeing a weakening of the tension between truth and falsehood that underpins the concept of a 'lie'. That could explain why confronting the propaganda with the facts – the normal critical response, in an earlier generation – no longer works to discredit the liars. The widespread partisan acceptance of the quickly fabricated 'stolen election' lie in late 2020, despite its prompt rejection by US courts, is a remarkable illustration.

But we need to go further. These distortions involve a complicity between the power-holders and their supporting constituencies – the 'base', as journalists now call it – that excludes counter-argument. An identity of interest is called into existence, which did not pre-exist the distortions. In that respect, the classical concept of ideology expounded by Lukács and Mannheim and adopted by many feminist scholars, which supposed a pre-existing interest that was expressed by the ideological framework, no longer applies. If that is correct, a critical response needs to go further than the unmasking of interests that classical ideology-critiques attempted. The only effective response is constitutive, the *making* of knowledge in other and more adequate forms.

New Configurations of Patriarchal Power

What are the wider conditions for these difficulties with meaning and truth? Feminist research has revealed the many facets of the power structure sustaining women's subordination. In the 1970s the term 'patriarchy' was revived in Global-North feminism to name this structure. In the 1990s queer theory popularized the idea of a heteronormative gender 'binary'. Both terms have their uses, but both drift towards a static understanding of gendered power and culture. It is crucial to recognize that the gender order is historically dynamic, and that power structures are constantly being re-configured.

Economic changes are among the drivers of these reconfigurations. The last generation has seen a stunning financialization of capitalist economies. Most wealth no longer takes the material form of dark satanic mills and their sooty satanic machines. Rather, wealth is mainly held in the form of financial instruments – stocks, bonds, pension fund entitlements, futures contracts and a marvellous array of derivatives. These entities have neither colour nor smell, and no permanent home, though they can be accessed via the glass towers in the financial districts of Manhattan, Frankfurt, Chicago, Shanghai, Tokyo or São Paulo. Here they are packaged and traded. This work is done overwhelmingly by men, in heavily masculinized workplaces – formerly noisy 'pits', now computerized trading rooms – supported by other masculinized professions ranging from corporate law to computer engineering.

Some of these assets have a traceable relationship to the factories, but for most, the connection is remote. The value of a financial asset is what the market says it is, i.e. the amount for which the asset can currently be sold in the masculinized milieu of the financial markets. To understand how the markets work, it is not enough to know the legal forms of financial property. One must also understand the electronic technology through which it is held and traded, the computer-based algorithms that embody the trading strategies, and the workforce that actually operates the system (Stark 2009; Zaloom 2006). A new form of patriarchal power, mostly anonymous and impersonal and with enormous effects – dramatized by the 2007–2008 global financial crisis but working constantly – now sits in a central part of the international economy.

Private wealth, though the legal basis of this industry, has over time become strikingly collectivized, in the form of transnational corporations and the financial markets just described. Both of these main forms operate constantly across national boundaries: to a striking extent, wealth has been sent offshore. The transnational corporation operates across jurisdictions to minimize taxes. Large personal or family fortunes extensively use tax havens. Wealth in circulation through financial markets is now a large part of what ties the global economy together.

Beginning with the Pinochet dictatorship in Chile in the 1970s, the development strategies of most regimes around the Global South, which formerly aimed at local industrialization and balanced development, have been replaced by the search for export staples that give comparative advantage in global markets. (This is the story behind the abandoned steelworks in Newcastle: the company that built and operated them, BHP, gave up on manufacturing and reverted to being an export-oriented mining company; it now trades coal, iron ore, copper and petroleum in international markets.) This neoliberal development strategy has tied economies in the postcolonial world much more closely to the institutions of the Global North, since restructuring has been combined with the deregulation and opening of local markets to transnational firms, and the growth of international debt on a massive scale.

Putting all this together, compared with 1973 when the United Nations published its first report on 'multinational corporations', the economy that shapes everyday life has become incomprehensible to most of the people who work in it, and has moved, to an increasing extent, beyond the control of elected governments.

Yet the effects of this incomprehensible economy are tangible. Enormous wealth has accumulated at the top of the income scale. In most countries, economic inequality grew steeply from the 1970s to the beginning of the new century – the trend that made Piketty's *Capital in the Twenty-First Century* a best-seller. As neoliberal policy regimes were installed, income taxes were cut and relative spending on public services – infrastructure, education, health and housing – has declined. These were the services that were expected to give social legitimation to capitalist states in the post-Second World War decades. The gendered shift of resources here is notable. Women collectively depend more on transfers through the state, while men collectively depend more on market incomes. There has been an *economic* gender backlash, though one that is rarely named or called to account.

Anti-union measures and casualization of workforces have weakened worker protections and bargaining power. In many developing countries the informal or 'grey' economy, where there is no job security and few social services, accounts for half of all economic activity. The end of the Cold War brought no peace dividend. Military spending has remained high, about 1,917 billion dollars worldwide in the year 2019, directing resources into strongly masculinized institutions with a vested interest in ideas about threat, attack and defence.

There are, then, perfectly good reasons for widespread feelings of uncertainty and fear. In this environment, right-wing politics – funded by the privileged classes who control a rising proportion of the social wealth – have responded quite effectively with a combination of force and fantasy.

The force is expressed in growing state authoritarianism, in policing which increasingly takes a paramilitary shape, and in massively increased surveillance (from the epidemic of CCTV in Britain to the new facial recognition technology in China). The fantasy is basically about inciting fear and directing it towards outside enemies or stigmatized internal groups. We have seen the continuing war on drugs, the new war on terror, incitement of Islamophobia and hatred of refugees, 'border protection' and vigorous revivals of racism, homophobia and misogyny. Samuel Johnson once called patriotism 'the last refuge of the scoundrel'; now it seems to be the first refuge. Concern with economic justice is not on the agenda. A number of new-right regimes maintain the neoliberal agenda of cuts in taxation and further privatization of public assets, moves which straightforwardly *increase* the level of inequality.

Re-imagined authoritarian nationalism takes many forms, of course, but a persistent element is a recuperative masculinity politics. This attempts to roll back the gains that feminist and homophile politics have made over the past two generations. Recuperative masculinity politics often uses the rhetoric of defending 'the family'. The right-wing leader becomes a symbolic protector for those who are fearful of further change, whether towards gender justice, ethnic pluralism or economic equality.

It isn't the poor who provide the bulk of support for the new authoritarianism. Research on 'why Trump won' in 2016 concentrated on his unorthodox appeal to the 'white working class', yet most of his votes came from existing Republican voters – i.e. groups privileged in terms of race, gender and class. Yet ethno-nationalism can recruit or intimidate substantial numbers of women, working-class men and even racial minorities. Ethno-nationalism is the note most constantly sounded by the contemporary right, from Xi to Putin to Johnson to Morrison. Once they are in the saddle, they have no commitment to public interest or common good that would stop a new-right regime using the familiar techniques of intimidation, voter suppression, patronage, harassment of opposition, heavy-handed policing and bribery to keep themselves in power.

Feminist Knowledge Work

It may seem a long jump from these grim scenes to the quiet world of epistemology, but there is a connection. The central achievement of feminist knowledge-making, over centuries and continents, has been to contest Big Lies. Feminist research as well as activism challenged the core stories of patriarchal ideology that defined women as deficient in intelligence, morality, creativity, loyalty, public-spiritedness or any other capacity that defined human worth. As the contemptuous title of a Mozart opera put it, *Così fan tutte* – women are all like that.

Like the gender order as a whole, gender ideology changes over time. The stories told in public by right-wing politicians now are less likely to emphasize women's innate inferiority. Rather, spokesmen maintain that feminism is obsolete, since discriminatory laws have now been abolished and equal opportunity reigns. (Apart from laws against abortion, to which populist conservatism clings with some fervour.) Alternatively, it is claimed that women have now gained so many legal privileges that it is men who are the disadvantaged sex.

There is a religious strand in this politics (Garbagnoli and Prearo 2017). An international 'anti-gender' campaign, which combines homophobia, anti-feminism and hostility to trans groups, has significantly widened the old slander against homosexual men that they prey on children. The charge of corrupting children or being a threat to children is now made by right-wing publicists against sex education, anti-bullying programmes (such as the Australian 'Safe Schools' programme), gay marriage, gay and lesbian parenthood, and feminist reform of any area of the school curriculum. Creepy memes about 'gender whisperers' in schools are circulated by no less than the current Prime Minister of Australia (Butson 2018).

But has feminism created its own difficulty in answering such claims? There is a strand of thought that sees feminism itself as helping to erode a straightforward concept of truth. Critiques of patriarchal ideology have shown, sometimes in numbing detail, how men's dominance in society, and dominance in specific disciplines of natural sciences and humanities, have resulted in self-serving doctrines and biased research. In proposing alternatives, feminists have long emphasized women's distinctive perspectives on the world, and the need to include emotion and embodiment in our account of knowledge (Crowley and Himmelweit 1992; Harding 2008).

Feminist thought has emphasized the standpoint of the knower as an influence on what is known. When that insight is combined with the deconstructionist approach to language that has been influential for queer theory, and the anti-normativity that has been equally influential for queer activism, it is possible to conclude there is no objective knowledge and no shared truth. This is a complaint often made by anti-feminist writers.

Feminism as the struggle for gender justice does not logically imply a culture where every group, or even every individual, claims their own truth. But in the context of the United States particularly, with its powerful individualism and its entrenched rights of private property, this slide can easily occur. Such difficulties are not easily resolved, especially in a time when the political momentum remains with the authoritarian-nationalist right. But perhaps we can see a direction in which solutions can be found.

The moment of *critique* is only one side of feminist approaches to knowledge. There is also the moment of *knowledge-making*, the building, weaving, germinating and nurturing side. In this element of knowledge work, encounters with the world are transformed into concepts and understandings, and made available for learning, use and new investigation. I see this as a parallel to the institution-building approach that Elaine Unterhalter (2007) takes to global social justice in feminist education; and to the ontoformativity that Susan Rudy (2019) finds in lesbian experimental writing.

A more complete understanding, then, emphasizes that knowledge-making is a social process, indeed a labour process involving a workforce, whether formal or informal (Connell 2019). As we know from studies of academic disciplines, that workforce is gendered in specific ways (such as the masculinization of the workforce in mathematics, which feeds into the masculinization of finance mentioned earlier). The notion of a 'standpoint' is a first approximation to analysis of the workforces producing different forms of knowledge and culture, and making use of them in professional life.

In this light, we can read discussions of 'feminist methods' not just as providing abstract criteria for knowledge, but also as descriptions of a workforce – perhaps, a workforce yet to be assembled – capable of working in different ways from the currently dominant academic and research institutions.

The emphasis on collective work, rather than a star system, in feminist discussions speaks to the logic of collective action that is fundamental to the research-based knowledge formation. The emphasis on embodied knowledge and the importance of emotion in knowledge work argue for a workforce that is not just gender-equal but that also is prepared to put a full range of human responses into knowledge-making. The ways to broadcast the findings of such research practice might look very different from the emotionally arid, hyper-specialized academic journals of today. The demand for socially relevant knowledge production, if it is not to become cover for corporate, authoritarian or military control of research, implies a democratic process of making decisions about the resources that enable research to be carried forward.

Developing a workforce and working collectively is not compatible with a purely anti-normative model of radical action. The knowledge project requires norms of honesty, justice, co-operation and corrigibility, to enable a social learning process to happen on a large scale.

Education and the Gender Order

Feminist strategies in education have centred on schooling for girls and literacy campaigns for adult women. Remarkable successes have been gained, especially where the agenda meshed with the economic development plans of postcolonial states. The excellent 2003 UNESCO report, *Gender and Education for All*, gave evidence of a global move towards parity, though it also noted gender disparities remaining. Literacy has increased massively, and educational participation by girls and young women now exceeds that for boys and young men in many parts of the world.

Though the subject curriculum is typically conservative in its definitions of content, and has been deeply patriarchal in the past, there have been real gains in making curricular materials more inclusive. Women now figure in history lessons once populated only by kings and conquerors. Drama lessons have become a vehicle for working through gender dilemmas. There is active work on making STEM fields more welcoming for girls and women, though we still have a long way to go in this area.

Feminist educational thought has been less engaged in strategizing for the education of boys, though there have been many declarations about the issue. While any privilege for boys and men remains, it is easy to understand feminists' reluctance to direct even more resources their way. But gender is interactive, it is a matter of relationships, not sealed-off silos. The education of boys and men matters for the lives of girls and women. I think feminist educational thinkers are right to take a robust interest in this field, as women in the school-teaching workforce do on a daily basis.

This requires thinking about the changes in gendered power that I sketched earlier. For instance, the 'breadwinner' image of masculinity is increasingly obsolete, given the widespread casualization of workforces, a changed balance of educational qualifications between women and men, and altered family structures. Its ghost still haunts the 'family values' rhetoric of the political right. But even in Japan, where the 'salaryman' model provided a classic instance of hegemonic masculinity, contestation and change have been visible for a generation (Roberson and Suzuki 2003). Familiar hierarchies of masculinities are now in question in many places. There was a majority vote for 'gay marriage' in Australia in 2017, in a kind of referendum actually initiated as a culture-wars manoeuvre by the political right. This victory speaks to the changed, if not yet revolutionized, position of gay men in popular culture (and hopefully, though less clearly, the changed position of lesbian women).

The strategies of feminist educational work, therefore, cannot remain static. If education is basically the nurturing of capacities for practice (Connell 1995), it must take into account the changing circumstances of practice. Feminist educators have indeed thought about the capacities for practice in women's lives that the education of girls should support – capacities for work and earning, for making decisions and exercising rights, for care, love and solidarity. We need to think in the same way about men's lives and the education of boys. Men too need capacities for work, decision-making, care and solidarity. We know this is possible because, contrary to patriarchal ideology, a vast body of research demonstrates that the psychological characteristics (including learning capacities) of women and men as groups are actually very similar (Connell 2021).

But – and this is crucial for educators – there can be huge differences in the circumstances in which boys and girls, and different groups of boys and girls, develop these capacities. Here, as well as gender hierarchy, the malign consequences of colonization, ethnic and caste exclusion, and class exploitation come into play. They shape life in schools and colleges, and informal learning contexts too. They influence who holds power in education systems, who makes policy, and how the teaching workforce is educated. This is the terrain of the real political struggles that are involved in democratizing education for the future.

In building educational projects adequate to the world we now live in, the knowledge resources of the Global South are needed (Epstein and Morrell 2012). Mainstream curricula in school and university systems are not in any simple sense 'Western knowledge'. However, they do mostly derive from a knowledge formation in which the elite institutions of the Global North have hegemony, while other sources of authority are marginalized (Reiter 2018). This represents a massive loss of capacity for global education. We cannot afford this, and the situation is gradually being altered by postcolonial scholarship, decolonial and anti-racist curriculum projects, Indigenous Knowledge movements and more. As I argued earlier, it is in the *making* of knowledge that the most effective responses to lies and distortions can be found. One implication is we need much wider participation in the making of knowledge. Democratic knowledge movements exist, and are important, for instance in environmental action. A legitimate goal of education is to expand the citizen workforce capable of critique and knowledge-making. The wealth of feminist thought and knowledge from the Global South is a strong, currently underused, resource for this work.

The capacities we seek to develop in education are collective as much as they are individual. Ultimately they involve the development of new capacities for action by society as a whole. This is easy to imagine with the familiar idea of technological change, but the point applies just as strongly to changing social relations – among them, gender relations. We can collectively, rather than individually, build new gender orders.

That is, indeed, the real significance of the authoritarian nationalist movements discussed earlier in this chapter. Though critics speak of 'backlash' and the movements themselves speak of 'restoring tradition', it is in fact *new* patriarchies that they are building. This involves new institutional arrangements and new pinnacles of power, and among the consequences are more insecurity and a pervasive corruption of culture.

Happily there is no guarantee that their agenda will succeed. We can do better! If the perspective of this chapter is right, struggles for gender justice and struggles for truth are fundamentally connected. That can be frightening, but it can also be inspiring. Resources for the combined struggle can be found all over the world.

References

Butson, Tyron (2018), '"Gender whisperers": Scott Morrison criticised for "hateful" tweet about trans students' [Television program], *SBS News*, SBS Television. Available online: https://www.sbs.com.au/news/gender-whisperers-scott-morrison-criticised-for-hateful-tweet-about-trans-students (accessed 8 November 2019).

Connell, Raewyn (1995), 'Transformative labour: Theorizing the politics of teachers' work', in Mark. B. Ginsburg (ed), *The Politics of Educators' Work and Lives*, 91–114, New York: Garland Publishing.

Connell, Raewyn (2019), *The Good University*, London: Zed Books.

Connell, Raewyn (2021), *Gender: In World Perspective*, 4th ed., Cambridge: Polity Press.

Crowley, Helen and Susan Himmelweit (eds) (1992), *Knowing Women: Feminism and Knowledge*, Cambridge: Polity.

Epstein, Debbie and Robert Morrell (2012), 'Approaching southern theory: Explorations of gender in South African education', *Gender and Education*, 24 (5): 469–82.

Gander, Kashmira (2018), 'Both sides of the science' *Newsweek*, 12 July. Retrieved from: https://www.newsweek.com/kelly-craft-new-us-ambassador-canada-climate-change-stance-both-sides-science-1248596 (accessed 8 November 2019).

Garbagnoli, Sara and Massimo Prearo (2017), *La croisade 'anti-genre': Du Vatican aux manifs pour tous*, Paris: Textuel.

Hofstadter, Richard (1964), *The Paranoid Style in American Politics and Other Essays*, New York: Vintage.

Harding, Sandra (2008), *Sciences from below: Feminisms, Postcolonialities, and Modernities*, Durham: Duke University Press.

Piketty, Thomas (2014), *Capital in the Twenty-First Century*, Cambridge, MA: Harvard University Press.

Reiter, Bernd (ed) (2018), *Constructing the Pluriverse: The Geopolitics of Knowledge*, Durham and London: Duke University Press.

Roberson, James E. and Nobue Suzuki (eds) (2003), *Men and Masculinities in Contemporary Japan: Dislocating the Salaryman Doxa*, London: Routledge Curzon.

Rudy, Susan (2019), 'Gender's ontoformativity, or refusing to be spat out of reality: Reclaiming queer women's solidarity through experimental writing', *Feminist Theory*, 21 (3): 351–65. Retrieved from: https://doi.org/10.1177/1464700119881311

Stark, David (2009), *The Sense of Dissonance: Accounts of Worth in Economic Life*, Princeton: Princeton University Press.

UNESCO (2003), *Gender and Education for All: The Leap to Equality*, Paris: UNESCO.
Unterhalter, Elaine (2007), *Gender, Schooling and Global Social Justice*, London: Routledge.
Zaloom, Caitlin (2006), *Out of the Pits: Traders and Technology from Chicago to London*, Chicago: University of Chicago Press.

4

Something Resembling 'Truth': Reflections on Critical Pedagogy in the New 'Post-truth' Landscape

Sondra Hale

Timothy Snyder, in his 2017 book *On Tyranny*, eloquently warns that 'To abandon facts is to abandon freedom. If nothing is true, then no one can criticize power because there is no basis upon which to do so. If nothing is true, then all is spectacle.'

Introduction

Timothy Snyder's statement above and related ones were going through my mind when I was revisiting Hannah Arendt's *The Origins of Totalitarianism* where she said that 'The ideal subject of totalitarian rule is not the convinced Nazi or the dedicated communist, but people for whom this distinction between fact and fiction, true and false, no longer exists' (Arendt 1951: 474). It seems, in the 'post-truth' era (if we accept that term), we have encountered just such totalitarian leaders and those who are convinced by them. As many of you know, one of Donald Trump's advisors, Kellyanne Conway, when asked by the press about some of Trump's statements which were shown to be lies, referred to them as 'alternative facts'.[1]

Even *Time Magazine* entered the business of truth-questioning with a 2017 cover theme that asked 'Is Truth Dead?'[2] Truth or 'facts' seem to be on everyone's mind. A 2018 play which opened on Broadway based on a book by John D'Agata

---

I have borrowed part of my title from a show at the Broad Museum, Los Angeles, 10 February to 13 May 2018—'Jasper Johns: Something Resembling Truth'.

was titled *The Lifespan of a Fact*. A new book by Michiko Kakutani, former book editor of *The New York Times*, has offered us *The Death of Truth: Notes on Falsehood in the Age of Trump*. In it she blames postmodernism and deconstruction (which she says are favourites of the left) for giving a model to the right-wing. Quote, 'The postmodernist argument that all truths are partial (and a function of one's perspective) led to the related argument that there are many legitimate ways to understand or represent an event' (Kakutani 2018). One result, she claims, has been the displacement of reason by emotion (2018). *New York Times* columnist, David Brooks, interviewed students at various elite US universities, and soon got the idea that this generation has very low expectations. One student remarked that 'we don't even have a common truth'. Another claimed that 'we don't even have a common set of facts' (in Brooks 2018).

It is not new for scholars and others to question the 'hard facts' of history and other fields. The late historian, Hayden White, in the early 1970s, saw history as storytelling and deemed all stories to be fiction. He argued that historical meaning is imposed on historical facts through storytelling (White 1973). Of course, I could go on and on, but I am simply trying to make the point that the universalism of 'truth' and the validity of the concept of 'post-truth', when brought into focus, are on shaky ground, but arguably not only for the reasons we have been led to believe. As we know, the *Oxford English Dictionary* assigned 'post-truth' the 2016 Word of the Year, defining it as 'denoting circumstances in which objective facts are less influential in shaping public opinion than appeals to emotion and personal belief'.

My purpose in this chapter is to discuss the phenomena arising from an era which is rampant with questions about what is true and what isn't, why it is important to us educators and community activists beyond the obvious, why it is, to some extent, a gendered phenomenon, and if we have strategic pedagogies with which to intervene. Additionally, some of the other major questions I ask in this chapter are whether or not it is counter-productive in this era to see the notion of 'truth' as fragmented, ambivalent and negotiable. As a teacher[3] in a number of settings I have been unsettled when challenged in the classroom and in community settings with counter-facts or ideas that I know or think I know to be patently false. Do I have the tools, methods and critical pedagogical strategies such as Freirean and feminist tools to deal with 'post-truth', as well as the wisdom to deal with the populist atmosphere that pervades? I am asking if we are equipped to negotiate 'truth' and 'facts' with our students/mentees, or are we to end up teaching entirely with metaphors? In the end, are we overlooking the possibility that this populist challenge to prevalent, established and mainly

Western/white/male hegemonic knowledge production espoused in our educational institutions and elsewhere may be a decolonizing and democratizing process at work?

Clearly, with the rise of both right-wing and left-wing populism in a number of Western countries and beyond, many people and groups are rejecting the status quo, claiming to speak for 'the people', and are therefore raising a number of questions about the 'facts' and ideas taught to them in schools, mainstream media, community and state – questions to which we in education, perhaps, are most obliged to respond. There is no doubt that this is a crisis, not only for education with its already dubious neoliberal tilt, but also for theorists of critical pedagogy, for teachers/facilitators in both institutional settings and in community settings, for women inside and outside of these settings, and for relativists in various disciplines, such as some in anthropology.

Since I first started thinking about this chapter, the world has been engulfed by, arguably, the most devastating pandemic ever. This pandemic has now been written about so much that it is difficult to capture anything new or helpful for us teachers/mentors. There is no doubt that Western institutions of learning at all levels have been turned upside down. The problems are more than having to teach remotely and learn a pedagogy that accommodates, more than depriving students of sociability, of full curricula, and turning evaluations upside down, and the like. It's hard to visualize or imagine what the post-pandemic will be like – perhaps both destructive and creative. Do we have the politics, tools and wisdom to take this on?

To be in a classroom or giving a community presentation of some sort, and have someone contradict what one has claimed, citing social media sources or something they heard from others whom they see as more like them or watched on YouTube – that is, having someone challenge one's 'received truth' – can be a stunning moment for most educators. Women professors, after all, had only just begun in the last few decades to gain credibility as significant knowledge producers. One is already on shaky ground if one tries to argue that what the student has gleaned from elsewhere is a 'non-truth', most especially if that 'truth' is based on the student's own experience.

Let me share a story from my first year of teaching at Unity High School for Girls in Khartoum, Sudan in the early 1960s. I was a new English teacher but I had agreed to be a substitute for a couple of days in a senior geography class. I began my session with a geography cliché – holding up a globe, in the belief that visuals are strong pedagogical tools – and saying that the world is round, expecting to build from there. A student from India whose family was living in Khartoum nearly bolted out of her chair with her hand up. I was momentarily pleased because I thought she was going to remind me that the earth is really spherical. She said, 'But Mrs Hale,[4] the world is *not* round'. I gave her a pleased smile, but she continued with, 'The world is flat'. After some pause, I had little choice, it seemed, because of my not wanting to humiliate one of my brightest students, so I sputtered something like, 'Yes, Anjali, there are many interpretations, but today let's pretend the world is round; let's use it as a metaphor'. She seemed stimulated by that idea, and we went on.[5] But one can see that this incident is still haunting me – even fifty years later.

Certainly in the past and arguably even more so today, teachers of evolution, climate science, ideas about when a foetus becomes a human, etc. might often encounter responses similar to Anjali's. This is an age-old problem for the classroom teacher or community mentor, especially in very strongly religious areas. There is nothing new in my story. But what *is* new is the changed landscape in which teachings of the sort I just mentioned are being challenged – not only by contrary religious teachings or alt-right sources – that has always been the case – but also by what the students or community members have learned, not only on the internet and from populist sources, but also from many of our leaders. Context is everything – but it is a constantly changing context.

Certainly such experiences raise many dilemmas for me, as someone who has been experimenting with postcolonial and postmodernist ideas and who has tended to question the concept of 'truth' in my classes and community work. I am, as well, someone who already has had a strong propensity for self-subverting and deconstructing everything, including 'truth', at the same time that I am a leftist activist who seeks a kind of 'truth' in liberation, freedom or insurrection, whether or not this truth is grounded or metaphorical (a seeming contradiction). As an activist I also came under the sway of speaking truth to power, a leftist cliché. But Margaret Atwood brings us up short by insisting: 'if you're going to speak truth to power, make sure it's the truth' (Atwood in Sawyer 2020).

My propensity to deconstruct such absolutes as truth, reason, authenticity, logic, legitimacy, neutrality, positivism and universality make such a methodology of deconstruction central to my pedagogy. Among other methodologies and approaches dealing with truth and untruths or 'post-truth' in the twenty-first century, I look to methods I have used and to the living fieldwork that I have carried out over many decades, as well as using 'feminist process', personalized methodologies and pedagogies, and oral histories in various forms in interactive classrooms and community settings. Furthermore, I refuse to disengage from the politics that come to my door as part and parcel of my teaching and research, and refuse to set myself at a distance in both mentoring and ethnographic encounters. One of my goals has been to motivate my students (and myself) to be in the midst of it all, or the 'exact middle of a living story', to quote the poet Dylan Thomas. Perhaps I have to trust my students more as they explore this new landscape that technology has brought us. After all, once we have taken part of the journey together, I need to learn to trust them to plunge into that living story. But is it that simple, or is one plunging into idealism in a time of crisis?

For this chapter, I mused about some of these pedagogies, theories and methodologies that I have held dear, but nonetheless often subverted; and I have contemplated if these are some of the ideas I want to carry forward in this era. I have also been asking myself for many years, with considerable anxiety, when we are using critical or liberatory pedagogy, how we can abide by the protocols of the neoliberal institutions where some of us teach, and still be accountable to our students, ourselves and our politics. How can someone like me, who is still experimenting with postmodern, postcolonial, and decolonial thought, embrace the concept of 'Truth' (with a capital 'T') as contrasted to 'untruth' or 'post-truth'? Although thinking in terms of post-truth might be a method for interrupting the Modernist agendas, I wonder if these strategies lead us anywhere. And how does any of this relate to gender? Is this post-truth era more difficult for feminists/women teachers/mentors than it is for men? My inclination is to say yes... but would this argument lead us into essentializing men and women, the former as authoritarian and dogmatic, not self-critical and not self-interrogating at every turn, in contrast to the latter, women, who have more emotional and experiential tools at our disposal, are more flexible, etc. That leads to a discussion of forms of knowledge.

Forms of Knowledge

As a research academic, a mentor and an active feminist, I am profoundly interested not only in pedagogy, but also in forms and sources of knowledge and the way it is produced. I am especially interested in the ways in which women, in particular, have produced unrecognized, subversive and subjugated forms of knowledge production, not to mention, knowledge as resistance. Further, I try to ascertain the ways in which we can innovate with these knowledges; and the ways in which we can transmit these knowledges through 'critical pedagogy', a self-examination that happens simultaneously with any transmission of knowledge. Where do the populist forms of knowledge in the 'post-truth' era fit into these categories? Such are our epistemological questions.

As we know, we transmit knowledge in very diverse ways, from our technologies to arts, literature and culture; from propaganda and storytelling to silence and body language; from letter-writing to collecting memories. And now, most famously through the internet and social media. That is quite an archive!

Even though we may be aware of all of these forms of transmission, still we most conventionally and narrowly think of the transmission of knowledge as a process of teacher-to-student through the written and spoken word. However, as we know from Freire and feminist methodologists, pedagogy is not only a linear process in which we pass on knowledge, or receive it. Something can happen to the knowledge in the process of the transmission; innovation can occur, and thus, change knowledge in the process. Therefore, we need to consider the ways in which we change not only the listener/viewer or the student, and the curriculum, but also ourselves in the process, because of what the listener/viewer/student might be giving back and/or the explicit commitment to actively transforming knowledge formation (as non-linear) through feminist pedagogies. Add to that complicated process the fact that the context is surely changing with every moment.

Some Notes on the Erstwhile 'Feminist Process' of Our Golden Years

Before we go any further, following are some notes on the erstwhile 'Feminist Process' of our golden years in the United States, Western Europe and Australia, because these are some of the tools we might still need or can revise to accommodate the changing environment. By the mid-to-late 1980s, with the work of such pioneers of feminist pedagogy as Frances Maher (1985), Renate Duelli Klein (1987), Jane Kenway and Helen Modra (1989) and Nancy Schniedewind (1987), the projects were designed to focus on 'sisterhood, anti-elitism, leaderless consciousness-raising groups and the power of collective decision-making and activity' (Howe and Ahlum 1973). Duelli Klein underscored consciousness-raising as a centrepiece method. She subsumed under consciousness-raising an 'interactive teaching and learning [...] being "other" [...] in the Women's Studies classroom; and the issue of power (asymmetrical teacher-student relations, and the matter of the authority of the teacher)' (Duelli Klein 1987: 189–98). However, most of us feminist teachers at that time thought of consciousness-raising as a given, and as a consequence, is still under-theorized. According to Kenway and Modra, we do not know exactly what happens in the classroom when feminist studies students, for example, engage in it (1989: 8). Furthermore, consciousness-raising suggests that there is an unknowing, perhaps ignorant subject who needs to be taught and brought into the light, so to speak – quite contrary to Freire's thinking, as well as to the ideas of many feminist pedagogical scholars who have since critiqued such assumptions about 'consciousness-raising'. We all had to be in the picture. As early as 1987 Sandra Harding helped steer us away from positivism and put us (the teacher, the ethnographer, the interviewer etc.) into the picture. Schniedewind (1987) forwarded five process goals, borrowing somewhat from the liberatory pedagogics: mutual respect, trust and community; shared leadership; cooperative structures; integration of cognitive and affective learning; and action.[6]

Following are some of the elements out of which emerged liberatory and critical pedagogies. I have had to conflate them. Many of us are familiar with and work within foundational feminist pedagogies, and some of us work within a Freirean framework. Many of these practices that I mention below are combinations of the ones I know best and have used frequently. The 'list' is not exhaustive. These practices might be recognizable to many of us who use them to facilitate different kinds of groups, not just the feminist or ethnic studies classrooms. For example, we might apply some as guidelines for small-group dynamics in some peoples' movements. Others might see the guidelines as deriving from revolutionary Chinese groups set up for criticism/self-criticism; or as informal rules in grassroots activism and in radical Non-government Organization (NGO) activities. Some might see them as applying twenty-first century challenges to the state and to neoliberalism by the contemporary anarcho/non-hierarchical insurrections.

However, I am mentioning these following feminist and Freirean practices as pedagogical strategies as among the ways of building change into the process. These are practices that advocate: generating the student/participant as subject, with knowledge emanating from her/him; applying self-disclosure as a way of using self as subject – later often referred to as 'situating', 'positioning', 'locating' ourselves or intervening with the self; I sometimes think of it as modelling. Some feminist scholars have advocated teaching and/or facilitating through question-asking: the self as inquirer. I had attempted to interject the experiential into theory and practice. Not all of us were successful in deconstructing a singular/essentialized 'voice', and recognizing the dynamism of 'Otherness' and 'alterity'. While facilitating self-definition, we analysed labelling, naming, renaming, appropriating and reappropriating. As I said at the start, some of these various teaching techniques were used, not as singular methods, but as combinations of them, such as fusing teaching and critical consciousness-raising, likewise integrating dialogue with presentation. Feminist and Freirean mentors were always trying to create space for the traditionally silenced. One way to accomplish that was by validating everyone's experience. One of the most difficult practices was positively integrating pain and hostility into the classroom/group/community process, which, of course, differs with each new context and space. Along the way, we interjected, challenging the claims of neutrality and value-free process in positivism and empiricism, and the resultant abstracting away of the researcher as a discrete unit. Demonstrating the practice of building on each other's ideas and working in collaboration is one of the more difficult strategies to put into practice, at least it has been for me. The high value placed on competition that dominates much of Euro-American societies undermines collaboration. Another practice that is difficult to convey is fusing not only self-knowledge and social knowledge with our everyday lives, or relatedly, fusing self-knowledge and social knowledge. We can simply encourage students/mentees to use their knowledge in everyday life and everyday politics. Perhaps more importantly, to quote Freire, 'Through dialogue, the teacher-of-the-students and the students-of-the-teacher cease to exist...' as a binary (1970: 67). Freire also insisted strongly to subvert the banking system of education (where the student is a receptacle and knowledge is deposited) and replacing it with the partner-teachers or what some feminist educators refer to as 'teacher as midwife'[7] (Belenky, Goldberger and Tarule 1986: 217–19).

In addition to the practices above, Harris and Andrews (1989) underscored interaction; cooperation and trust; connected, holistic thought; intuition and insight; and closely related empathy; joining feeling and thinking; and social responsibility. Mary Belenky et al. (1986), in *Women's Ways of Knowing*,[8] singled out 'connected education'. One can almost see some of these works as preludes to Sara Ahmed's *Living a Feminist Life* (2017).

The authors of many of the feminist and Freirean pedagogical strategies mentioned above are, with few exceptions, white, which makes it seem as if these practices were totally white-dominated.[9] Fortunately, that is definitely not the case. By the late 1980s and all through the 1990s (and still today) influential African American and other feminist scholars of colour intervened and interrupted the hegemonic narrative of both white men and women. However, even before the late 1980s Gloria Anzaldúa was to write *Borderlands* (1987) one of the most influential books on feminist theories and practices, causing many of us to rethink the classroom. Indeed, although the 1980s may have been a pedagogic zenith for some, it was only a few years later in 1994 that bell hooks urged us to consider the idea of teaching as 'transgression', and joined some others in proclaiming the idea that education should be the practice, not only of resistance, but of freedom (1994). I argue that hooks was putting many of our ideas – both white feminists and feminists of colour – all together for us to forge into the classroom.

In 1989 African American scholar, Patricia Hill Collins, attracted a great deal of attention in academia. She outlined a strategy that involved using elements and themes from Black women's culture and traditions and infusing them with new meaning. She forwarded the idea of 'rearticulated consciousness' and stressed concrete experience as a criterion of meaning; the use of dialogue in assessing knowledge claims; the ethic of caring; and the ethic of personal accountability (1989).

It goes without saying that these theorists greatly influenced the way many of us teach today, as well as our ideas about what should or can go on in the classroom. As we would expect, these ideas of the 1980s and 1990s led to new and some more radical approaches to the classroom and outside in the community. We in Critical Education, Feminist Studies, Sexuality Studies, and Ethnic Studies are all still using some of these strategies in our teaching and community work and have enhanced our pedagogies with new methods, and a younger generation of feminist pedagogues have taken up these ideas, deconstructing them and raising new challenges (as in the examples in this collection). Assuming this, can we ask if the older practices are still effective or are they the products of an idealistic era?

As we know, many more recent and, arguably, more radical approaches have taken front stage in recent years. Many radical educators use Freire and expand on his ideas, taking us to social justice spaces, life-long learning, new forms of activism that spill over into the classroom, not to mention the decolonization process of Indigenous feminist scholars and others, arguably originating and reaching its strongest statements in two very different locations – South Africa and Latin America.

Some feminists and others, such as contemporary anarcho-activists, also herald teaching in radical learning spaces. We see, for example, the writers in the book edited by Robert Haworth and John Elmore, *Out of the Ruins: The Emergence of Radical Informal Learning Spaces* (2017), and myself and Gada Kadoda (2017) as part of our ongoing studies of facilitating radical ideas about social justice in safe informal spaces. One also thinks of Kathleen Weiler (1991),

Peter McLaren (1995) and later, Henry Giroux (2011), Carlos Torres (2014), Penny Jane Burke (2016) and some of the authors in an entire 2017 issue of *Occasional Papers* from the University of Newcastle, Australia (e.g. essays by Burke and Misiaszek, Burke and Gyamera, and Hale and Kadoda). Also, new pedagogical ideas emerged from the essays in a recent co-edited special issue of *Teaching in Higher Education on Gender, Post-truth Populism and Higher Education Pedagogies*, co-edited by Burke and Ronelle Carolissen (2018). Works on the pedagogy of caring and studies of digital feminist activism also pushed us forward. The pioneer Kenway is working on elite institutions, interjecting notions about class, which, for all of our talk about intersectionality, always seems to fall between the cracks of feminist teaching (Kenway et al. 2015). There is no doubt that we have developed a great many ideas and pedagogic strategies, but will they be enough for us to face the onslaught of lies and untruths so prevalent today in social media and other sources?

A Note from a 'Recovering Anthropologist': Aligning Ethnographic Methods and Classroom/Community Pedagogies

It may seem abrupt to move from feminist and Freirean pedagogical strategies to something like ethnography, but my meshing these is an attempt to explore further both ethnographic methods and feminist pedagogic practices, e.g. accountability.

In my field of research I try to interrupt modernist agendas using oral history, ethnography, auto-ethnography, self-study and memory retrieval in my quest to find methodologies and pedagogies with which to challenge the hegemonic narratives.

However, a conundrum may very well develop in ethnographic fieldwork by generating a situation in which a mentor is interacting with a student who is the narrator of her/his own life – holding centre stage, as it were – but expressing what the mentor sees as an 'untruth'. To put it in the Sudanese context of interviewer/interviewee, for example, when there are class and/or racial differences, or when the interviewer or mentor historically represents the colonizer, and the narrator/interviewee sees her/himself as the colonized, and might, in fact, without having the terminology, see her/himself as attempting to decolonize the research arena (or the classroom) – it may not be appropriate for the interviewer/mentor to expect to be equally affirmed. I asked rhetorically in a 1991 essay if it is logical for me, a white Western feminist mentoring or interviewing a Sudanese woman, for example, to expect to be considered as I see myself, when I may represent so many other categories to her (Hale 1991)? My self-identity might be as a leftist, progressive, and racially enlightened human rights and women's rights activist, etc. But she may only see me as a white Western privileged symbol of colonialism.

Is there anything that can be or should be done about this conundrum? Can any mentor/researcher avoid imposing what we have become? Can we/ should we be different from who we are? Especially considering that we and the world around are constantly changing. If we are committed to a particular pedagogy, theory or methodology, and are engaged in praxis, is it authentic (a term always to be interrogated) to be or do otherwise, i.e. attempt to be different from who we are? Don't we want to be more than conduits of the student's story, or the interviewee's version of history? Might we also aspire to be interpreters, dialogists, or even collaborators? At some point in this process do we become cultural imperialists, working at odds with someone who considers her/himself to be a decolonizer, either consciously or unconsciously?

So much of what anthropologists do 'in the field' is, to a large extent, contrived. That intense centrepiece method referred to as 'participant-observation' is usually a staged performance in which the researcher and researched are characters in a play. The interviewer sets up the situation and then participates in it. Being and doing are important both to the narrator in an interview or student in the classroom, and to her feminist interpreter. It is possible, however, that the small but significant degree of distance demanded in conventional participant-observation shields the interactional and intersubjective interpreter of another woman's life from false assumptions of mutuality. At the same time, for the most part in the 'feminist interview', the closeness and intersubjectivity remain artificial and temporary, frustrating expectations and potentially creating tensions among different feminisms. Are we able to question the same issues in a mentoring situation – one in which the teacher/mentor sets up the situation and then participates in it? Is that what we are doing with many of the strategies named above as feminist and/or Freirean? Even in various forms of liberatory pedagogy, for the most part, the closeness and intersubjectivity may remain artificial and temporary.

What some mentors/interviewers are starting to realize is that people who have traditionally been the subjects of study in research or merely the receptacles of 'knowledge' in the classroom, are generating their own knowledge and are intervening, interrupting, unsettling and subverting that knowledge which we have historically referred to as 'truth'.

All of this adds up to my hesitation or even reluctance to use not only conventional research methods and methodologies, or conventional pedagogical strategies, but also even some feminist or Freirean practices in participating with Sudanese and other African and Middle Eastern women, or my interlocutors in the United States. As my drive towards political solidarity and liberatory agendas grows, my anxiety about what and how to be in this context increases. My not-totally satisfactory and hopefully temporary solution has been to self-subvert my every academic move and to hold myself accountable at every turn.[10] I am not sure, however, that this solves the problem of our students or mentees subverting what we say in the classroom or community settings based on populist notions of 'truth'. Are Western feminist notions about mutuality, bonding, solidarity and 'dreams of a common language' (again borrowing from Adrienne Rich (1978)) demolished by what could be called a decolonizing of education, or knowledge? Look at that contradiction!

Where Are We Now?

Stanley Aronowitz claims that 'We need a radical imagination'.[11] Most of us feminist facilitators/educators would agree with that. Henry Giroux says we need individual and collective agency (2011). Yes, but neither of these positions takes us as far as we may want to go. Raewyn Connell (2019) offers a vision of 'the good university'. We could back up and tend to Paulo Freire or Judy Rohrer's ideas (1970, 2018) about listening and sharing what is in the room. Nonetheless, even if we were to be successful in affecting these radical visions, the obstacles in this particular political climate may still seem insurmountable. We are being asked to do more than just respond to alt-right populism, the growing pitfalls of neoliberal education, and the populist renditions of the Truth. Furthermore, we have to ask if the expanded notion of gender (i.e. not only LGBT, but LGBTQIA+) and the rise of Indigenous scholarship, in particular, as well as taking into consideration the increased numbers and diversity in our classrooms and in our big-city communities, have made some of these pedagogical and process strategies obsolete, or at least impractical, or not enough. Especially since some traditionalists won't let go, won't embrace digital pedagogy, for example. Besides, most of our neoliberal institutions hold us back unless we are talking about money-making projects (Connell 2019). In addition, we have to query if we can apply *any* of these pedagogical strategies that I have mentioned while teaching within the institutions of authoritarian societies – such as Sudan,

China, Iran and the like. Or, in so many Western institutions where students are being treated like customers, trained to buy privilege (Connell 2019). Are we dreaming, or, are these critical pedagogical strategies more relevant now in the 'post-truth' era than ever before? Perhaps with a bit more flexibility, more self-reflexivity...

I would like to suggest the idea (not entirely mine, and not new) that all along part of the problem with some of the feminist pedagogical strategies has been that they have often been practices/rules generated by one group and then imposed on the 'Other' in the name of egalitarianism and community. It goes something like this: one group develops and learns the rules and doles them out to the 'invitees', the 'newcomers', the 'uninitiated' (see Hale and Kadoda 2017 for an example). Besides, the process often does not happen on a level playing field.

Some Concluding Remarks on Critical Pedagogy

My main direction in this chapter, if not already apparent, is to move forward with the practices that we already have, those being developed, and those on the horizon to create a breakthrough in the post-truth era, as idealistic as that sounds.

If we turn the classroom or community workshop into a Freirean (1970) and feminist environment imbued with local knowledges by centring and empowering the student, by teaching through example, modelling criticism/self-criticism, listening and respecting, building on each other's ideas, by all of us challenging and questioning everything, by linking theory to action and analysing through self-reflexivity, by experimenting with connectedness in all ways, then maybe we could have a plan to propel democratizing and decolonizing.

We could try discussing among ourselves in a safe space a set of 'post-truth' assertions transported to the group by others within the group. One strategy is to agree that all of us (the confluence of students and teachers) write letters to each other (Burke 2017) about some of these supposedly post-truth bits of knowledge. Groups could work together to 'self-correct', negotiate truth, make explicit the context and note how that context is changing every minute. If we can help each other see the ambivalent and fragmented qualities of 'truth', we might change each other in the process. To paraphrase Rohrer again – it's all in the room (2018).

Perhaps it would help if we were more self-critical about some of our own assumptions that the internet and social media are phenomena that we need to contradict, counter, challenge or 'offset' and try to understand what is happening with regard to women, people of colour, queers, queers of colour, transgender and non-binary people, First Nation and Indigenous people, the disabled, and many people of the Global South, etc. Sometimes those who have trained and taught in conventional schooling take on resistance to the internet as an accepted part of our pedagogy. The disdain we exhibit towards digital pedagogy or e-learning may only result in quelling attempts to decolonialize knowledge. In the end, if we continue on this path, we may be overlooking, albeit, thwarting the possibility that what we are seeing in this so-called 'post-truth' era is a populist challenge to prevalent, established and Western/white/male hegemonic knowledge production espoused in our educational institutions and elsewhere; that we are impeding what may be a decolonizing and democratizing process at work.

Above I discussed some strategies partially based on feminist notions of inclusiveness and connectedness and on Freirean ideas. Perhaps we can go further and rely on ideas from the works of Ernst Bloch (1986 [1959]) or Jack Halberstam (2011) to consider developing methods that might facilitate our playing a role in building the unfinished human (including ourselves), to think of hope as a methodology, or part of the not-yet revolution, that is, a movement to help set the conditions for producing a new life, the hope of finding freedom. As Sayegh and Shafei suggest, 'Pedagogy, then, becomes a life practice located in scholarship, discourse making, and pushing for material and theoretical ground' (2018: 337). Or, as they further suggest, we can turn our tensions into 'pedagogical moments' (2018: 337). Perhaps the best we can do at this point in our journey is to participate in equipping young people with the feeling that they may be on a journey in their lives, one in which they strive to own their own life-long education. Let's join in the various projects of decolonizing, in my case, as a White/Western academic from an elite institution, who would heartily participate in these projects to the best of my limited abilities and my unlimited possibilities.

Notes

1 See Wikipedia entry on Alternative Facts, available at: https://en.wikipedia.org/wiki/Alternative_facts
2 *Time Magazine,* 3 April 2017.
3 In this chapter, I am uncomfortable having used the terms 'teacher' or 'mentor' because of not only the hierarchy associated with them, but also the uni-directional

suggestion. I sometimes use 'facilitator'. For the most part I try to draw only a slight distinction between those who facilitate gatherings in community settings and those who teach or mentor in the classroom.

4   'Mrs Hale' is not a title I have used, but Unity High was a school run by the Church of England, i.e. very formal.
5   Thomas L. Friedman had not yet written *The World is Flat: A Brief History of the Twenty-First Century*.
6   Clearly in this section I am skipping and jumping over significant feminist pioneers (e.g. Lugones and Spelman, Lusted, and Connell).
7   However, I don't think that such a gender-laden term as 'midwife' is helpful.
8   Perhaps we can forgive the essentialism of that title.
9   One reason why we might have that impression is because the institutions where these pedagogical practices were most likely to be present, i.e. in women's studies programmes, were fairly consistently white for many years.
10 Nadine Naber examines my accountability (2014).
11 Aronowitz is a sociologist at the Graduate Center of the City University of New York. He is the co-managing editor of *Situations: Project of the Radical Imagination* and a board member of the Institute for the Radical Imagination.

References

Ahmed, Sara (2017), *Living a Feminist Life*, Durham, NC: Duke University Press.
Anzaldúa, Gloria (1987), *Borderlands/La Frontera: The New Mestiza*, San Francisco: Aunt Lute Books.
Arendt, Hannah (1951), *The Origins of Totalitarianism*, New York: Schocken Books.
Belenky, Mary B., Clinchy N. Goldberger and Jill Tarule (eds) (1986), *Women's Ways of Knowing: The Development of Self, Voice, and Mind*, New York: Basic Books.
Bloch, Ernst ([1959] 1986), *The Principle of Hope*, London: Basil Blackwell.
Brooks, David (2018), 'A Generation Emerging from the Wreckage', *New York Times*, 27 February: A19.
Burke, Penny Jane, Gill Crozier and Lauren Ila Misiaszek (2016), *Changing Pedagogical Spaces in Higher Education: Diversity, Inequalities and Misrecognitio*, London: Routledge.
Burke, Penny Jane (2017), 'Constructing a radical world of imagination through feminist (writing) methodologies and praxis', *Occasional Papers*, Issue 02: XX–XX14-21, Newcastle, Australia: Centre of Excellence for Equity in Higher Education.
Burke, Penny Jane and Gifty Gyamera (2017), 'Exploring the impact of neoliberalism on female academics in universities in Ghana', *Occasional Papers*, Issue 2: 56–67. Newcastle, Australia: Centre of Excellence for Equity in Higher Education.

Burke, Penny Jane and Lauren Ila Misiaszek (eds) (2017), 'Introduction to the international network on gender, social justice and praxis', *Occasional Papers*, Issue 2: 2–13. Newcastle, Australia: Centre of Excellence for Equity in Higher Education.

Burke, Penny Jane and Ronelle Carolissen (eds) (2018), Special Issue, 'Introduction: gender, post-truth populism, and higher education pedagogies', *Teaching in Higher Education*, 23 (5): 543–7.

Connell, Raewyn (2019), *The Good University: What Universities Actually Do and Why It's Time for Radical Change*, London: Zed Books.

Freire, Paulo (1970), *Pedagogy of the Oppressed*, New York: Seabury Press.

Friedman, Thomas L. (2005), *The World Is Flat: A Brief History of the Twenty-first Century*, New York: Farrar, Straus and Giroux.

Giroux, Henry (2011), *On Critical Pedagogy*, New York: Bloomsbury Academic.

Halberstam, Jack (2011), *The Queer Art of Failure*, Durham, NC: Duke University Press.

Hale, Sondra (1991), 'Feminist method, process, and self-criticism: Interviewing Sudanese women', in S. Gluck and D. Patai (eds), *Women's Words: The Feminist Practice of Oral History*, 121–36, Bloomington: Indiana University Press.

Hale, Sondra (2019), 'The connections between education and power in the liberatory feminist classroom: Appreciating and critiquing freire', in C. A. Torres (ed), *The Wiley Handbook of Paulo Freire*, 379–88, Hoboken, NJ: Wiley-Blackwell.

Hale, Sondra and Gada Kadoda (2012), 'The changing nature of political activism in Sudan: women "Activists" as catalysts in civil society' [conference presentation], International South Sudan and Sudan Studies Association, Bonn, Germany, 23–25 July.

Hale, Sondra and Gada Kadoda (2017), 'Chronicle of collaboration: Toward creating justice spaces in Sudan', *Occasional Papers*, Issue 2: 34–53. Newcastle, Australia: Centre of Excellence for Equity in Higher Education.

Harding, Sandra (1987), *Feminism and Methodology*, Bloomington: Indiana University Press.

Harris, Judith, JoAnne Silverstein and Dianne Andrews (1989), 'Educating women in science', in Judith G. Touchton, Carol S. Pearson and Donna L. Shavlik (eds), *Educating the Majority, Women Challenge Tradition in Higher Education*, New York: American Council of Education.

Haworth, Robert H. and John M. Elmore (eds) (2017), *Out of the Ruins: The Emergence of Radical Informal Learning Spaces*, Oakland: PM Press.

Hill Collins, Patricia (1989), 'The social construction of Black feminist thought', *Signs*, 14 (4): 745–73.

hooks, bell (1994), *Teaching to Transgress: Education as the Practice of Freedom*, New York and London: Routledge.

Howe, Florence and Carol Ahlum (1973), 'Women's studies and social change', in A. Rossi and A. Calderwood (eds), *Academic Women on the Move*, 393–423, New York: Sage.

Kadoda, Gada and Sondra Hale (2013), 'Contemporary urban youth movements and the role of social media in Sudan' [unpublished conference workshop paper presentation], 14th Mediterranean Research Meeting on Social Media, Urban Movements and Grass-Roots Creativity in the Mediterranean during the Crisis, Mersin, Turkey, 20–23 March.

Kakutani, Michiko (2018), *The Death of Truth: Notes on Falsehood in the Age of Trump*, New York: Harper Collins.

Kenway, Jane and Helen Modra (1989), 'Feminist pedagogy and emancipatory possibilities', *Critical Pedagogy Networker*, 2 (2/3): 2–14.

Kenway, Jane, Johannah Fahey, Debbie Epstein, Aaron Koh, Cameron McCarthy and Fazal Rizvi (2015), *Class Choreographies: Elite Schools and Globalization*, London: Palgrave Macmillan.

Klein, Renate Duelli (1987), 'The dynamics of the women's studies classroom: A review essay of the teaching practice of women's studies in higher education', *Women's Studies International Forum*, 10 (2): 187–206.

Maher, Frances (1985), 'Pedagogies for the gender balanced classroom', *Journal of Thought*, 20 (3): 48–64.

McLaren, Peter (1995), *Critical pedagogy and Predatory Culture: Oppositional Politics in a Postmodern Era*, London and New York: Routledge.

Naber, Nadine (2014), 'Sondra Hale's ethnographic accountability', in A. Basarudin and K. Shaikh (eds), *Scholar, Mentor, Activist: Sondra Hale's Transnational Feminist Commitments*, Special Issue of the *Journal of Middle East Women's Studies*, 10 (1): 128–32.

Rich, Adrienne (1978), *The Dream of a Common Language*, New York: W. W. Norton.

Rizvi, Fazal (2015), *Class Choreographies: Elite Schools and Globalization*, London: Palgrave Macmillan.

Rohrer, Judy (2018), '"It's in the room": Reinvigorating feminist pedagogy, contesting neo-liberalism, and trumping post-truth populism', *Teaching in Higher Education: Critical Perspectives*, 23 (5): 576–92.

Sawyer, Miranda (2020), 'Margaret Atwood: "If you're going to speak truth to power, make sure it's the truth"', *The Guardian*, 12 September. Available at: https://www.theguardian.com/lifeandstyle/2020/sep/12/margaret-atwood-if-youre-going-to-speak-truth-to-power-make-sure-its-the-truth

Sayigh, Ghiwa and Yasmin Shafei (2018), 'Feminisms in tension at the "feminism in crisis?" conference', *Journal of Middle Eastern Women's Studies*, 14 (3): 333–7.

Schniedewind, Nancy (1987), 'Feminist values: Guidelines for a teaching methodology in women's studies', in Ira Shor (ed), *Freire for the Classroom*, 170–9, New Hampshire: Boynton & Cook.

Snyder, Timothy (2017), *On Tyranny: Twenty Lessons from the Twentieth Century*, London: Bodley Head.

Torres, Carlos Alberto (2014), *First Freire. Early Writings in Social Justice Education*, New York: Teachers College Press.

Torres, Carlos Alberto (ed) (2019), *Wiley Handbook on Freire*, Hoboken, NJ: Wiley-Blackwell.

Weiler, Kathleen (1991), 'Freire and a feminist pedagogy of difference', *Harvard Educational Review*, 61 (4): 449–75.

White, Hayden (1973), *Metahistory: The Historical Imagination in Nineteenth-Century Europe*, Baltimore: Johns Hopkins Press.

Part Two

Feminism and Education

5

Situating the Feminist Classroom: Between Free Speech and Media Myth

Nicola Rivers

Feminism currently occupies complex and contested terrain in multiple Western contexts, entangled with the rise of populist and post-feminist rhetoric that positions it as both *passé* and irrelevant, yet simultaneously dangerous and subversive. Whilst women's rights are now seemingly *en vogue* and championed by an increasing number of celebrities across multiple media platforms, leading to the emergence of the fourth wave of feminism (Cochrane 2013; Rivers 2017) and the rise of so-called 'neoliberal feminism' (Rottenberg 2018), there has also been a notable resurgence of what Sarah Banet-Wiser has termed 'popular misogyny' (Banet-Wiser 2018: 2). This populist backlash against the emerging fourth wave of feminism plays out across political rhetoric, popular culture and, notably for those of us engaged in feminist pedagogy, across university campuses. As the fourth wave of feminism finds itself caught between a complex, contested popularity and an increasingly hostile populism, the role of feminist pedagogy becomes ever more vital. The feminist classroom is the space to critique, expose and resist insidious narratives that are both anti-education and actively seek to undermine feminist gains. With arguments raging over the role of the contemporary university, this chapter explores how feminism is situated in key debates surrounding free speech and censorious students, currently shaping the perception and provision of higher education.

Within the neoliberal university, where education is viewed as a commodity that can be bought, and students are positioned as 'consumers', courses are increasingly ranked on a series of metrics ostensibly designed to allow students greater insight into the supposed 'value' of their degree. Gender studies, and associated fields within the humanities and social sciences that focus on studying elements of human identity such as race and sexuality, have been much derided as offering little 'value' to students. Noting the impact that this neoliberal landscape has had on certain disciplines, Yvette Taylor and Kinneret Lahad describe this as 'a critical and particularly vulnerable moment in academia' where '[g]lobal capitalism and the growing focus on the sciences lead many universities to adopt market driven models, with numerous departments, mostly within the humanities and social sciences, being closed down' (Taylor and Lahad 2018: 1–2).

In populist narratives courses within the humanities and social sciences are regularly assailed and described as 'Mickey Mouse' degrees or soft subjects, presented as offering students little to no benefit in the purported 'real world'. In an article published by *The Huffington Post,* Lukas Mikelionis takes specific aim at gender studies programmes, claiming 'Mickey mouse degrees are rightfully smack talked down but at least we can defend them on the basis they still teach something remotely valuable and attract a talented bunch. Alas, I cannot say the same about gender studies' (2015: para. 1–2). He goes on to claim that '[t]he evident ludicrousness of gender studies as an academic subject means attracting numerous talented people is off the table' arguing the 'requirements to get into gender studies programme is dumped down [*sic*], and the content is designed to pander very specific groups of people, for the sake of survival' (Mikelionis 2015: para. 7). Mikelionis's attempted 'smack talk' of gender studies offers a critique of the lack of intellectual merit – apparently evident in both the students and the subject – but also presents a post-feminist analysis whereby he expresses supposed concern for otherwise 'high-achieving women who are being radicalized, victimized and then deceived into studying subjects like gender studies' (Mikelionis 2015: para. 10). Of course this argument undermines his previous point that gender studies programmes are failing to attract any talented students in the first place, but it does serve to further a post-feminist position whereby women are presented as high-achieving individuals held back only by a victim mentality fostered by feminism. Within the academy gender studies programmes have also come under attack, being referred to under the pejorative umbrella term of 'grievance studies' (Pluckrose, Lindsay and Boghossian 2018: para. 2), with claims being made about the lack of rigour expressed in the study of such disciplines. The moniker 'grievance studies' apparently signals the propensity for encouraging students to take a divisive view of society predicated on identity politics, or the understanding of certain groups as victimized or subjected to unequal treatment based on their identity.

Yet despite their apparent lack of relevance, importance or impact, such disciplines are not being left to die a quiet death at the hands of market forces, but have also drawn ire from rising right-wing governments. In Hungary, for example, funding for gender studies programmes has been withdrawn based not only on the supposed lack of worth these courses offer, but, somewhat paradoxically, also on the apparent threat they pose to national values. In 2018, Hungarian prime minister Viktor Orban revoked accreditation and withdrew funding for two gender studies programmes, issuing a statement asserting that, 'The government's standpoint is that people are born either male or female, and we do not consider it acceptable for us to talk about socially constructed genders rather than biological sexes' (Oppenheim 2018: para. 3). Far from being out of touch with 'real' world issues then, gender studies programmes are instead seen to be potentially dangerous sites of subversion, encouraging students to question established norms and pushing the boundaries of 'acceptable' debate.

More recently, critical race theory has also found itself at the heart of political debates in both the UK and United States, with Members of Parliament (MPs) aligning it with protest movements such as Black Lives Matter. In a much-publicized speech in the Houses of Parliament, Conservative MP Kemi Badenoch asserted 'Any school which teaches these elements of critical race theory, or which promotes partisan political views such as defunding the police without offering a balanced treatment of opposing views, is breaking the law' (Shand-Baptiste 2020: para. 9). As with attacks on gender studies programmes taking a post-feminist position to argue for their irrelevance, and the potential harm caused by supposedly encouraging women to see themselves as victims, Badenoch sought to undermine critical race theory on similar grounds, claiming it as 'an ideology that sees my blackness as victimhood'. Donald Trump's administrations also spoke out against federal funds being used to support teaching critical race theory, suggesting it is 'un-American propaganda' (Victor 2020: para. 1). Again, critical race theory is presented as both outdated and wrong, yet dangerously subversive.

Of course, despite the supposed threat posed by the study of critical race theory, apparently rendering it worthy of outlawing or censorship, the idea of schools or universities overrun with courses dedicated to furthering students' understanding of the role of race can only be considered, in the language of the day, as 'fake news'. In fact, in the UK context, a recent British Sociological Association report (Joseph-Salisbury, Ashe, Alexander, and Campion 2020) stressed that often race and ethnicity are 'taught as an add-on or specialist module, rather than a fundamentally integrated part of the curriculum' (2020: 6). Nonetheless, the perception in popular imagination persists, fuelling the idea of university campuses as radically left-wing, or the frontline of what has been dubbed, the 'culture wars' (Giroux 2005).

However, despite the current heightened political and media interest in what happens on university campuses and across the education sector, such arguments and debates are not new. As Susan Giroux writes, the 'culture wars' can be traced back to the 1980s and 1990s and are a right-wing response to what she suggests could be seen as universities' 'multicultural turn' (Giroux 2005: 315). Of course, Giroux is quick to stress that such a 'turn' was in principle rather than practice, and that despite the 'limp endorsement' of ideals such as 'non-discrimination' and 'diversity', these commitments failed to materialize (2005: 315). However, Giroux also highlights how institutional use of the language of diversity and inclusion, even if not realized, nonetheless fuelled conservative rhetoric about radicalized university campuses. The circulation of these debates within mainstream political and popular discourse then produces a misrepresentation of the education sector, feeding into the political and populist myth of the contemporary university as out of touch with ordinary people or a hotbed of left-wing activism. Although, as Giroux wryly observes, '[i]f we assent, for the moment, to the conservative view of the university as a hotbed of radical thought, we would have to admit that, thus far, it has been devastatingly ineffectual' (2005: 319). Nonetheless, universities find themselves caught in the unenviable and seemingly impossible position of being presented as both the driving force for radical social change, and lumbering institutions held in sway to neoliberal market forces and government sanctioned directives and metrics.

Paradoxically, despite criticism of universities coming from centralized government sources like Badenoch and Trump, such pronouncements ironically further a sense of distrust with the establishment, positioning those who make these statements as rogue outsiders prepared to tell the uncomfortable truth. This feeds into a political populism, fuelling what Tom Nichols has diagnosed as the 'death of expertise' in his 2014 article of the same name, and subsequent book, *The Death of Expertise: The Campaign Against Established Knowledge and Why It Matters*. Nichols laments the turn against expertise and established knowledge, seemingly primarily because of the challenge it presents to his assertion that, as an expert, he can and should expect that his 'opinion holds more weight than that of most other people' (2014: para. 1). However, his work is certainly not a robust defence of universities as he currently sees them. In fact, Nichols lays at least some of the blame for public distrust in expertise with universities themselves, characterizing them as 'soft' (2017) and run by academics enslaved by the whims of students.

Despite purportedly different aims then, with academics from within the academy mourning the death of expertise and politicians celebrating this expediency, each discourse amounts to the same thing: the questioning of what takes place on university campuses, what counts as knowledge and, critically, who gets to decide. Feminist classrooms and critical race theory courses are thus caught in a double-sided attack. Criticized from 'outside' by politicians who are ostensibly seeking to protect students – and perhaps more pertinently, the status quo – from unwanted exposure to gender studies, or critical race theory, which is forced upon them by academics and their left-wing agenda, and from within as lacking academic rigour or bowing to student demands in terms of diversifying the curriculum. Again, gender studies and critical race theory are somehow simultaneously outdated or irrelevant forms of expertise linked to 'soft' science and derided within the academy, mocked by the publication of spoof articles, and yet also a threat to social orthodoxy and cohesion. What critical race theory and feminist pedagogy have in common then, alongside their demonization by conservative or right-leaning governments, is an attempt to examine race and gender in relation to the structural confines and pressures of culture, history and the law. Crucial to both is an acknowledgement that race and gender will shape our lived realities to some extent.

Contemporary students find themselves caught in a similar paradox; frequently presented as 'snowflake millennials' lacking the resilience and ambition to thrive in the modern world, yet simultaneously accused of threatening the survival of free speech or liberal democracy through the use of 'trigger' warnings and 'no-platforming' (Webster and Rivers 2018). As with all of these debates, arguments around free speech on university campuses, or what is currently referred to as 'cancel culture', are not new, in fact, there has been a no-platform policy for racists and fascists implemented by the UK Students Union since 1974. Although presently being afforded increasing public attention and column inches in mainstream media, questions about the limits on debate placed by students, or the rights of lecturers to express what could euphemistically be described as 'controversial' or 'unpopular' opinions (and less euphemistically as racism, homophobia and sexism), have circulated for at least the last forty years. Again, much of the discussion has centred around the caricature of university campuses as overtly left-wing or liberal – with the focus often being on issues around diversity and inclusion – and attempting to stifle the expression of conservative or right-wing views.

Media headlines have gleefully reported sensationalist stories about censorious students. In 2015, for example, Goldsmiths, the University of London's Welfare and Diversity officer, Bahar Mustafa, achieved notoriety in the national – and to a lesser degree, international – press, for her attempts to organize a Black, Asian,

Minority Ethnic and non-binary people only event on campus. News outlets from across the political spectrum, from *The Guardian* to *The Daily Mail* were quick to run stories questioning the merits, or even validity, of Mustafa setting up such an event. Headlines such as 'Anger after white people and men are banned from "anti-racism" rally at British university by its own student union DIVERSITY OFFICER' (Harding 2015), revelled in the apparent controversy and irony of the supposedly 'racist' and 'sexist' diversity officer discriminating against white students, and fuelling what Hamilton Carroll has referred to as the perception of white injury (Carroll 2014).

The notion that creating a safe space for Black, Asian and Minority Ethnic students, as well as those who identify as non-binary, to meet and discuss their experiences was somehow beyond the remit of Bahar Mustafa's role as Goldsmiths Welfare and Diversity officer, or indeed in conflict with her position, was risible. However, such was the strength of feeling against Mustafa and her attempts to provide students with this space, that a change.org petition was created calling for Mustafa to be 'removed from Goldsmiths University in all aspects with police interaction and degree revocation' (Keene 2015: para. 1). This received in excess of 26,000 supporters, highlighting the popularity, if not credibility, of this position.

Andy Keene, the creator of the petition, argued that Mustafa was guilty of 'hate speech' (Keene 2015). He suggested this was evident both in the wording she used to promote the event, urging, if 'you're a man and/or white, PLEASE DON'T COME', and later in her posting a photograph of herself next to sign that read, 'No White-Cis-Men Pls'. Not content with seeking that Mustafa be removed from her post at Goldsmiths, Keene argued that the 'seriousness' of Mustafa's 'crime' could warrant the involvement of the European courts on charges of 'inciting racial hatred and genocide' (Keene 2015: para. 8). The Metropolitan Police confirmed that Mustafa was interviewed under caution following a complaint, however, Keene was unsuccessful in his attempts to get Mustafa removed from her position. A separate vote conducted by the university failed to get sufficient support to force a referendum, and thus she held her post. No criminal charges have been brought against her. Nonetheless, Mustafa's case was presented as an example of the apparent problem of identity politics overrunning UK university campuses, and the seemingly inevitable fallout from a left-wing preoccupation with so-called 'grievance studies'. However, the very fact that organizing a small, on-campus event that excludes those who frequently hold the most power in our society – white, cisgender men and women – made the news at all, in fact highlights what a rarity this kind of action is.

Debates around no-platforming have also been particularly prevalent in contemporary feminism too, often coming to the fore on university campuses. Students at Cardiff University, for example, sought to have Germaine Greer's invitation to speak there rescinded due to her hostile perspective on trans people. Similarly, Julie Bindel was banned from an event taking place at Manchester University following concerns expressed that her views may 'incite hatred towards, and exclusion of [...] trans students' (Whibly 2015). More recently still, although not linked to universities, columnist Suzanne Moore resigned her position at *The Guardian*, citing bullying by her colleagues there and censorship over her views on trans women, claiming that contemporary feminism has lost its way or is newly divided.

However, defence for Moore has come from the perhaps unlikely ally of the right-wing paper, *The Spectator*, with Scottish Editor, Alex Massie suggesting *The Guardian* would be 'diminished' without her. Aligning those that complained about Moore's column on the grounds that it perpetuated a hostile environment for trans people, and specifically those working at *The Guardian*, with infantile and censorious students, Massie writes:

> 'I read something in the paper and disagreed with it' now often seems to be considered some kind of assault upon the person, rather than being something you should expect – and even look forward to. Perhaps this should not surprise for when personal is political and when identity is the basis for politics a mere difference of opinion – or even emphasis – becomes a hostile act. Such things must be policed. Which might be fine on campus but the adult world is supposed to be marginally more robust.
>
> (Massie 2020: para. 5)

This is a curious defence of Moore, whose own explanation of leaving the paper is rooted in her commitment to the idea that the personal is political and, indeed, stressed that: '[t]he truth is I never fitted in at the *Guardian*. The personal is political the moment you don't feel clean enough' (Moore 2020).

In an attempt to co-opt Moore's resignation to further serve debates around free speech and censorious students then, Massie empties the situation of its political content, and in so doing undermines the complexity of contemporary feminisms. Massie's simplistic and reductive argument is seemingly that all speech is good speech. At best, feminist debates over what constitutes a woman are dismissed as generational (Rivers 2017), at worst, entirely ignored. Rather than acknowledging the seriousness of the mounting criticism against Moore's position on the inclusion of trans women within women-only spaces,

Massie aligns those complaining with the easily assailable 'snowflake' student, again feeding into dominant narratives of university campuses as overrun by 'woke' millennials intent on limiting free speech and creating classrooms that are 'safe spaces'. Such a view of students not only refuses to engage with the very real concerns they raise, but also presents a homogenizing and clearly unrepresentative view of the student body, and millennials in general. As Alison Winch, Jo Littler and Jessalynn Keller have argued: '[m]illennials are not a homogeneous group, and their socioeconomic and cultural location is dependent on gender, race, ethnicity, disability, sexuality, religion and place' (Winch, Littler and Keller 2016: 563).

Sara Ahmed has argued, students' concerns – whether real or imagined – are more easily dismissed by presenting the students themselves as overly-sensitive or demanding. Aligning students with what she has termed 'willful subjects' (2014), Ahmed argues: 'What protestors are protesting *about* can be ignored when the protestors are assumed to be suffering from too much will; they are assumed to be opposing something because they are *being oppositional*' (2015: para. 4). Ahmed also highlights a fundamental misunderstanding in mainstream media discussions of terms such as 'trigger warnings' and 'safe spaces' as they relate to students. Far from being a sign that debate or difficult discussions have been abandoned at the demands of the sensitive and censorious student, the inclusion of 'trigger warnings' and creation of 'safe spaces' exist precisely so these discussions can still take place. As Ahmed stresses: 'safe spaces are another technique for dealing with the consequences of histories that are not over [...]. The real purpose of these mechanisms is to enable difficult conversations to happen' (2015: para. 23).

Nonetheless, the idea that universities have succumbed to the demands of censorious – and frequently feminist – students persists in the public imagination. Yet a recent report from the Policy Institute at King's College London (Grant, Hewlett, Nir and Duffy 2019) found that only 12 per cent of students had heard of incidents of this freedom being threatened frequently at their own university, and 46 per cent had never heard of any instances on campus. Demonstrating the longevity of these concerns – if not their validity – Stanley Fish's collection of essays, *There's No Such Thing as Free Speech: And It's a Good Thing Too*, cites a 1991 survey, *Campus Trends*, as concluding that 'despite "anecdotal accounts" "problems are not widespread." Ninety per cent of all institutions report no "controversies over the political or cultural content of remarks made by invited speakers"' (Fish 1994: 53–4). Fish's point, however, was not that there was no debate taking place, or even that there was no cause for debate, but rather he questioned the terms of discussion surrounding free speech, and the assertion that it is the political left seeking to limit what can be said or taught.

Fish questioned what advocates of free speech were actually seeking, noting that on all sides of the debate parameters are drawn around what can or can't be said in public spaces, and that the rationale for these decisions is, of course, inherently political. And yet the very notion of being political was, and indeed still is, often framed as an accusation, and seen as an indication of a biased or partisan approach to speech. This accusation is most frequently levelled at a left-wing that are accused of having abandoned rational thought in favour of political correctness or bowing to the demands of identity politics. As Fish stresses, 'what we have here, then, is not, as has been advertised, a brave resistance to politics by the apolitical rationality but rather an argument between two forms of politics, or if you prefer, two forms of political correctness' (1994: 56).

The framing of advocates of free speech as rational and politically neutral casts them as defenders of uncomfortable truths, whilst positioning those arguing for limits on who and what should occupy public discourse as partisan and political. Those who would limit free speech are presented as overly sensitive at best, and at worst, hiding from arguments they know they can't win. As Ahmed has argued, students demanding a say over who does and does not take up valuable space and resources on university campuses are thus not portrayed as engaged and critical independent thinkers – which would surely be the ideal type – but rather as 'snowflakes' frightened of honest debate and challenge.

What is so useful about Fish's earlier intervention into debates on free speech is his illuminating the role of politics and the limits placed on freedom of expression across political divides. How else to read Badenoch's assertion that critical race theory has no place on UK campuses, or Trump's threat to withdraw federal funds from institutions that continue to offer critical race theory in their classrooms, than as an attack on free speech on university campuses? This is despite Badenoch's Conservative values more commonly aligning with the argument for wholly unfettered freedom of expression. Indeed, her pronouncements on the illegality of critical race theory came after Education minister, Gavin Williams, announced a Higher Education Restructuring Regime requiring institutions to 'demonstrate their commitment to academic freedom and free speech' in order to benefit fully from government support following the COVID-19 pandemic. Similarly, Donald Trump has frequently taken to Twitter to threaten to withdraw funds from institutions he sees as limiting freedom of expression, for example, in 2017 asking the presumably rhetorical question of: 'If UC Berkeley does not allow free speech and practices violence on innocent people with a different point of view – no federal funds?' (Bay Area News Group 2017). It seems then even the staunchest defenders of academic freedoms and freedom of expression are happy to place limits on these ideals when it is they who are being offended.

Yet more recently – and somewhat disappointingly – in an apparent attempt to defend the position of the university in post-truth and populist times, Fish has also fallen into blaming students for imperilling the place of experts. Despite having written compellingly about the misconceptions surrounding the place of politics on university campuses, and the influence of this on debates surrounding free speech, Fish now decries what he describes as the 'rhetoric of virtue' and students as 'virtue monitors' (Fish 2019: 78). Writing on students he dismissively suggests: '[i]n short, they don't want to learn anything' (2019: 77). In an assessment of the student population that bears remarkable similarities to the caricatures so skilfully illustrated by Ahmed – as the consuming, complaining, over-sensitive or censorious type (Ahmed 2015) – Fish takes particular aim at 'activist students (situated largely on the left) who lobby for a role in the formation of the curriculum and in the choice of texts to be included in the syllabus of a particular course' (Fish 2019: 73). Rather than seeing this as evidence of students' engagement with what they study, whereby they are demonstrating an admirable awareness of the way social inequalities have historically shaped, and continue to shape the accepted canon of knowledge and the content of course syllabus, he instead presents this as a refusal to learn.

However, Fish also maintains that much of what is characterized in media discussions as infringements of free speech on campus, have little to do with free speech at all, and instead revolve around the questions of professionalism and what the university is for. Fish's response to the increasingly hostile political environment that universities find themselves operating in is to retreat from politics. He argues:

> Of course it is true that universities are politically *situated*: everything about them, from their incorporation to their funding, their tax status, and the state services they rely on, is enmeshed in politics. But that is quite different from saying that those who work inside universities should conduct themselves as political actors. It is one thing to be embedded in a structure made possible by political activities; it is quite another to be acting as a political agent within that structure. The first is unavoidable; the second, I think, is to be avoided no matter what the temptation.
>
> (2019: 86)

This argument appears to be predicated on survival – as Fish asserts 'the university that rigorously distances itself from politics will be at once true to its mission and more likely to prosper politically' (87) – but it is clearly not survival for all. Sacrificed on the altar of Fish's ideal university would surely be gender studies programmes, and courses including critical race theory, for fear of seeming too 'political'. It also hints at a nostalgia for an imagined university of the past, described by Fish as 'the life of disinterested contemplation' (77) where the politics of the day presumably held no influence over who was doing the contemplating or what was contemplated.

Defunding the feminist classroom, or banning the teaching of critical race theory does not just signal a retreat from politics though, but rather a retreat from reality. Far from being a hotbed of left-wing activism, arguably universities are nowhere near radical enough. Universities UK, for example, have just seen fit to publish a report specifically intended to deal with 'the widespread evidence of racial harassment found on university campuses' by the Equality and Human Rights Commission (UK Universities 2019). The turn to a right-wing populism and the associated calls of 'fake news' and post-truth, as Marie Moran and Jo Littler contend, are not simply a 'cultural backlash' but are at least in part fostered by a neoliberal attack including 'the eroding of public institutions required for a functioning democracy' and the 'hollowing out or serious undermining of: an inclusive and objective media' and 'an education system fostering critical thinking' (Moran and Littler 2020: 866). What is needed on university campuses is more critical race theory, and more feminist classrooms, not less. From accusations of silencing, and arguments over the boundaries of free speech, to questions over the value of education and the importance of expertise in an apparently 'post-truth' society, a commitment to teaching feminist and critical race theory demonstrates a commitment to an understanding of education as transformative. To rework Giroux's earlier cited assertion that 'if we assent, for the moment, to the conservative view of the university as a hotbed of radical thought, we would have to admit that, thus far, it has been devastatingly ineffectual' (Giroux 2005: 315), it's perhaps time we got a little better at it.

References

Ahmed, Sara (2014), *Willful Subjects*, Croydon: Duke University Press.
Ahmed, Sara (2015), 'Against students', *The New Inquiry*. Available online: https://thenewinquiry.com/against-students/

Banet-Wiser, Sarah (2018), *Empowered: Popular Feminism and Popular Misogyny*, Croydon: Duke University Press.

Bay Area News Group (2017), 'Trump tweets at UC Berkley no free speech no federal funds?', *East Bay Times*, 2 February. Available online: https://www.eastbaytimes.com/2017/02/02/trump-tweets-at-uc-berkeley-no-free-speech-no-federal-funds/

Bindel, Julie (2015), 'No platform: My exclusion proves this is an anti-feminist crusade', *The Guardian*, 9 October. Available online: https://www.theguardian.com/commentisfree/2015/oct/09/no-platform-universities-julie-bindel-exclusion-anti-feminist-crusade

Carroll, Hamilton (2014), *Affirmative Reaction: New Formations of White Masculinity*, Croydon: Duke University Press.

Cochrane, Kira (2013), 'The fourth wave of feminism: Meet the rebel women', *The Guardian*, 10 December. Available online: http://theguardian.com/world/2013/dec/10/fourth-wave-feminism-rebel-women

Fish, Stanley (1994), *There's No Such Thing as Free Speech… And It's a Good Thing Too*, Oxford: Oxford University Press.

Fish, Stanley (2019), *The First: How to Think about Hate Speech, Campus Speech, Religious Speech, Fake News, Post-truth, and Donald Trump*, New York: One Signal Publishers.

Giroux, Susan Searls (2005), 'From the "Culture Wars" to the conservative campaign for campus diversity: Or, how inclusion became the new exclusion', *Policy Futures in Education*, 3 (4): 314–26.

Grant, Jonathan, Kirstie Hewlett, Tamar Nir and Bobby Duffy (2019), *Freedom of Expression in UK Universities*. Available online: https://www.kcl.ac.uk/policy-institute/assets/freedom-of-expression-in-uk-universities.pdf

Harding, Eleanor (2015), 'Anger after white people and Men are banned from "anti-racism" rally at British university by its own student union DIVERSITY OFFICER', *The Daily Mail*, 23 April. Available online: http://www.dailymail.co.uk/news/article-3051977/Anger-anti-racism-rally-banned-white-people-attending.html

Joseph-Salisbury Remi, Stephen Ashe, Claire Alexander, Karis Campion (2020), *Race and Ethnicity in British Sociology*. Available online: https://es.britsoc.co.uk/bsaCommentary/wp-content/uploads/2020/06/BSA_race_and_ethnicity_in_british_sociology_report_pre_publication_version.pdf

Keene, Andy (2015), 'Bahar Mustafa should be removed from Goldsmiths University in all aspects with Police interaction and degree revocation'. Available online: https://www.change.org/p/expel-bahar-mustafa-from-goldsmiths-university-for-criminal-misconduct-bahar-mustafa-should-be-removed-from-study-at-goldsmiths-university (accessed 15 June 2015).

Massie, Alex (2020), 'Suzanne Moore's departure is a sad day for the Guardian', *The Spectator*, 17 November. Available online: https://www.spectator.co.uk/article/suzanne-moore-s-departure-is-a-sad-day-for-the-guardian

Mikelionis, Lukas (2015), 'Forget Mickey Mouse degrees, gender studies is the new non-degree', *The Huffington Post*, 23 January. Available online: https://www.huffingtonpost.co.uk/lukas-mikelionis/forget-mickey-mouse-degre_b_6507658.html?

Moore, Suzanne (2020), 'Why I had to leave the Guardian', *UnHerd*, 25 November. Available online: https://unherd.com/2020/11/why-i-had-to-leave-the-guardian/
Moran, Moran and Jo Littler (2020), 'Cultural populism in new populist times', *European Journal of Cultural Studies*, 23: 857–73.
Nichols, Tom M. (2014), 'The death of expertise: The campaign against established knowledge and why it matters', *The Federalist*. Available online: https://thefederalist.com/2014/01/17/the-death-of-expertise/
Nichols, Tom M. (2017), *The Death of Expertise: The Campaign against Established Knowledge and Why it Matters*, Oxford: Oxford University Press.
Oppenheim, Maya (2018), 'Hungarian Prime Minister Viktor Orban bans gender studies programmes', *The Independent*, 25 October. Available online: https://www.independent.co.uk/news/world/europe/hungary-bans-gender-studies-programmes-viktor-orban-central-european-university-budapest-a8599796.html
Pluckrose, Helen, James A. Lindsay and Peter Boghossion (2018), 'Academic grievance studies and the corruption of scholarship', *Areo Magazine*. Available online: https://areomagazine.com/2018/10/02/academic-grievance-studies-and-the-corruption-of-scholarship/
Rivers, Nicola (2017), *Postfeminism(s) and the Arrival of the Fourth Wave*, Cham: Palgrave Macmillan.
Rottenberg, Catherine (2018), *The Rise of Neoliberal Feminism*, Oxford: Oxford University Press.
Shand-Baptiste, Kuba (2020), 'The government has no intention of taking racism seriously – and it is using MPs of colour to avoid criticism', *The Independent*, 22 October. Available online: https://www.independent.co.uk/voices/critical-race-theory-racism-kemi-badenoch-black-history-month-bame-discrimination-b1227367.html
Taylor, Yvette and Kinneret Lahad (eds) (2018), *Feeling Academic in the Neoliberal University: Feminist Flights, Fights and Failures*, London: Palgrave.
Universities UK (2019), *Tackling Racial Harassment in Higher Education*. Available online: https://www.universitiesuk.ac.uk/policy-and-analysis/reports/Pages/tackling-racial-harassment-in-higher-education.aspx
Victor, Ray (2020), 'Trump calls critical race theory "un-American." Let's review', *The Washington Post*, 2 October. Available online: https://www.washingtonpost.com/nation/2020/10/02/critical-race-theory-101/
Webster, David and Nicola Rivers (2018), 'Resisting resilience: Disrupting discourses of self-efficacy', *Pedagogy, Culture and Society*, 27: 523–35.
Whibly, Sarah (2015), 'SU bans Julie Bindel from speaking at Uni free speech event', *The Tab*. Available Online: http://thetab.com/uk/manchester/2015/10/06/su-bans-julie-bindel-from-speaking-at-uni-13938
Winch, Alison, Jo Littler and Jessalyn Keller (2016), 'Why "Intergenerational feminist media studies"?', *Feminist Media Studies*, 16 (4): 557–72.

6

Persistence, Patience and Persuasion: Critical Reflections on Creating Space for Indigenous Content in Australian University Curricula

Susan Page

Aboriginal and Torres Strait Islander people should be aware that this chapter contains the names of deceased persons

Prologue

Until recently, many Australians would have been more familiar with the names of First Nations peoples of North America than Indigenous Australians. Raised on a diet of American television we absorbed the names of Native American nations without fully realizing the connection between our own Indigenous peoples and those that we were consuming through entertainment. One of my favourites, F Troop, reinscribed colonial relations and reinforced the colonial hierarchy despite the hapless soldiers often being outwitted by the local Native American tribe. Little that we saw hinted at theft of land or more sophisticated notions such as sovereignty or agency (Tahmahkera 2014). Generations have grown up consuming Disney films, which, despite recent attempts, continue to stereotype Indigenous peoples (Sandlen and Garlen 2017). Now, at least, many Australians can identify the traditional custodians of the Country on which they live or work (or attend school). Globalized media and entertainment mean that Australians are in close contact with the (largely Western dominated) world.

The Black Lives Matter movement largely caught Australia's attention, not in 2015 when Dunghutti man David Dungay Junior gasped 'I can't breathe' from his prison cell but when George Floyd, an African American man in the United States, uttered the same thing as police knelt on his neck on a city street in 2020. In a breathtaking example of silencing, as people took to the streets across the United States, our Australian prime minister, Scott Morrison spoke to the media to express his relief that such things – the deaths of Black people in police custody – did not happen in his country (Anthony 2020). It may have seemed to Morrison, a relatively safe thing to assume, but it reflects an ongoing, casual ignorance of Indigenous matters in the broader Australian society. He perhaps did not hear the wheels of activism grinding to life in his own cities and towns as Aboriginal people and supporters gathered to remind the nation that Australian Black lives also matter. While the Australian protests were in sympathy with global issues, the focus was on the more than 400 Aboriginal deaths associated with custody since 1999 when a national inquiry investigated the apparent inequity of Aboriginal deaths in judicial circumstances (*The Guardian* 2020).

These two vignettes outline two issues which form the national context for the work of creating space for Indigenous content in university curricula; the first briefly outlines one factor contributing to many Australians being unaware of Indigenous histories and cultures and the second points to the highly politicized nature of the work.

Introduction

Australian universities and those in colonized nations such as Canada (Battiste, Bell and Findlay 2002; Schaefli et al. 2018) and New Zealand (Jones 2009; Pitama et al. 2018) are increasingly seeking to ensure that university students engage with Indigenous Knowledges and develop cultural capability. Consequently, universities in Australia have progressively focused on embedding Indigenous content in disciplinary curricula. This sharpening of intent is not related to increased demand by students for Indigenous studies major streams but rather is being driven by recognition that university graduates can contribute to addressing current socioeconomic inequity through workforce participation. While not all university graduates will work specifically in Indigenous contexts, many will likely progress to professional roles (Carroll 2015), in which they potentially make decisions directly or indirectly affecting Indigenous peoples and communities, risking reproduction of the current inequitable status quo. In a world where truth is increasingly under pressure, and post-truth ideas are dependent less upon factual accuracy and are more reliant on emotion and belief (Horsthemke 2017), giving voice to Indigenous truths is challenging.

Much of the truth of Indigenous history and culture and, indeed, colonialism, remains too often unknown, hidden and silenced in disciplinary curricula (Bodkin-Andrews, Page and Trudgett 2018). This disciplinary 'ignorance' could simply be explained as a gap in knowledge or, as Sullivan and Tuana (2007) suggest, as a more systematic unknowing designed to reproduce racial oppression. The history wars (Macintyre and Clark 2003), which deeply contested the colonial origins of the Australian nation, including major issues of contention such as massacres of Indigenous peoples (Hooper et al. 2020) or the removal of Indigenous children as genocidal (Robinson and Paten 2008) might be one such example. An intellectual contest between historians spilled over into a fierce political debate about what truths should be told in our school classrooms and whether the achievements of white colonialists outweighed the violence of the conquest of Indigenous Australians (Parkes 2007). Years of teaching Indigenous studies and recent work to embed Indigenous perspectives in all degrees across an institution, lead me to conclude that many non-Indigenous Australians continue to be unaware of the extent of colonial violence *or* the rich Aboriginal and Torres Strait Islander histories that have shaped our nation. These curricula absences lead critical race theorists to refer to the curriculum as a White masterscript, recreating and reproducing graduates in its own image (Ladson-Billings 1998). This curriculum dominance is changing in Australian universities, though, spurred by Indigenous scholarly and community activism, and an increasing recognition, particularly in the professions, that this absence in curricula is problematic. Despite many professions already including discipline-relevant Indigenous perspectives (Bullen and Roberts 2018; Kickett, Hoffman and Flavell 2014), the magnitude of this task cannot be underestimated.

In this chapter, I critically reflect on my experience as an Aboriginal academic, in the context of my now long experience teaching Indigenous Studies in Australian universities, with a focus on my more recent experience as the leader of a university's Indigenous Graduate Attribute (IGA) project. While a range of practical and theoretical aspects of the project have been written about elsewhere, here I take the opportunity to consider three key challenges of this work: persistence, persuasion and patience. I use these descriptors purposely because they can be characterized as challenges, but they can also be embodied as qualities and conducted as acts. For example, the need to regularly persuade others of the need for Indigenous content in curriculum can be demanding, yet it requires significant persuasive abilities in frequent episodes of persuasion. This chapter begins by establishing the broader context of Australian Indigenous higher education and outlining the IGA project, before further elaborating on the three challenges and how they might act to address ignorance, (re)animate silences and (re)fill absences.

Indigenous Higher Education

There is a tendency, when considering Aboriginal and Torres Strait Islander peoples in higher education, to refer to comparisons with similar non-Indigenous cohorts, resulting in statements of deficiencies or gaps. Statistics reflect under-representation and poorer retention outcomes for Indigenous students and little percentage increases of Indigenous staff over decades. However, those numbers do not fully reflect gains made in Indigenous education. Numerical analyses also obscure the enduring leadership of Indigenous peoples who have driven change over decades (Holt and Morgan 2016; Page, Trudgett and Sullivan 2017), despite being 'outnumbered' in a higher education system dominated by Western modes of organization and disciplinary epistemology. Indeed, many universities also now have senior Indigenous staff (Trudgett, Page and Coates 2020), including leadership appointments commonly in Pro Vice-Chancellor Indigenous positions and most universities have some Indigenous outcomes included in institutional strategic documents (Moreton-Robinson, Walter, Singh and Kimber 2011), both illuminating previously invisible work and actively countering the prevailing mainstream dominance. Over the last decade, there have been significant increases in the numbers of Indigenous students enrolling to study at Australian universities. While the profile is changing, Indigenous students remain more likely to be mature-aged and female. These mature-aged women are often already skilled workers who return to university to take up opportunities for education that were not available to them as young women, due to previous exclusionary educational practices (Plater et al. 2015), or due to issues such as child raising or the need to work to support families (Bennett, Uink and Van den Berg 2020). Women also dominate the Indigenous staff profile with more than two-thirds of staff identifying as female (Thunig and Jones 2020).

Despite these gains, universities remain sites of challenge for Indigenous staff, and students at all levels. Undergraduate student retention remains persistently below that of their non-Indigenous counterparts (Behrendt et al. 2012) and a cluster of issues including experiences of racism (Oliver et al. 2013), financial pressure (Behrendt et al. 2012) and feelings of isolation in largely white institutions (Kinnane 2014) continue to be reported. As well, Indigenous students notice the lack of Indigenous content in curricula, and are concerned that Indigenous Knowledges are not valued in the academy (Rochecouste et al. 2014) or even more worrying, that taught Indigenous content is incorrect (Cameron and Robinson 2014). Postgraduate students report similar issues. Financial pressures continue, students can experience cultural isolation and disruption of community networks (Barney 2013), and research students can have difficulty finding Indigenous supervisors for their research (Trudgett 2011). As well, many of the gains driven by Indigenous staff come at the cost of additional burdens of responsibility for Indigenous students, responding to enquiries and needs of non-Indigenous staff (Page and Asmar 2008) and the ongoing effects of working in environments where white privilege continues to be a source of oppression for Indigenous people (Fredericks 2009; Thunig and Jones 2020).

One key recent development is the establishment of a national strategic focus on Indigenous outcomes, in key areas of tertiary education, such as student success, research and workforce, as well as including Indigenous content in the curriculum. Universities Australia, the peak body for Australian universities, in collaboration with a longstanding Indigenous higher education advocacy group, the National Aboriginal and Torres Strait Islander Higher Education Consortium, produced a comprehensive strategic document, the *Indigenous Strategy 2017–2020* (Universities Australia 2017). The strategy commits all universities to having Indigenous content in the curricula. Indigenous scholars have championed this national commitment; however, it is a 'double-edged sword'. It is likely that much of the challenge of this work will fall to Indigenous staff, and particularly to female staff, who are in the majority (Liddle 2013). A common approach to embedding Indigenous content in curriculum has been through graduate attributes.

Leading an Indigenous Graduate Attribute Project

Graduate attributes have been a response to sustained technological change and employer demands for highly skilled graduates for the contemporary workforce (Bridgstock 2009; Kalfa and Taksa 2015). While initially the soft skills of communication and working with others were common features of curricula designed to meet employability needs, more recently a new generation of skills, aimed at enhancing graduates' abilities to be productive contributors to social cohesion (Barrie 2007), such as intercultural and international skills (Clifford and Montgomery 2014), and sustainability (Milutinovi and Nikoli 2014), have emerged. The development of Indigenous Graduate Attributes was seen as an effective mechanism through which widespread Indigenizing of curriculum could be achieved, to buttress the development of Indigenous curriculum in the health disciplines over almost two decades (see, for example, Dudgeon et al. 2016; Phillips 2004; Virdun et al. 2013) and more recently other professional disciples like law (Wood 2013) and education (Hart et al. 2012). However, not all disciplines have embraced the need for Indigenous-focused curriculum (Anning 2010; Howlett et al. 2013) and while the institution-wide focus that graduate attributes bring can be seen as a 'win', this success brings a fresh set of challenges.

There are two key, but separate challenges of Indigenizing curriculum through the mechanism of graduate attributes. First, a graduate-attributes approach draws this curriculum work into institutional quality frameworks, which Bullen and Flavell (2017) argue is not well-placed to manage the challenges of this work. For example, the resistance of students whose negativity can be reflected in evaluations of teaching and the paucity of non-Indigenous academics who are capable or confident to develop the required curriculum (Wolfe et al. 2018). Second, the generic nature of graduate attributes can mean that the relevance of specific attributes are taught and developed outside of the disciplinary context and yet, as Jones (2009) discovered, apparently generic skills such as problem-solving have different meaning and application in different disciplines. Arguably, to have meaning and to produce cultural capability in graduates, Indigenous curriculum has to be connected to the learner's discipline or degree (Page et al. 2019a). The silence and invisibility of Indigenous matter in many disciplines (Bodkin-Andrews et al. 2018) entrenches this challenge and is one reason Indigenous academics are called on to take up the bulk of this work. Non-Indigenous academics do not have to become experts, rather they need to be 'knowledgeable and receptive' (Bessarab 2015: 2) and prepared to work through any discomfort in order to 'know' rather than 'unknow'.

For the last two decades I have been teaching Australian Indigenous Studies to both Indigenous and non-Indigenous undergraduate students. I am Aboriginal Australian and trace my ancestry through my father's family. Like many Indigenous teachers, I teach because I am committed to the discipline but also because I hope that through my teaching, students will have a better understanding of Indigenous peoples, that they will combat racism (Hollinsworth 2016) and work more effectively to enhance outcomes for Indigenous people (Asmar and Page 2009). More recently, I led an Indigenous Graduate Attributes (IGA) project at an Australian university. The university not only was committed to ensuring that all graduates developed Indigenous professional capability, but also understood that this work would likely require Indigenous leadership to be successful. Our all-Indigenous Australian team led the IGA project from its beginning in February 2015 until the end of 2018.

Part of what this work requires is institution-wide change in both culture and practice because, as Dervin (2016: 78) notes, acquiring knowledge about another culture does little to expose underlying 'hegemony, hierarchies, and power differentials'. Notably, organizational change often fails to be implemented fully or sustainably for a variety of reasons, including staff resistance (Georgalis et al. 2015). In this case social justice and inclusiveness were already explicit in the university's curriculum, policies and strategies, and embedded in the culture of the institution (Page, Trudgett and Bodkin-Andrews 2019a). In this context, staff resistance was not overt; however, academic staff concerns about capacity and knowledge and getting things wrong were common. While the university was poised for the implementation of the Indigenous Graduate Attribute project in many respects, at the practical level of designing curriculum, there was considerable work to do. Much of this work involves sensemaking (Eckel and Kezar 2003) which ensures that all staff, both academic and professional, consider Indigenized curriculum to be part of the routine work of the institution and know how their practice contributes to the overall goal.

A major part of sensemaking is the ongoing conversations, which contribute to 'new mental models' (Eckel and Kezar 2003: 40) required for transformational and sustained change. For me, these conversations occurred after the presentations in the many workshops I facilitated, and often in individual meetings with colleagues who sought my advice on how to Indigenize their particular curriculum. This ongoing discourse helped to build a shared understanding of the project, to manage concerns about the crowded curriculum and build the enthusiasm so critical for effective change (Mader, Scott and Razak 2013). Patience, persistence and process are key concepts in organizational change (Johnson-Grau et al. 2016).

Indigenous Knowledges may be characterized as gifts or hospitality (Bullen and Flavell 2017). Sharing and the notion of reciprocity are common aspects of Indigeneity, yet Kuokkanen (2008) cautions that the gift of Indigenous Knowledges to the academy are not infinite and should not be taken to granted. Below I reflect on my own experiences, considering my previously published work in the area of Indigenous graduate attributes and Indigenized curriculum, from a fresh perspective using the framework of three challenges. I have summarized these challenges in terms of three key ideas – persuasion, patience and persistence.

Persuasion, Patience and Persistence

Having set the context, I now outline three challenges in my work. The first challenge is persuasion. This challenge requires the ability to overcome resistance in both students and colleagues. The second challenge – patience – is about taking time – both in curriculum and with people. The third challenge – persistence – follows the first two and is the most difficult and the one without which the others do not count. I bring to my work a theoretical arsenal which means I can identify racism in its many forms, and I can recognize white fragility or label a micro-aggression (DiAngelo 2011), but these are events that happen outside of me. They are critical concepts I use to understand what is happening around me and these notions name things that happen to Indigenous academics (Thunig and Jones 2020). The tools *I use* in response, though, are what I want to discuss here. They are not the same tools everyone uses, although most would use them in some way or another. The way I use these tools is related to both my Knowledge and my personal approach. My approach though, is not only individual; it is part of a broader political struggle (Cormier 2007) in which I seek to contribute to collective anti-racist actions. When I use persuasion, for example, it will likely involve questions that might lead to alternative ways of thinking or reframing (Bolman and Gallos 2010) or it might involve sharing alternative possibilities. My way is not the only way; however, they are qualities and acts that I have seen repeated over many years. While these skills are likely to be deployed differently, I would argue that at their heart these are tools Indigenous academics use frequently and reflexively, tactically taking advantage of the tools at our immediate disposal to enact 'world-shaping power' (Cormier 2007: 2).

Persuasion

I use persuasion to describe a discursive approach rather than as a power-coercive tactic (de Freitas and Oliver 2005). Persuasion is often the antidote to an event or a response to a situation. The skill of persuasion can be required in a range of circumstances, both individual and institutional, at times requiring more effort than others. Descriptors such 'white privilege' and 'white fragility' (DiAngelo 2011; Flynn 2015) have taken hold, specifically reflecting observed student behaviours as well echoing the fraught space of Indigenous teaching more generally. Hostility, anger and disengagement mark out the resistant student and are recurring responses to Indigenous studies curriculum that teachers perennially encounter (Asmar and Page 2009). Staff can also exhibit behaviours redolent of privilege and whiteness. These are situations where skills and acts of persuasion must combine.

Persuasion is most obviously required when negotiating with non-Indigenous students or colleagues, but it can also be necessary to use it with Indigenous colleagues. Powers of persuasion may be required not just in response to resistant students in the classroom, but can be necessary to address colleagues who are not convinced that Indigenous content in their curriculum is needed. It may be required at institutional level to convince a committee of the need for policy change to support Indigenous curriculum implementation or for example to create an award to recognize staff achievement. Conversely, sometimes I find myself persuading Indigenous colleagues that their work is valuable and valued, although it may seem invisible in their school, department, faculty or university.

Persuasion may be required to support colleagues who do not think there is space in their curriculum or who want to embed Indigenous curriculum into their courses but who do not quite know how. These conversations involve discussions about possibilities, about resources that might be sought or approaches that could be taken. They often entail taking an interest in discipline areas which are out of my area of expertise. On other occasions persuasion is required to help manage fear. Student resistance behaviour can occur outside of the classroom, most commonly through written, anonymous, difficult to respond to and negative teaching evaluations. As noted above, there is a cluster of problems associated with this type of resistance including the effects on teacher confidence (Gair 2016), and the wider implications of poor teaching evaluations on programmes and faculties (Gair 2016; Hollinsworth 2016). Some of my work is persuading teachers (and administrators) to continue rather than be immobilized by occasional negative feedback. Theoretical tools such as White fragility or the notion of privilege are useful beginning points for understanding often complex human behaviour, but it is the persuasive conversations that challenge students' thinking (Thorpe and Burgess 2016) and open dialogue between staff.

Patience

Patience, along with traits such as openness, respect and curiosity, are considered important for student learning (Spelt et al. 2009) but is less often considered as a teacher trait or considered necessary for organizational change. The academy is a place and space where patience is not necessarily considered as a virtue. If we think of space in terms of temporality and time rather than simply as a geographic and concrete entity, this makes more sense. Learning in higher education is usually conceptualized and operationalized as linear in time (Bennett and Burke 2018). A semester begins, then unfolds week by week and ends with exams or final assessment, via a forward trajectory. Rarely is a student or staff member able to go back once the forward momentum begins. University timetables are often overtly governed via the passage of hours (lectures and tutorials), weeks (semesters) and years (time taken to complete a degree), and increasingly for academic staff, in terms of workload formulas, performance and productivity requirements, or availability of casual teaching hours (Leathwood and Read 2020). Time, however, can also be considered more temporally as in how we experience time. Time becomes something we spend, use or indeed waste. Some of my time is spent in conversations with colleagues and students. I deploy that time patiently.

Hoy (2012) argues that time can be considered from different vantage points, sociological, scientific and philosophical and makes the interesting distinction between universal time and the human experience of time. This is a useful distinction for me as I consider my use of patience in my IGA work. Patience is more than time, there are (at least) additional elements such as giving and respect, but these are underpinned by time and in the institutional context time is the most visible and accountable factor. I am often thanked for being *generous* with my time, perhaps reflecting a recognition of the 'gift'. If I think of the institution's time, I am aware of what Adam (2003) calls clock time, or the commodification of time that represents money in respect to my salary (the idea that time is money) and the increasing compression and control of time. Consequently, I worry about whether I am I using my time wisely, if conversations are a useful way to spend my time, or if I am I am simply *wasting* time. These reflections are associated with feelings of guilt, being rushed, and can be a source of stress.

Using my conversations with academic colleagues as a point of reference, the topics we discuss are very similar and they fall into two major categories. First, the fear of getting 'things' wrong and second, a lack of confidence in whether Indigenous curriculum is something the individual should be doing (Gair 2007). Addressing my reflexive self, on balance, I make appointments for an hour rather than half an hour. Although the topics of conversation are similar, each individual experiences them in their own way. It is difficult to know at the outset whether the time will be 'wasted' or how many of those single hours it will take for confidence to build or understanding to develop. In this respect, I consider the time spent as an investment, recognizing that any productivity gains, within the Western constraints of modern educational spaces (Stein 2019), in this deeply interpersonal work, require patience.

Persistence

Persistence is both the overarching and underpinning factor, without which patience and persuasion remain weakly valent individual acts with limited capacity to galvanize change. The ability to persist and the act of persisting in the face of adversity and indifference is critical. Persistence has been the key to creating space, initially for Indigenous people in universities (Holt and Morgan 2016) and more recently for advocating for change in curriculum. The need and desire to persist stems from anger and a strong sense of injustice but also from hope; for recognition, for equality and for opportunity. Thirty years ago a Royal Commission into Aboriginal Deaths in Custody called for better education of non-Indigenous people in relation to Indigenous Australian history and culture (Johnston 1991) as a remedy to the gross neglect and negligence experienced by Indigenous Australia through judicial process (Marchetti 2005). The evocation for non-Indigenous Australians to have greater awareness of the entangled histories (Nakata 2007) of Indigenous and non-Indigenous Australians, has subsequently reverberated through a range of recent higher education reports and policy documents. For example, a review of Australian higher education (Bradley et al. 2008) in the late 2000s made recommendations for the federal government to consider measures to both access to, and outcomes of, tertiary education for Indigenous Australians. This review led to a trio of reports ranging from a comprehensive report on Indigenous outcomes in higher education (Behrendt et al. 2012), to specific areas such as growing the Indigenous higher education workforce (Indigenous Higher Education Advisory Council 2011) and developing Indigenous curriculum (Universities Australia 2011). What is not immediately evident when considering such reports is the work required to gather the evidence or to make the required arguments. This is where the persistence of Indigenous people, academics – and our allies – is required.

No opportunity is forgone. Each of the reports noted above critically developed considerable bodies of evidence, illuminating the results of government and institutional inertia; too few Indigenous students, insufficient Indigenous staff, inadequate cultural competency of university staff or invisibility of Indigenous matters in disciplinary curriculum. Incrementally, momentum has gathered with each fresh layer of evidence pointing to the under-representation of Aboriginal and Torres Strait Islander peoples, which sits at the very heart of inequity in Australian Higher Education, fuelled by the persistence of Indigenous Australians, bit individually and collectively, over generations.

At an individual level persistence manifests as the capacity to return to teaching Indigenous studies classes knowing that there will be resistant students, racist comments and misinformation to address (Hollinsworth 2016). Like Ground Hog Day, each year, each semester delivers a fresh set of learners who will not know that you have heard these same arguments regularly or be unaware of the hurt that can be caused by even inadvertent racism (Thorpe and Burgess 2016). Indigenous academics feel the strain (Asmar and Page 2009; Thunig and Jones 2020) and are sometimes captive to university quality and workload processes, which fail to account for the nature of this work (Bullen and Flavell 2017). Resolve is required to have the same conversation with different colleagues, justifying the need to Indigenous curriculum despite existing national and institutional policy commitments, knowing that it is often the second or third conversation which causes a shift in thinking that will ultimately result in change. When these conversations were part of my role leading the IGA project, taking that time seemed justifiable. It is less so for Indigenous academics who are attempting to develop their own careers while juggling the dual demands of servicing the needs of (some) unknowing non-Indigenous colleagues and the teaching of Indigenous studies where they are confronted with (and by) resistant or racist students.

Despite the familiarity of interactions, I see these discussions and each of these challenges and qualities as critical to reframing thinking, building understanding and entrenching Indigenous curriculum into the fabric of an institution. While Indigenous leadership of such projects is desirable, the burden of developing and teaching Indigenous curriculum should not be singular.

References

Adam, Barbara (2003), 'Reflexive modernization temporalized', *Theory, Culture & Society*, 20 (2): 59–78.
Anning, Berice (2010), 'Embedding an Indigenous graduate attribute into University of Western Sydney's courses', *Australian Journal of Indigenous Education*, 39 (2): 40–52.
Anthony, Thalia (2020), 'I can't breathe!' Australia must look in the mirror to see our own deaths in custody', *The Conversation*, 2 June: Available online: https://theconversation.com/i-cant-breathe-australia-must-look-in-the-mirror-to-see-our-own-deaths-in-custody-139848 (accessed 2 June 2020).
Asmar, Christine and Susan Page (2009), 'Sources of satisfaction and stress among Indigenous academic teachers: Findings from a national Australian study', *Asia Pacific Journal of Education*, 29 (3): 387–401.

Barney, Katelyn (2013), '"Taking your mob with you": Giving voice to the experiences of Indigenous Australian postgraduate students', *Higher Education Research & Development*, 32 (4): 515–28.

Barrie, Simon C. (2007), 'A conceptual framework for the teaching and learning of generic graduate attributes', *Studies in Higher Education*, 32 (4): 439–58.

Battiste, Marie, Lynne Bell and L. M. Findlay (2002), 'Decolonizing education in Canadian universities: An interdisciplinary, international, indigenous research project', *Canadian Journal of Native Education*, 26 (2): 82–95.

Behrendt, Larissa, Steven Larkin, Robert Griew, Particia Kelly (2012), *Review of Higher Education Access and Outcomes for Aboriginal and Torres Strait Islander People – Final Report*, Canberra: Commonwealth of Australia.

Bennett, Anna and Penny Jane Burke (2018), 'Re/conceptualising time and temporality: an exploration of time in higher education', *Discourse: Studies in the Cultural Politics of Education*, 39 (6): 913–25.

Bennett, Rebecca, Bep Uink and Chanelle van den Berg (2020), 'Educating Rita at the cultural interface: Exploring intersections between race and gender in the experiences of Australian Aboriginal women at university', *Diaspora, Indigenous, and Minority Education*, 15 (2): 84–98.

Bessarab, Dawn (2015), 'Changing how and what we do: The significance of embedding Aboriginal and Torres Strait Islander ways of knowing, being, and doing in social work education and practice', *Australian Social Work*, 68 (1): 1–4.

Bradley, Denise, Peter Noonan, Helen Nugent and Bill Scales (2008), *Review of Australian Higher Education: Final Report*, Canberra: Commonwealth of Australia. Available online: www.deewr.gov.au/he_review_finalreport

Bodkin-Andrews, Gawaian, Susan Page and Michelle Trudgett (2018), 'Shaming the silences: Indigenous graduate attributes and the privileging of Aboriginal and Torres Strait Islander voices', *Critical Studies in Education*, 63 (2): 232–60.

Bolman, Lee G. and Joan V Gallos (2010), *Reframing Academic Leadership*, San Francisco: John Wiley & Sons.

Bridgstock, Ruth (2009), 'The graduate attributes we've overlooked: Enhancing graduate employability through career management skills', *Higher Education Research and Development*, 28 (1): 31–44.

Bullen, Jonathan and Helen Flavell (2017), 'Measuring the "gift": Epistemological and ontological differences between the academy and Indigenous Australia', *Higher Education Research & Development*, 36 (3): 583–96.

Bullen, Jonathan and Lynne Roberts (2018), 'Driving transformative learning within Australian Indigenous Studies', *The Australian Journal of Indigenous Education*, 48 (1): 12–23.

Cameron, Shaun and Ken Robinson (2014), 'The experiences of Indigenous Australian psychologists at university', *Australian Psychologist*, 49 (1): 54–62.

Carroll, David (2015), *Beyond Graduation 2014. A Report of Graduates' Work and Study Outcomes: Three Years after Course Completion*, Melbourne: Graduate Careers Australia Ltd.

Clifford, Valerie and Catherine Montgomery (2014), 'Challenging conceptions of western higher education and promoting graduates as global citizens', *Higher Education Quarterly*, 68 (1): 28–45.

Cormier, Harvey Jerome (2007), 'Ever not quite: Unfinished theories, unfinished societies, and pragmatism', in S. Sullivan and N. Tuana (eds), *Race and Epistemologies of Ignorance*, 59–76, Albany: State University of New York Press.

De Freitas, Sara and Martin Oliver (2005), 'Does e-learning policy drive change in higher education?: A case study relating models of organisational change to e-learning implementation', *Journal of Higher Education Policy and Management*, 27 (1): 81–96.

Dervin, Fred (2016), *Interculturality in Education: A Theoretical and Methodological Toolbox*, London: Springer.

DiAngelo, Robin (2011), 'White fragility', *International Journal of Critical Pedagogy*, 3 (3): 54–70.

Dudgeon, Pat, Dawn Darlaston-Jones, Gregory Phillips, Katrina Newnham, Tom Brideson, Jacquelyn Cranney, Sabine Hammond, Jillene Harris, Heather Herbert, Judi Homewood and Susan Page (2016), *Australian Indigenous Psychology Education Project (AIPEP): Curriculum Framework*, Perth, WA: University of Western Australia.

Eckel, Peter D. and Adrianna Kezar (2003), 'Key strategies for making new institutional sense: Ingredients to higher education transformation', *Higher Education Policy*, 16 (1): 39–53.

Flynn Jr, Joseph (2015), 'White fatigue: Naming the challenge in moving from an individual to a systemic understanding of racism', *Multicultural Perspectives*, 17 (3): 115–24.

Fredericks, Bronwyn (2009), 'Look before you leap: The epistemic violence that sometimes hides behind the word inclusion', *Australian Journal of Indigenous Education*, 38 (S1): 10–16.

Gair, Susan (2007), 'Pursuing Indigenous-inclusive curriculum in social work tertiary education: Feeling my way as a non-Indigenous educator', *Australian Journal of Indigenous Education*, 36 (2): 49–55.

Gair, Susan (2016), 'Critical reflections on teaching challenging content: Do some students shoot the (white) messenger?', *Reflective Practice*, 17 (5): 592–604.

Georgalis, Joanna, Ramanie Samaratunge, Nell Kimberley and Ying Lu (2015), 'Change process characteristics and resistance to organisational change: The role of employee perceptions of justice', *Australian Journal of Management*, 40 (1): 89–113.

The Guardian, (2020), *Deaths Inside: Indigenous Australian Deaths in Custody*, online database. Available online: https://www.theguardian.com/australia-news/ng-interactive/2018/aug/28/deaths-inside-indigenous-australian-deaths-in-custody (accessed 4 January 2021).

Hart, Victor, Susan Whatman, Juliana McLaughlin and Vinathe Sharma-Brymer (2012), 'Pre-service teachers' pedagogical relationships and experiences of embedding indigenous Australian knowledge in teaching practicum', *Compare: A Journal of Comparative and International Education*, 42 (5): 703–23.

Hollinsworth, David (2016), 'Unsettling Australian settler supremacy: Combating resistance in university Aboriginal studies', *Race Ethnicity and Education*, 19 (2): 412–32.

Holt, Leanne and Robert Morgan (2016), 'Empowering Aboriginal aspirations in Australian university structures and systems', *Higher Education Research and Development*, 39: 96–105.

Hooper, Greg, Jonathan Richards and Judy Watson (2020), 'Mapping colonial massacres and frontier violence in Australia: "The names of places"', *Cartographica: The International Journal for Geographic Information and Geovisualization*, 55 (3): 193–8.

Horsthemke, Kai (2017), '"#FactsMustFall"?–education in a post-truth, post-truthful world', *Ethics and Education*, 12 (3): 273–88.

Howlett, Catherine, Jo-Anne L. Ferreira, Monica. M Seini and Christopher J. Matthews (2013), 'Indigenising the Griffith school of environment curriculum: Where to from here?', *Australian Journal of Indigenous Education*, 42 (1): 68–74.

Hoy, David Couzens (2012), *The Time of Our Lives: A Critical History of Temporality*, Hong Kong: MIT Press.

Indigenous Higher Education Advisory Council (2006), *Partnerships, Pathways and Policies, Improving Indigenous Education Outcomes*, Conference Report of the Second Annual Indigenous Higher Education Conference, 18–19 September, Canberra: Australian Government.

Indigenous Higher Education Advisory Council (2011), *National Indigenous Higher Education Workforce Strategy*, Canberra: IHEAC.

Johnson-Grau, Glen, Susan G. Archambault, Elisa S. Acosta and Lindsey McLean (2016), 'Patience, persistence, and process: Embedding a campus-wide information literacy program across the curriculum', *The Journal of Academic Librarianship*, 42 (6): 750–6.

Johnston, Elliot (1991), *Final Report of the Royal Commission into Aboriginal Deaths in Custody*, Canberra: Australian Government Publishing Service.

Jones, Anna (2009), Redisciplining generic attributes: The disciplinary context in focus, *Studies in Higher Education*, 34 (1): 85–100.

Kalfa, Senia and Lucy Taksa (2015), 'Cultural capital in business higher education: Reconsidering the graduate attributes movement and the focus on employability', *Studies in Higher Education*, 40 (4): 580–95.

Kickett, Marion, Julie Hoffman and Helen Flavell (2014), 'A model for large-scale, interprofessional, compulsory cross-cultural education with an indigenous focus', *Journal of Allied Health*, 43 (1): 38–44.

Kinnane, Stephen, Judith Wilks and Katie Wilson (2014), *Can't be What you Can't See: The Transition of Aboriginal and Torres Strait Islander Students into Higher Education: Final Report 2014*, Sydney: Office for Learning and Teaching.

Kuokkanen, Rauna (2008), 'What is hospitality in the academy? Epistemic ignorance and the (im) possible gift', *The Review of Education, Pedagogy, and Cultural Studies*, 30 (1): 60–82.

Ladson-Billings, Gloria (1998), 'Just what is critical race theory and what's it doing in a nice field like education?' *International Journal of Qualitative Studies in Education*, 11 (1): 7–24.

Leathwood, Carole and Barbara Read (2020), 'Short-term, short-changed? A temporal perspective on the implications of academic casualisation for teaching in higher education', *Teaching in Higher Education*: 1–16.

Liddle, Celeste (2013), 'Strategies for inclusivity: Indigenous women and the academy', *Agenda*, 21: 24–5.

Machetti, Elena (2005), 'Critical reflections upon Australia's royal commission into Aboriginal deaths in custody', *Macquarie Law Journal*, 5: 103–25.

Macintyre, Stuart and Anna Clark (2003), *The History Wars*, Melbourne, Australia: Melbourne University Press.

Mader, Clemens, Geoffrey Scott and Dzulkifli Abdul Razak (2013), 'Effective change management, governance and policy for sustainability transformation in higher education', *Sustainability Accounting, Management and Policy Journal*, 4 (3): 264–84.

Milutinovic, Slobodan and Vesna M. Nikoli (2014), 'Rethinking higher education for sustainable development in Serbia: An assessment of Copernicus charter principles in current higher education practices', *Journal of Cleaner Production*, 62: 107–13.

Moreton-Robinson, Aileen, Maggie Walter, David Singh and Megan Kimber (2011), *On Stony Ground: Governance and Aboriginal and Torres Strait Islander Participation in Australian Universities, Review of Higher Education Access and Outcomes for Aboriginal and Torres Strait Islander People*. Retrieved from https://docs.education.gov.au/system/files/doc/other/moreton-robinson_et_al_2011.pdf

Nakata, Martin (2007), 'The cultural interface', *The Australian Journal of Indigenous Education*, 36 (5): 2–14.

Oliver, Rhonda, Judith Rochecouste, Debra Bennell, Roz Anderson, Inala Cooper, Simon Forrest and Mike Exell (2013), 'Understanding Australian Aboriginal tertiary student needs', *The International Journal of Higher Education*, 2 (4): 52–64.

Page, Susan and Christine Asmar (2008), 'Beneath the teaching iceberg: Exposing the hidden support dimensions of Indigenous academic work', *The Australian Journal of Indigenous Education*, 37 (S1): 109–17.

Page, Susan, Michelle Trudgett and Corrinne Sullivan (2017), 'Past, present and future: Acknowledging Indigenous achievement and aspiration in higher education', *HERDSA Review of Higher Education*, 14: 29–51.

Page, Susan, Michelle Trudgett and Gawaian Bodkin-Andrews (2019a), 'Creating a degree-focused pedagogical framework to guide Indigenous graduate attribute curriculum development', *Higher Education*, 78 (1): 1–15.

Page, Susan, Michelle Trudgett and Gawaian Bodkin-Andrews (2019b), 'Tactics or strategies? Exploring everyday conditions to facilitate implementation of an Indigenous graduate attributes project', *Journal of Higher Education Policy and Management*, 41 (4): 390–403.

Parkes, Robert J. (2007), 'Reading history curriculum as postcolonial text: Towards a curricular response to the history wars in Australia and beyond', *Curriculum Inquiry*, 37 (4): 383–400.

Phillips, Gregory (2004), *CDAMS Indigenous Health Curriculum Framework*, Melbourne, Australia: Vic Health Koori Health Research and Community Development Unit.

Pitama, Suzanne G., Suetonia C. Palmer, Tania Huria, Cameron Lacey and Tim Wilkinson (2018), 'Implementation and impact of indigenous health curricula: A systematic review', *Medical Education*, 52 (9): 898–909.

Plater, Suzanne, Julie Mooney-Somers and Jo Lander (2015), 'The fallacy of the bolted horse: Changing our thinking about mature-age Aboriginal and Torres Strait Islander university students', *The Australian Journal of Indigenous Education*, 44 (1): 59–69.

Robinson, Shirleene and Jessica Paten (2008), 'The question of genocide and Indigenous child removal: The colonial Australian context', *Journal of Genocide Research*, 10 (4): 501–18.

Rochecouste, Judith, Rhonda Oliver and Debra Bennell (2014), 'Is there cultural safety in Australian universities?', *International Journal of Higher Education*, 3 (2): 153–66.

Sandlin, Jennifer A. and Julie C. Garlen (2017), 'Magic everywhere: Mapping the Disney curriculum', *Review of Education, Pedagogy, and Cultural Studies*, 39 (2): 190–219.

Schaefli, Laura, Anne Godlewska, Lisa Korteweg, Andrew Coombs, Lindsay Morcom, and John Rose (2018), 'What do first-year university students in Ontario, Canada, know about First Nations, Métis, and Inuit peoples and topics?', *Canadian Journal of Education*, 41 (3): 689–725.

Spelt, E. J., H. J. Biemans, H. Tobi, P. A. Luning and M. Mulder (2009), 'Teaching and learning in interdisciplinary higher education: A systematic review', *Educational Psychology Review*, 21 (4): 365–1330.

Stein, Sharon (2019), 'Beyond higher education as we know it: Gesturing towards decolonial horizons of possibility', *Studies in Philosophy and Education*, 38 (2): 143–61.

Sullivan, Sharon and Nancy Tuana (2007), 'Introduction', in S. Sullivan, and N. Tuana (eds), *Race and Epistemologies of Ignorance*, 1–10, Albany: State University of New York Press.

Tahmahkera, Dustin (2014), *Tribal Television: Viewing Native People in Sitcoms*, Chapel Hill: UNC Press.

Thorpe, Katrina and Cathie Burgess (2016), 'Challenging lecturer assumptions about preservice teacher learning in mandatory Indigenous Studies', *The Australian Journal of Indigenous Education*, 45 (2): 119–28.

Thunig, Amy and Tiffany Jones (2020), '"Don't make me play house-n*** er": Indigenous academic women treated as "black performer" within higher education', *The Australian Educational Researcher*, 48(3): 397–417.

Trudgett, M. (2011), 'Western places, academic spaces and Indigenous faces: Supervising Indigenous Australian postgraduate students', *Teaching in Higher Education*, 16 (4): 389–99.

Trudgett, Michelle, Susan Page and Stacey Kim Coates (2020), 'Talent war: Recruiting Indigenous senior executives in Australian Universities', *Journal of Higher Education Policy and Management*, 43 (1): 110–24.

Universities Australia (2011), *National Best Practice Framework for Indigenous Cultural Competency in Australian Universities*, Canberra, ACT: Universities Australia.

Universities Australia (2017), *Indigenous Strategy 2017–2020*, Canberra, ACT: Universities Australia.

Wolfe, Naomi, Loretta Sheppard, Peter Le Rossignol and Shawn Somerset (2018), 'Uncomfortable curricula? A survey of academic practices and attitudes to delivering Indigenous content in health professional degrees', *Higher Education Research & Development*, 37 (3): 649–62.

Wood, A. J. (2013), 'Incorporating indigenous cultural competency in the broader law curriculum', *Legal Education Review*, 23 (1): 57–81.

Virdun, Claudia, Joanne Gray, Juanita Sherwood, Tamara Power, Angela Phillips, Nicola Parker and Debra Jackson (2013), 'Working together to make Indigenous health care curricula everybody's business: A graduate attribute teaching innovation report', *Contemporary Nurse*, 46 (1): 97–104.

7

Anti-feminist Misogynist Shitposting: The Challenges of Feminist Academics Navigating Toxic Twitter

Xumeng Xie, Idil Cambazoglu, Bárbara Berger-Correa
and Jessica Ringrose

Introduction

Gender-trolling is a specific form of online violence where entangled forms of abuse including misogyny, (hetero)sexism, racism, nationalism, transphobia and anti-feminism coalesce to create new forms of gendered knowing and being online steeped in hate (Mantilla 2013; Ringrose 2018). We apply the concept of gender-trolling in this chapter to explore an episode where our own digital feminist pedagogies on Twitter were attacked and patrolled by an angry mob of trolls. We want to position the Twitter trolling event in the context of post-truth populism where groups are struggling and fighting to gain visibility in the on/offline sphere and at the same time delegitimize other knowledge and groups, and ultimately aiming to drive other voices and views offline and out of the online public space (Salter 2018). In order to demonstrate our argument, we look in depth at the trolling episode, which involved an attack on tweets regarding a Masters level session that was exploring arts-based methodologies in sex education, specifically making Play-Doh genital models.

As we explore, anti-feminist, misogynist and right-wing conservative discourses manifested in the Twitter troll attack take four broad pathways. The first tweet trail we follow was aimed at lambasting feminist academia as part of a crisis of education and putting legitimate academia at risk. Secondly, the trolls positioned Professor Ringrose's account as a parody as a mode of defamation, to delegitimize her authority in the public domain. Thirdly, we found a defensive response to the idea of 'clitoral validity' reproducing phallogocentrism that sought to reinforce penile advantage and men's sexual superiority over women through derogatory comments about women and vulvas as well as sexualized attacks on Ringrose herself. And finally, and relatedly, we found moral panics about childhood innocence positioning sexuality education as risky, inciting hysteria around the Play-Doh genitals as evidence of sexual degradation of children by feminist academics. Taken together these four discursive tweet pathways display and disseminate anti-feminist and misogynist ideologies to delegitimate social justice discourses and control and police such voices in digital public space (Salter 2016).

The original tweet made over 200,000 impressions indicating its widespread visibility as an object of ridicule by the trolls. We will argue that platforms like Twitter magnify and amplify these discourses, by algorithmically promoting troll swarms. Twitter's main corporate goal is user engagement by any means, whatever hashtags/topics that can attract postings are what constitute their trending topics (Burgess and Baym 2020). Online performances of hate and discrimination are hence implicitly endorsed by the Twitter platform (Marwick and Lewis 2017) since the machine learning tools created to detect codes of direct threat and violence do not necessarily pick up the swarming activity, the momentum through which attacks occur in a pile-up. As we noted, the connected aim of the trolls operating in the network is to intimidate and threaten feminist accounts off the platform. Indeed, as part of the trolling, the geolocation of the tweet and Professor Ringrose was discussed (akin to doxxing) to threaten and incite fear (Jane 2016), leading to Professor Ringrose having to make a police report. Yet the attack was judged by the police as bullying rather than hate because direct threats of sexual violence were not detected, and responsibility for intervention was deflected back to Twitter reporting systems. The Twitter reporting, however, had little effect. In our conclusions we will, therefore, argue that universities need to be thinking about these digital politics of hate. In the context of this volume, trolling is important in relation to politics of truth and voice, who can speak and gain legitimacy, and how hate and misogyny are mobilized to silence feminist voices (Banet-Weiser 2018) in the post-truth context. If feminist academics are to be taking up positions of visibility and thus becoming likely subjects to ongoing episodes of abuse and reputational defamation, what must their institutions do to manage this risk and protect academics (Ringrose 2018)?

Techno-politics of Online Hate

The first point we wish to make is how platform-specific affordances (boyd 2014) and platform vernaculars (Gibbs et al. 2015) of social media platforms facilitate online discriminatory and oppressive performances. Twitter as a platform provides a vehicle to create vast networks of loosely associated online communities that follow one another based on shared feelings/affects and ideas (Papacharissi 2015). In the case of anti-feminism and misogyny, these are values of defensive anxiety around (particularly angry, white) men losing privilege and entitlement (Kimmel 2015) and a deep attachment to heteropatriarchy (Ging 2019). We will argue phallogocentric value systems seek to maintain women in a subordinate position to masculinity politically and psychosocially through digital tactics of control, harassment and abuse, aiming to drive women back to the private sphere (Pateman 1988, in Salter 2016). Such tactics are performed on Twitter through (male-dominated) linguistic and behavioural patterns and homosocialization central to the dissemination of misogyny and anti-feminism which seek to legitimize masculine superiority over women/femininities (Pascoe 2007).

Our starting point to work with social media is understanding an entwined relation between the online and offline domains, in a way that gendered power dynamics, inequality and discrimination in wider society are reproduced and often amplified in social media (Mendes et al. 2019; Ringrose 2018). Such exclusionary and discriminatory digital (gendered) performances are being carried out as multiple forms of 'technology-facilitated violence' (Ging and Siapera 2018: 516) such as cyberharassment, cyberbullying, doxxing, flaming, and (gender-)trolling (Jane 2014, 2016; Mantilla 2013; Salter 2018). These forms of violence are often sexualized (Powell and Henry 2017) seeking to sexually denigrate women, with women constituting disproportionate victims of online hate and violence (Moloney and Love 2018; Pew Research Center 2017) while the perpetrators are mostly white, cis-gender, heterosexual, privileged, middle-class men (Vera-Gray 2017).

The affordances of social media enable alliances between different social groups united in beliefs and demands for male supremacy. In this respect, Ging (2017) develops the notion of 'manosphere' to demonstrate how heterogeneous, toxic, masculinist, alt-right internet sub-cultures unite in their fight against feminism and gender equity (Ging 2019). Moreover, the influence of online abuse and violence extends far beyond the digital sphere, causing the victims stress, danger, anxiety and suicidality (Mendes et al. 2019; Moloney and Love 2018). The ongoing risk of violence, harassment and/or abuse requires marginalized groups to 'bargain' with digital patriarchy by compromising their feelings and opinions often going as far as removing themselves from the platforms (being cancelled) for fear of further abuse (Regehr and Ringrose 2018). As put by Dragiewicz et al. (2018), these misogynistic and anti-feminist tactics alter patterns of social media use, fundamentally disciplining women and regulating the online visibility of progressive gender politics.

One of the central tactics of Twitter trolling and swarming we analyse in this chapter is 'shitposting' which is an internet strategy to bait viewers to posts through outrageous claims including hate and abuse, to provoke emotional reactions in users (Evans 2019). As we will explore, shitposting is a joined-up tactic of trolling and particularly gender-trolling, where followers pile up with immediate, reactive and often highly offensive content. The platform's hate detection mechanisms fail because it does not detect nuanced use of human language (Zhang and Luo 2019) nor does it grasp the affective modulations (Massumi 2015) of interlinked group-networked practices which rely on volumes of shitposting. In this way, trolling violence is underestimated and reporting to either the platform or police gains little traction.

Research (Herring et al. 2002) on experiences of trolling suggests crucial differences between trolling and other acts of hate and harassment online (e.g. flaming or insulting). One major difference is that trolling is often identity-based and interlinked with sexism and racism (Ortiz 2020; Sundén and Paasonen 2020). When trolling tactics are addressed to a specific gender, as Mantilla (2013: 563) argues, the 'generic forms of online trolling' become 'gendertrolling' because they express anti-feminist, misogynistic, homophobic, transphobic, with white supremacist and other elements of far-right conservative forms of hate (Marwick and Lewis 2017). Moreover, gender-trolling should be understood as a more dangerous form of harassment and violence for the possibility to experience it across various platforms simultaneously and its adoption of language of (gender-based) hate and insults to actualize collective coordinated effort aimed to 'purge' the internet from women and feminists (Mantilla 2013).

Given all this, the costs of becoming a #TrendTopic on a platform like Twitter seems harder for women as they face the manoeuvres of digital sexual violence throughout the net (Ortiz 2020; Powell and Henry 2017) designed to cancel their voices. As we argue in our conclusions, therefore, there is a need for feminist activism and scholarship to rethink and recontextualize gender-trolling within a post-truth era where the techno-political background of online gendered-hate is being reconfigured through regulations of online speech designed to police and silence feminism and social justice.

Pandemic Pedagogy and Its Discontents

In 2021, the Masters module Gender, Sexuality and Education that we co-teach was running in an online format via Zoom. The session on youth sexuality and relationship and sex education was the midpoint of the ten-week module and the start of a conceptual move from theoretical foundations of gender, sexuality and feminisms to putting theories into feminist praxis. Building on the research-policy-practice relationships that Professor Ringrose activates as part of her academic advocacy work, one of her key collaborators, the School of Sexuality Education (SSE) charity, was invited to the module for the third year running to deliver a session that demonstrates a workshop taught in secondary school using Play-Doh to create genitals. The session is run by a medical doctor who is also a sex education facilitator in secondary schools. In previous runs of the module, the workshop has focused solely on creating vulvas as a way of prioritizing feminine body parts given the lack of consideration of female sexual pleasure in global sex education (Allen 2013). The session's goal is to theorize and materialize empowerment and understandings of sexual and reproductive organs and sexual pleasure, with a focus on the exploration of the clitoris which has been neglected globally in sex education practice (Hirst 2012). Purposefully focusing on exploring the clitoris, the session works to explain that anatomically correct images of the clitoris were not created till 1981, showing how heteropatriarchal, Western, male-dominated science and medicine has neglected women's health and well-being in profound ways (Ringrose et al. 2019; Russo 2017).

As we all joined into the session on 9 February, however, we were suddenly instructed to also include diagrams and modelling time devoted to creating the penis as well as the vulva/clitoris, which was not planned. Including the penis in the modelling session created a different dynamic in several ways than in the previous years. First, as some of the students rightly pointed out, it reinforced a binary idea of genitals rather than fully considering intersex and other issues explored in the module. What we would come to understand later, moreover, is that producing Play-Doh penises would eventually be read as juvenile, disgusting, perverted and more. But none of this occurred to us as we worked our way through the impromptu session. Proud of the way the session had proceeded despite the limitations of Zoom online-only engagement (fatigue, glitches, disembodiment), Professor Ringrose used some of the Play-Doh genital images that students were asked to capture and upload onto an interactive digital teaching space (with students' consent) as well as a selfie to make an Instagram post about the teaching session. Mindful of potential hate and toxicity that Twitter can attract she then put four of the six images (minus her selfie) onto Twitter.

The following day the tweet was picked up by @oldandrewuk, an account with almost 20,000 followers, linked to an educational blog run by Andrew Old, titled 'Scenes from the battlefield: Teaching in British Schools'. The disparaging tweet read (Figure 7.1): 'Next time somebody asks if it's worth getting an MA in education, pass this on.'

This tweet started to generate negative comments and shortly thereafter Professor Ringrose posted a second tweet (Figure 7.2): 'Some men are seriously threatened by play-doh vulvas! My Tweet has gone viral with Twitter trolls who think that women's sexual empowerment does not belong in the classroom! Guess What? Your aggressive digs just make us feminists stronger! Please retweet if you agree! 👍♡🌈

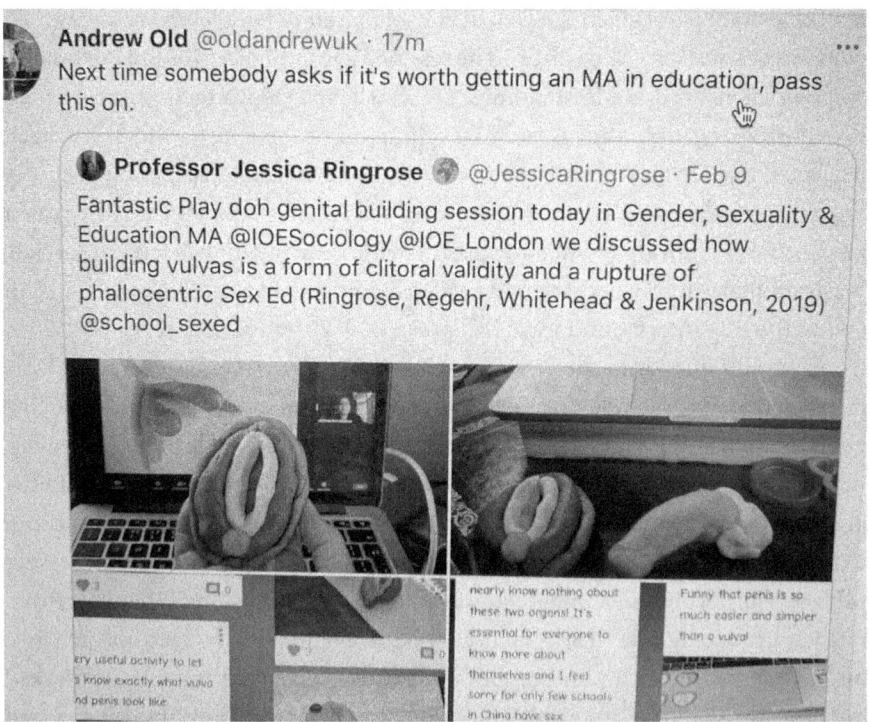

Figure 7.1 Andrew Old responding to Prof. Ringrose's first Tweet here.

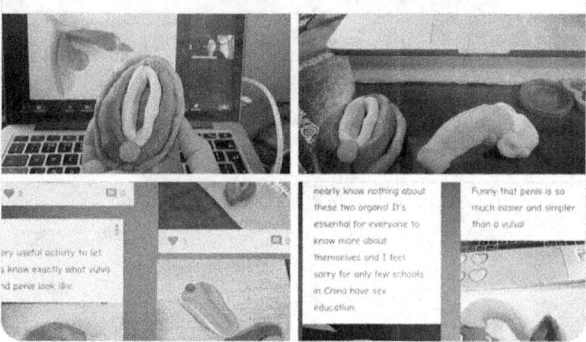

Figure 7.2 Screenshot of Prof. Ringrose's two Tweets here.

From here the Twitter activity escalated. Perhaps the tweet calling out the trolls struck a nerve and shortly afterwards the first tweet was picked up and quoted by a known anti-feminist, misogynist and, we would argue, shitpost catalyst Peter Lloyd @suffragentleman invoking Professor Ringrose's account as a 'parody' to their followers (Figure 7.3): 'This is NOT a parody! It's a real tweet from a gender studies professor at University College London @ucl.'

138 Gender in an Era of Post-truth Populism

Figure 7.3 Peter Lloyd's first Tweet (parody account) here.

Shortly after this tweet, Peter Lloyd tweeted a response to one of the images showing a student's comments around their experiences of building a penis ('Funny the penis is so much easier and simpler than the vulva') saying 'Really? Given that most women can't orgasm through sex alone, I think it's men who have the last laugh' (Figure 7.4). This smack of shitposting is designed to galvanize their followers into binary thinking around the penis and vulva, with

Peter Lloyd ✓ @Suffragentleman · 1m
Replying to @JessicaRingrose

"Funny that the penis is so much easier and simpler than the vulva".

Really? Given that most women can't orgasm through sex, I think it's men who have the last laugh.

Figure 7.4 Peter Lloyd's second Tweet (responding to student's comment) here.

an evolutionary psychology discourse of penile superiority and male sexual dominance over women (Ging 2019).

Unpacking Shitposts: Four Twitter Pathways of Hate

Using feminist critical discourse analysis (Lazar 2005), we investigate the discursive themes in 180 trolling replies and quoted retweets. These replies showed a convergence of online communities coming together in response to Professor Ringrose's two tweets. All tweets have been strictly transcribed verbatim with all original emojis, punctuation, letter case and spellings left unchanged. As we proceed, we will explore the four interrelated discursive pathways of the tweets:

1. Education in a legitimacy crisis in need of correction.
2. Attacks on Professor Ringrose's account and feminist academia as a parody.
3. Masculinist projections of penile superiority debasing women's sexual pleasure and empowerment.
4. Moral panics about childhood innocence and sex education as perverted.

Through conceptualizing Twitter's affordance of visibility, we also unpack how tactics like gender-trolling, flaming and shitposting are being widely and strategically weaponized to shut down feminist public pedagogy in digital spheres

(Ringrose 2018) and to remove feminist discourses from online public space (Salter 2018). We shall reflect on how Twitter as a platform has failed to afford effective tools to tackle disinformation, gendered hate or abuse (also intersecting with racism, transphobia etc.), and tolerated or even amplified online hostility and 'toxicity' against women and feminism (Amnesty International 2018).

Feminist Academia as an Embodiment of Crisis in Higher Education

> Next time somebody asks if it's worth getting an MA in education, pass this on.

The first notable form of negative responses stemmed from Andrew Old's tweet (see Figure 7.1) designed to ridicule the legitimacy and seriousness of using Play-Doh as a teaching tool delivered in a Masters level class. Old's followers seem to hold themselves up as genuine academic authorities who are outraged at the legitimation and visibility of feminist academia:

> how is this worthwhile education at a university level?? my god, no wonder the western world is collapsing.

> This is close to the work of Newton, Darwin and Einstein. I'm gobsmacked at your incredible insights.

Another lamented the loss of 'true' academics saying 'once upon a time we had Benjamin Jowett' whom we discovered by googling was a theologian tutor at the University of Oxford in the 1800s. These tweets signal a rejection of feminist academia, a melancholic yearning for the 'classics' embodied by the old, white, male, conservative scholars who made 'real' contributions to knowledge, civilization and society compared to Professor Ringrose.

The rejection of feminist content was driven home through a populist, conservative and capitalist discourse of rights as taxpayers to justify their acts and carry out public shaming of high-profile feminist scholars to remove them out of online public space. Many posters bemoaned public money funding a feminist scholarship at a 'top' reputable university for example:

> University College London. Taxpayer funded. Let that sink in.

> Really hope you're a parody. Sadly, I fear you're serious and I'm paying for this 🐷 💩 through my taxes.

The conservative elitist discourse against feminist academia being funded by taxpayers also expressed itself as anti-intellectualism more generally. One account, for instance, denounced the Play-Doh activity as sickening:

> You spend your day making play doh penises when most of us are working hard and putting ourselves at risk. It makes me sick to my gut that you people are allowed to call what you do work. You are a disgrace. I hope you are not being funded by the taxpayer!!

In addition to rejecting academia as worthy or legitimate, posters also pointed to the idea of sex education as a direct cause of 'men becoming more feminine' and hence signalling 'a dying civilization'. In the tweet below a history of 'Greeks, Romans and Germans' was recounted as a warning of a crisis of masculinity, under the influence of feminist academia. It also manifested how anti-feminism has been racialized by online (white-)nationalists where 'a normative white masculinity' is 'both privileged and under attack' (Bjork-James 2020: 177) and demonstrated the entanglement of anti-feminism and (white-)nationalism.

> Obsession with gender and sexuality is a sign of a dying civilization, along with men becoming more feminine. Was happening to the Greeks before the rough and ready Romans extinguished them. Was happening to the Romans before the rough and ready Germans extinguished them.

Another thread saw nationalist and conservative fear of China as a rising political and economic power, which the dying civilization and failure of worthwhile academia in the UK was hastening. China was often presented in those tweets as a seemingly positive example of focusing on 'churning out engineers, doctors, scientists and innovators' to 'build a huge economy and empire' without having to introduce sex education to its population.

> 'AnD I FeEl soRrY fOr cHiNa wHeRe oNlY a FeW sChOoLs hAvE sEx eDuCaTiOn'

> Meanwhile china is churning out engineer's, doctors, scientists and innovators whilst Western unis are making cocks out of play doh.

> Meanwhile in China, a billion people still manage to procreate by copulation, despite never playing with plasticine. In between all this amatuer shagging they still manage to build a huge economy and empire.

However, the common reference to China was constructed based on a racist, Orientalist view seeing China as a distinct pre- or anti-feminist culture that prospered through 'amateur shagging'. The core of the tweeters' political agenda to recover the hierarchy of gender and race in the British Empire was buttressed by a masculinist, patriarchal and heteronormative notion that equates sex with (hetero-)sexual reproductive intercourse.

From Mocking to Anti-feminist Abuse

In similar tweets, Play-Doh genital building was ridiculed and mocked as 'nursery school activities' for young children such as 'ball pool' or 'sand pit'. Those narratives sought to suggest our teaching represented an infantilizing model of higher education. The delegitimization of the content took greater flight, however, with Peter Lloyd's tweet signalling 'parody' which seemed to unite the trolls to collectively patrol, mock and shame feminist accounts. Professor Ringrose has been called a parody by right-wing commentators in the past in coverage in *The Daily Mail*. Usually combined with sarcastic humour, such parodying is a form of homosocial banter (Haslop and O'Rourke 2020; Ringrose et al. 2021), a way of disparaging feminism and feminists through ridiculing and shaming them in a bid to harass them off the platform and cancel them from the digital public domain (Moloney and Love 2018; Regehr and Ringrose 2018; Ringrose 2018).

Following Peter Lloyd's invocation to parody there was a huge swathe of replies saying that 'you missed out "parody" in your bio' or 'Saturday Night Live alert'. In addition to simplistic mocking and repetitions of the teaching activity as a parody other related tweets tried to clarify that 'this is NOT parody' and expressed sarcasm as to how this could constitute 'serious academia':

> This would be funny if it wasn't considered serious academia for grown ups.
>
> @uclnews I wonder why I wasted 8 years doing a degree and PhD in theoretical physics when I could have been making a plasticine cunt…
>
> All for this. The more play-doh in higher education, the better. Can't have those big salaries going to waste. And yes, clitoral validity is a key issue in today's phallocentric society.

The sarcasm expresses a defensive rejection of arts-/play-based participatory feminist pedagogies while defending phallogocentric ideas of proper academic knowledge by undermining pedagogical hands-on methods that challenge the 'seminal' ideals of giving lectures as the only proper university teaching. Comparably, LEGO as a 'serious' (and masculine) play has also been used by academics in teaching and research (Gauntlett and Holzwarth 2006) without coming under attack. This indicated that it is the message of sexual empowerment that seems to irritate the trolls who reject a method of Play-Doh teaching, wishing to hold gendered power structures of masculinist knowledge and hierarchies in place. This is also apparent in tweets that attempted to discount sex education by juxtaposing it to physics or engineering, creating a binary illusion of feminist academia as not as 'legitimate knowledge' as 'hard' (objective) scientific disciplines (Massanari 2018). It is through joking that the trolling point to an alleged common sense of what is proper academic work. Massumi (2015) calls these processes 'affective modulation' where targeted repetition over time solidifies what is considered normal. Here we see how the social media vernacular of 'parody' creates a homosocial masculinity bond to unite the trolls (Gibbs et al. 2015). As the in-side joke repeats, the humour works to affectively conceal the truth claims into common sense, it shuts down complexity and critical thinking, which is what feminist pedagogy is promoting (Lawrence and Ringrose 2018).

Emojis also played an important part in doing shorthand 'emotion work' (Riordan 2017), and were included in many tweet replies to signal affective messages such as bullshit (🐂💩) in an earlier tweet and humour 'gold' in the following tweet.

> Thank fuck you're not furloughed or we'd all miss this clitoral validity gold 🤡🤡🤡

Here the poster references COVID-19 working conditions where the UK Government implemented a furlough scheme to mock Professor Ringrose still having a job. The clown emoji seems to have become a well-versed visual signifier for enabling viral mocking and derision. *Urban Dictionary* defines the clown emoji as an 'overused' tool 'to express something funny' but also to 'burn someone in insult form'.[1]

Heterosexist Defensiveness: Male Sexual Prowess against the Feminist Vulva

Biological essentialism, heterosexism and their heteronormalizing power are evidenced in another form of anti-feminist discourse articulating hostility towards feminist sex education. A range of tweets tried to sexualize the vulvas, relating them as either poor facsimiles of vulvas, to make offensive jokes about women's sexual organs or to parody identity politics and race-colour:

> I smell fish
>
> If your vulva is green, then you should improve your vulva hygiene.
>
> - My vulva is not multi-coloured. Am I abnormal? - Not if your vulva identifies as multi-coloured.

Other tweets refer to the penis through heterosexist in-side jokes. They use irony and laughter to heterosexualize the Play-Doh genital models and compare them to sex toys as the only knowable referent point for a model penis. For instance:

> Thanks but I'll stick with Fleshlight.
> Worst. Dildos. Ever.

It is through sarcastic humour that these tweets are trying to maintain the heterosexual order as the common sense (Massumi 2015), and to sexualize the genitals through a pornified male gaze as seen in the following poster who uses the phrase 'clitoral validity' from the original tweet to turn it into a heterosexual sex scene with 'the wife':

> I often ask the wife as I'm frantically validating her clitoris, 'is it valid yet, love?'

We see the tweeters as producing 'virtual manhood acts' (Moloney and Love 2018: 603) and their tweets also demonstrate traits of a 'baseline masculinity' (Pascoe 2007: 87) where male sexual strength, prowess and heterosexual-male superiority must be displayed against femininity. Accordingly, every attempt

Figure 7.5 Snowman meme.

and/or implication that *might* challenge the tenets of these masculine norms are belittled or mocked as a tactic of self-protection (Kimmel 2015) of 'fragile masculinity' shown in Figure 7.5.

In this tweet, a snowman penetrates a snow woman from behind with a snow-penis. The snow woman is face down on the ground and one of the snowman's arm is pinning her down while the other raising in a high five – presumably a homosocial salutation to the 'brothers' out there who identify with sexual domination over women. This tweet demonstrates how gender-trolling often occurs through using lad banter graphic language (Mantilla 2013) of images, memes and GIFs. The tweet is a graphic representation of penile masculine superiority used to put the feminist tweets about clitoral validity in their place, indicating that as part of the shitposting there is some deep reactive desire to disqualify any discourse of women's sexual empowerment. The use of sexualizing humour through images are explicitly used for justifying male superiority through *apparent* male sexual prowess. Other tweets sought to involve Professor Ringrose in the sexual *mise-en-scène*:

> She clearly has trouble achieving orgasm, and it's the fault of men.

Sending sexualizing graphic images and comments to Professor Ringrose constitutes a form of 'unwanted sexual attention' (Barak 2005) and harassment, and should be read as abuse in the guise of sarcastic humour. Notably, it was not recognizable to the police who reviewed the case, since the shitposters were aware of the law and reserved making explicit threats of sexual violence. Seen on a continuum of digital sexual violence (Powell and Henry 2017), these discourses, images and graphics create a form of digital lad banter and online sexual harassment (Haslop and O'Rourke 2020; Ringrose et al. 2021). The unwanted sexual attention, hence, becomes a viral tactic for justifying the male superiority and punishment of those women who express feminist ideas (Cole 2015; Jane 2014).

Going even further than casual sexual harassment a small proportion of tweeters posted explicitly Men's Rights Activist (Ging 2017) derived tweets with memes that denigrate Professor Ringrose.

> A wide selection of twats to be sure but the biggest must be you. (Meme in Figure 7.6 included in the tweet.)

Culturally associated with radicalized far-right conservative ideology (Hodge and Hallgrimsdottir 2020), the misogynistic meme in Figure 7.6 becomes particularly noteworthy since it portrays feminists as 'repellent'. The meme

THE SHOOMER

>body positive
>uses small penis insults
basic
thinks shes hilarious
omg I'm so fat
ham sandwich pussy
my vagina stinks
"dog mom"
alchoholic
can't hold a relationship
"if you want a queen, earn her"
"*feminist*" single
"I don't shave, if you don't like it 💅💅"
lmao I farted
>"meme queen"
>shares normie memes
no kids, but looks like she has 3.

Figure 7.6 Anti-feminist meme 'THE SHOOMER'.

as a form of accessible and graphic language is weaponized to quickly spread discontent, disinformation and exclusionary masculinist ideology, and to regulate the online sphere (Ging 2017; Hodge and Hallgrimsdottir 2020). We see a distinctive strand of digital 'witch hunt' (Siapera 2019) where women are persecuted and threatened with the aim of driving them off the online public space. For instance, one of the tweets mentioned the physical geolocation of Ringrose's (similar to doxxing) replying 'From "Woking" indeed... ' which appeared to communicate an implicit threat to incite fear over disclosing her address and at the same time intend a wordplay as a mockery or insult of 'wokeness'.

Feminist Sex Education as Perverting the Innocent Child

Other tweets displayed implicit and explicit mocking expressions of making Play-Doh genitals as perverted or mentally ill behaviours that need to be disciplined and rectified. Terms in this vein that were used to describe Professor

Ringrose included: idiot, moron, lunatic, pathetic, sick, fucked, nutty, damaged goods, pervert. Some posters mentioned that the activity was akin to what lads do at school and get in trouble for:

> I used to get a slap round the ear for doing this at school.

Several tweets like this one talked about how unfair it was that this practice was now being used by feminist academics, something that was out of step with normal and proper childhood educational settings. Other tweeters were more outraged by the practising of genital modelling with children, saying for instance 'they're just kids'. These tweets were organized around a protectionist discourse (Egan and Hawkes 2008) of imperilled childhood innocence (Garlen 2018), which further related to Professor Ringrose being called a pervert or 'grooming children':

> Keep away from my fucking grandkid you creeps
>
> This is absolutely disgusting, and deeply disturbing. How do they get away with this?!
>
> Absolutely preposterous. Beyond repulsion.
>
> Sick bastards. Leave kids the fuck alone and let them develop, naturally.
>
> Tender your resignation 'Prof' you complete and utter lunatic.

We see a conservative, puritan discourse on sexuality intertwined in these attacks, since our activity with Masters level students incurred concerns about exposure to sex education putting childhood innocence at risk and ideas that discussing genitals and sexuality with young people was 'disgusting' and 'beyond repulsion':

> I am a woman, and you sort are vile. You encourage the degrading of females. How stupid you are with the dopey empowerment and Feminist buzzwords stick your plastic sex toys and stay away from grooming children.

This poster invoked her identity 'as a woman' in order to legitimize herself as a protector of children and reject feminist ideas about 'empowerment' as actually 'degrading'.

Gender-Trolling as a Trap of 'Unwanted Visibility'

Having teased out the primary discourses manifested in the trolling episode in the previous sections, we now offer a conceptualization of gender-trolling in relation to post-truth politics to account for how gendered hate and violence has been facilitated and amplified in social network sites such as Twitter. Gender-trolling as a networked form of harassment has been picked up by anti-feminist and misogynistic online groups (Mantilla 2013; Marwick and Caplan 2018) and can be better understood if we consider the dynamic entanglement of a vast array of online feminist and anti-feminist discourses, affects and the platform specificity of Twitter.

The original tweet, which received over 200,000 impressions, exemplified how specific articulations of feminisms in an online public platform can initiate a huge connective backlash causing (im)possibilities for visibility of feminist pedagogy (Ringrose 2018). The concept of 'context collapse' (Marwick and boyd 2011: 114) demonstrates the challenge to manage one's digital performances on social media platforms which singularize and reduce the context of posting (to a limited number of characters) and reach unpredictable audiences to view/comment/attack. In our case, we are called upon to perform a public digital feminist pedagogy by our institution (Ringrose 2018) and yet this invokes a wide range of anti-feminist and misogynistic hostilities (Banet-Weiser 2018). Although they are not the intended audience, the trolls, fuelled by disinformation and misperceptions about (feminist) sex education and academia and moral panic logics, flooded the original tweet with male supremacist and conservative replies, emojis, GIFs and memes expressing disgust, scorn, anger and mockery.

Moving beyond the politics of making feminist issues visible in the mediascape ('clitoral validity' in this case), we also take account of online visibility as 'the potential audience who can bear witness' (boyd 2014: 11) which is intersected with the economy of (gendered-)visibility (Banet-Weiser 2018). Marwick and Lewis (2017) have pointed out that online hate groups and trolls have adopted some tactics such as memes, bots and networks to enhance the visibility of their messages. The feature of the Twitter platform allowed their replies to appear right under the original tweets which rendered the trolls and shitposts an exhibitive space out of the control of the original poster. In this regard, our feminist pedagogy to challenge both phallogocentrism and the patriarchy in current sex education practices was hijacked by the anti-feminist and misogynist troll mob.

In doing so, posters used various tech skills and known troll tactics out of the 'alt right playbook' (Ging 2021) such as: using satirist humour and irony in memes and GIFs; posting sexist and racist hate comments; publicly posting private information about the selected target(s) (e.g. location of Professor Ringrose); and disrupting meaningful, on-topic dialogue via posting with off-topic, marauding banter (e.g. shitposting) (Ortiz 2020). In this sense, the shitposting is distinctly anti-feminist and misogynistic, and these trolling tactics should be conceptualized as 'unwanted visibility' in terms of their intrusive presence in the context. More importantly, such 'unwanted visibility' is enabled and amplified by the Twitter platform and its algorithms of hate speech detection. Research on social media detection approaches enabled by machine learning and artificial intelligence showed that these are replicating racial and gendered bias (Caliskan et al. 2017; Carlson and Rousselle 2020). Our experiences mirrored these findings as misogynistic slurs such as 'cunt', 'slapper', 'bitch', went undiscovered and unremoved even in conversations reported, which contradicted Twitter's policy on hateful conduct to prohibit 'repeated and/or non-consensual slurs, epithets, racist and sexist tropes, or other content that degrades someone' (Twitter Help Center 2021). Also, because such trolling tactics do not operate through visible violent hate speech, even when reported they are not understood as causing (enough) harm by either the police or the platform to do anything. This is also part of the post-truth landscape to legitimate and normalize anti-feminist hatred.

Our theorization of gender-trolling as a form of 'unwanted visibility' also considers the relations between platform designs and how users perceive, understand and approach certain platforms (Bucher and Helmond 2018). For social media platforms that technologically feature machine learning and economically benefit from interactions with user-generated contents, the relation between the platform and its users is not at all unidirectional, since the platform influences and is influenced by its users. We noticed some trolls responding to Professor Ringrose's second tweet saying such as '8 hrs later and only 23 RT'. Those replies tried to quantify and measure and then delegitimate the visibility of Ringrose's tweet which noted that the former tweet had 'gone viral' with trolls and asked feminists in her own feed to retweet and show support for feminist work on women's sexual empowerment. The troll rejects the claim of visibility of virality, in an attention economy which to them signals feminists are having a reaction. Such quantification is based on the capitalist logic of social media interactions being translated into profitable and legitimating attention, which the trolls seek to cancel off the platform. Researchers have expressed concerns about social media platforms' encouragement of polarizing views and disputes for its (profit-)ability to turn such disputable contents into traffic and trends for the corporates to monetize while disregarding their social responsibility to deal with hate and abuse (Bartow 2009; Munn 2020; Shepherd et al. 2015).

Empirical research has evidenced how publicity and visibility have become a major challenge for feminists and women to negotiate on Twitter (Mendes et al. 2019). This hence creates a trap where on one hand public platforms like

Twitter are widely used to promote feminist visibility, and on the other hand feminists and women are being primary targets for trolls and other online abuse (Jane 2016). This adds to the precarity of practising feminist pedagogy online and hugely undermines women's parity of participation in public spaces, and also contradicts Twitter's claimed endorsement for public conversation and for protecting against hate speech. In addition to the problems with algorithms and designs that have built-in bias and normalized polarization and harassment, Twitter's current mechanisms of tackling hateful conducts shift the responsibilities to its users by asking them to report problematic and harmful behaviours or use blocklist as a form of self-care (Wheatley and Vatnoey 2020). The focus on individual-level responsibilization is insufficient to tackle trolling as a collective form of online abuse, with wide homosocial reach in the case of misogynist networks, and is totally inadequate in tackling the structural and systemic gender inequalities that are intrinsically intertwined within infrastructures of social media platforms like Twitter.

Concluding Remarks

In this chapter, we explored an online gender-trolling event targeted at Professor Ringrose in response to tweeting about Play-Doh genital building session conducted online for Masters students in the context of a global pandemic. We summarized the main discursive themes as categorized in four pathways: education in crisis; feminist academia as a parody; masculine penile superiority and moral panics about childhood innocence. We demonstrated the main goal of gender-trolling is to disrupt dialogues through using repetitive, systematic techniques such as 'luring into pointless and time-consuming discussion' (Herring et al. 2002: 372) which we identified as shitposting. Moreover, shitposting in this chapter was identified as anti-feminist and misogynist, as we also showed sarcastic humour was part of the affective spreads of digital lad banter (Haslop and O'Rourke 2020; Ringrose et al. 2021) with a goal of harassment to cancel women and feminists, and to silence their voices in online space. At the same time, they employ strategies of avoiding Twitter Artificial Intelligence (AI) hate speech detection and future legal consequences.

The affordance of visibility was discussed to explain how gender-trolling created a trap and obstacle for digital feminist pedagogy on Twitter. However, as mentioned previously, a reconceptualization of gender-trolling is needed for a more comprehensive definition (Ortiz 2020). Trolling is not only the digital performance of hate directed to a collectively chosen target (Ortiz 2020: 6) but also the enactment and reproduction of social inequity. Our definition of gender-trolling describes the act as a form of collective and identity-based online violence adopting sarcastic lad banter humour, interlinked with (white) cis-heteronormative masculinity and regressive far-right politics.

Our position on gender-trolling is both ethical and epistemological (Ringrose et al. 2019) since we are challenging the ways that recurrent forms of online abuse are shaping the possibilities for women and marginalized people to create expression and voice, to make truth claims and dialogue with audiences online and offline. Yet also, we are pointing at how online abuse, taking discursive and affective forms of hate, disgust and satirical humour, feed into post-truth politics through abusers' modulation and reshaping of what is (not) legitimate knowledge. Facing such a post-truth climate and invasive 'alt-right gaze' (Massanari 2018: 3), feminist researchers must carefully reconsider what online space means and does for conducting, disseminating and promoting gender-progressive academic work.

We close this chapter by emphasizing the need to consider gender-trolling as a structural inequity problem but also as gendered violence and hate crime. In a moment where misogyny is starting to be recognized legally as a hate crime in the UK (Dathan and Hamilton 2021), we are pushing for the recognition of gender-trolling as digitally mediated gendered abuse. Moreover, a multi-dimensional approach to addressing gender-trolling is urgently needed which moves beyond individual self-care/protection and calls for further public debate, and legal and institutional change. Stakeholders such as social media platforms must take measures to counter these abuses instead of continuing to amplify them for their profitability. Moreover, universities encourage both scholars and PhD students to disseminate their work via social media as representatives of the institutes. Yet any encounter with online abuse is easily framed as individual-based, avoiding the need for institutional intervention nor support to prevent or protect academics from these attacks. This problem reveals significant neglect of gendered power relations endemic to knowledge production and contributes to the entangled dynamics that push feminist scholars out of the public sphere.

Note

1   The original information can be accessed from *Urban Dictionary* at https://www.urbandictionary.com/define.php?term=%F0%9F%A4%A1+%28Clown+Emoji%29

References

Allen, Louisa (2013), 'Girls' portraits of desire: Picturing a missing discourse', *Gender and Education*, 25 (3): 295–310.

Amnesty International (2018), TOXIC TWITTER - A TOXIC PLACE FOR WOMEN, retrieved from: https://www.amnesty.org/en/latest/research/2018/03/online-violence-against-women-chapter-1/

Banet-Weiser, Sarah (2018), *Empowered: Popular Feminism and Popular Misogyny*, Durham: Duke University Press.

Barak, Azy (2005), 'Sexual harassment on the Internet', *Social Science Computer Review*, 23: 77–92.

Bartow, Ann (2009), 'Internet defamation as profit center: The monetization of online harassment', *Harvard Journal of Law & Gender*, 32 (2): 383–430.

Bjork-James, Sophie (2020), 'Racializing misogyny: Sexuality and gender in the new online white nationalism', *Feminist Anthropology*, 1 (2): 176–83. https://doi.org/10.1002/fea2.12011

boyd, danah (2014). *It's Complicated: The Social Lives of Networked Teens*, New Haven: Yale University Press. Retrieved from: http://journals.openedition.org/lectures/17628

Bucher, Taina and Anne Helmond (2018), 'The affordances of social media platforms', in J. Burgess, A. Marwick and T. Poell (eds), *The SAGE Handbook of Social Media*, 33–253, London: Sage. https://doi.org/10.4135/9781473984066.n14

Burgess, Jean and Nancy K. Baym (2020), *Twitter: A Biography*, New York, NY: New York University Press.

Caliskan, Aylin, Joanna J. Bryson and Arvind Narayanan (2017), 'Semantics derived automatically from language corpora contain human-like biases', *Science*, 356 (6334): 183–6. https://doi.org/10.1126/science.aal4230

Carlson, Caitlin Ring and Hayley Rousselle (2020), 'Report and repeat: Investigating Facebook's hate speech removal process', *First Monday*, 25 (2). https://doi.org/10.5210/fm.v25i2.10288

Cole, Kirsti K. (2015), '"It's like she's eager to be verbally abused": Twitter, trolls, and (en)gendering disciplinary rhetoric', *Feminist Media Studies*, 15 (2): 356–8.

Dathan, Matt and Fiona Hamilton (18 March 2021), 'Misogyny to be classed as hate crime from autumn', *The Times*. Retrieved from: https://www.thetimes.co.uk/article/misogyny-to-be-classed-as-hate-crime-from-autumn-ztkbztjwd

Dragiewicz, Molly, Jean Burgess, Ariadna Matamoros-Fernández, Michael Salter, Nicolas Suzor, Delanie Woodlock and Bridget Harris (2018), 'Technology facilitated coercive control: Domestic violence and the competing roles of digital media platforms', *Feminist Media Studies*, 18: 1–17.

Egan, R. Danielle and Gail L. Hawkes (2008), 'Endangered girls and incendiary objects: Unpacking the discourse on sexualization', *Sexuality & Culture*, 12 (4), 291–311.

Evans, Robert (15 March 2019), 'Shitposting, inspirational terrorism, and the Christchurch mosque massacre', *Bellingcat*. Retrieved from: https://www.bellingcat.com/news/rest-of-world/2019/03/15/shitposting-inspirational-terrorism-and-the-christchurch-mosque-massacre/

Garlen, Julie C. (2018), 'Interrogating innocence: "Childhood" as exclusionary social practice', *Childhood*, 26 (1): 54–67. https://doi.org/10.1177/0907568218811484

Gauntlett, David and Peter Holzwarth (2006), 'Creative and visual methods for exploring identities', *Visual Studies*, 21 (1): 82–91. https://doi.org/10.1080/14725860600613261

Gibbs, Martin, James Meese, Michael Arnold, Bjorn Nansen and Marcus Carter (2015), '#Funeral and Instagram: Death, social media, and platform vernacular', *Information, Communication & Society*, 18 (3): 255–68. https://doi.org/10.1080/1369118X.2014.987152

Ging, Debbie (2017), 'Alphas, betas, and incels: Theorizing the masculinities of the manosphere' *Men and Masculinities*, 22 (4). https://doi.org/10.1177/1097184X17706401

Ging, Debbie (2019). 'Bros v. Hos: Postfeminism, anti-feminism and the toxic turn in digital gender politics', in D. Ging and E. Siapera (eds), *Gender Hate Online*, 45–67, Cham: Palgrave Macmillan. https://doi.org/10.1007/978-3-319-96226-9_3

Ging, Debbie (15 April 2021), *Blackpilled: Incels, Evolutionary Psychology and the Failed Intimacies of Neoliberal Capitalism*. Retrieved from: https://www.youtube.com/watch?v=AFz5zlW7EtE&ab_channel=PostdigitalIntimacies

Ging, Debbie and Eugenia Siapera (2018), 'Special issue on online misogyny', *Feminist Media Studies*, 18(4): 515–24. https://doi.org/10.1080/14680777.2018.1447345

Haslop, Craig and Fiona O'Rourke (2020), '"I mean, in my opinion, I have it the worst, because I am white. I am male. I am heterosexual": Questioning the inclusivity of reconfigured hegemonic masculinities in a UK student online culture', *Information, Communication and Society*. https://doi.org/10.1080/1369118X.2020.1792531

Herring, Susan, Kirk Job-Sluder, Rebecca Scheckler and Sasha Barab (2002), 'Searching for safety online: Managing "trolling" in a feminist forum', *The Information Society*, 18 (5) 371–84. https://doi.org/10.1080/01972240290108186

Hirst, Julia (2012), '"Get some rhythm round the clitoris". Addressing sexual pleasure in sexuality education in schools and other youth settings'. In L. Allen, M. L. Rasmussen and K. Quinlivan (eds), *Interrogating the politics of pleasure in sexuality education: Pleasure bound*, 35–56, New York: Routledge.

Hodge, Edwin and Helga Hallgrimsdottir (2020), 'Networks of hate: The alt-right, "troll culture", and the cultural geography of social movement spaces online', *Journal of Borderlands Studies*, 35 (4): 563–80. https://doi.org/10.1080/08865655.2019.1571935

Jane, Emma Alice (2014). '"Back to the kitchen, cunt": Speaking the unspeakable about online misogyny', *Continuum: Journal of Media & Cultural Studies*, 28 (4): 558–70.

Jane, Emma Alice (2016), 'Online misogyny and feminist digilantism', *Continuum*, 30 (3): 284–97. https://doi.org/10.1080/10304312.2016.1166560

Kimmel, Michael (2015), *Angry White Men: American Masculinity at the End of an Era*, New York: Nation Books.

Lawrence, Emilie and Jessica Ringrose (2018), '@NoToFeminism, #FeministsAreUgly and misandry memes: How social media feminist humour is calling out antifeminism', in J. Keller and M. Ryan (eds), *Emergent Feminisms and the Challenge to Postfeminist Media Cultures*, 211–32, New York: Routledge.

Lazar, Michelle, M. (2005), *Feminist Critical Discourse Analysis: Gender, Power and Ideology in Discourse*, New York: Palgrave MacMillan.

Mantilla, Karla (2013), 'Gendertrolling: Misogyny adapts to new media', *Feminist Studies*, 39 (2): 563–70.

Marwick, Alice E. and danah boyd (2011). 'I tweet honestly, I tweet passionately: Twitter users, context collapse, and the imagined audience', *New Media & Society*, 13 (1): 114–33. https://doi.org/10.1177/1461444810365313

Marwick, Alice E. and Rebecca Lewis (2017), *Media Manipulation and Disinformation Online*, Data & Society Research Institute. Retrieved from: https://datasociety.net/wp-content/uploads/2017/05/DataAndSociety_MediaManipulationAndDisinformationOnline-1.pdf

Marwick, Alice E. and Robyn Caplan (2018), 'Drinking male tears: Language, the manosphere, and networked harassment', *Feminist Media Studies*, 18 (4): 543–59. https://doi.org/10.1080/14680777.2018.1450568

Massanari, Adrienne L. (2018), 'Rethinking research ethics, power, and the risk of visibility in the era of the "alt-right" gaze', *Social Media + Society*, 4 (2). https://doi.org/10.1177/2056305118768302

Massumi, Brian (2015), *Politics of Affect*, Cambridge: Polity Press.

Mendes, Kaitlynn, Jessica Ringrose and Jessalynn Keller (2019), *Digital Feminist Activism: Women and Girls Fight Back against Rape Culture*, Oxford: Oxford University Press.

Moloney, Mairead Eastin and Love, Tony P. (2018), 'Assessing online misogyny: Perspectives from sociology and feminist media studies', *Sociology Compass*, 12:e12577.

Munn, Luke (2020), 'Angry by design: Toxic communication and technical architectures', *Humanities and Social Sciences Communications*, 7, 53. https://doi.org/10.1057/s41599-020-00550-7

Ortiz, Stephanie M. (2020). 'Trolling as a collective form of harassment: An inductive study of how online users understand trolling', *Social Media + Society*. https://doi.org/10.1177/2056305120928512

Papacharissi, Zizi (2015), *Affective Politics: Sentiment, Technology, and Politics*, Oxford: Oxford University Press.

Pascoe, C. J. (2007), *Dude, You're a Fag*, Los Angeles: University of California Press.

Pateman, Carole (1988), *The Sexual Contract*, Oxford: Polity Press.

Pew Research Center (2017), *Online Harassment*. Retrieved from: https://www.pewinternet.org/2017/07/11/online-harassment-2017/

Powell, Anastasia and Nicola Henry (2017), *Sexual Violence in a Digital Age*, London: Palgrave.
Regehr, Kaitlyn and Jessica Ringrose (2018), 'Celebrity victims and wimpy snowflakes: Using personal narrative to challenge digitally mediated rape culture', in J. R. Vickery and T. Everbach (eds), *Mediating Misogyny: Gender, Technology, and Harassment*, 353–69, New York: Palgrave.
Ringrose, Jessica (2018), 'Digital feminist pedagogy and post-truth misogyny', *Teaching in Higher Education*, 23 (5): 647–56. https://doi.org/10.1080/13562517.2018.1467162
Ringrose, Jessica, Katilyn Regehr and Sophie Whitehead (2021), 'Wanna trade?': Cisheteronormative homosocial masculinity and the normalization of abuse in youth digital sexual image exchange, *Journal of Gender Studies*, 1–19.
Ringrose, Jessica, Sophie Whitehead, Kaitlyn Regehr and Amelia Jenkinson (2019), 'Play-Doh Vulvas and Felt Tip Dick Pics: Disrupting phallocentric matter(s) in Sex Education', *Reconceptualizing Educational Research Methodology*, 10 (2–3): 259–91. https://doi.org/10.7577/rerm.3679
Riordan, Monica A. (2017), 'Emojis as tools for emotion work: Communicating affect in text messages', *Journal of Language and Social Psychology*, 36 (5):549–67. https://doi.org/10.1177/0261927X17704238
Russo, Naomi (2017), 'The still-misunderstood shape of the clitoris', *The Atlantic*. Retrieved from: https://www.theatlantic.com/health/archive/2017/03/3d-clitoris/518991/
Salter, Michael (2016), 'Privates in the online public: Sex(ting) and reputation on social media', *New Media & Society*, 18 (11): 2723–39. https://doi.org/10.1177/1461444815604133
Salter, Michael (2018), 'From geek masculinity to Gamergate: The technological rationality of online abuse', *Crime Media Culture*, 14 (2): 247–64.
Shepherd, Tamara, Alison Harvey, Tim Jordan, Sam Srauy and Kate Miltner (2015), 'Histories of hating', *Social Media + Society*, 1 (2): 1–10. https://doi.org/10.1177/2056305115603997
Siapera, Eugenia (2019), 'Online misogyny as witch hunt: Primitive accumulation in the age of techno-capitalism', in D. Ging and E. Siapera (eds), *Gender Hate Online*, 21–43, Cham: Palgrave Macmillan. https://doi.org/10.1007/978-3-319-96226-9_2
Sundén, Jenny and Susanna Paasonen (2020), *Who's Laughing Now?: Feminist Tactics in Social Media*, Cambridge, MA: MIT Press.
Twitter Help Center (31 March 2021), *Twitter's Policy on Hateful Conduct*. Retrieved from: https://help.twitter.com/en/rules-and-policies/hateful-conduct-policy
Vera-Gray, F. (2017), 'Talk about a cunt with too much idle time: Trolling feminist research', *Feminist Review*, 115 (1): 61–78. https://doi.org/10.1057/s41305-017-0038-y
Wheatley, Dawn and Eirik Vatnoey (2020), '"It's Twitter, a bear pit, not a debating society": A qualitative analysis of contrasting attitudes towards

social media blocklists', *New Media & Society*, 22 (1): 5–25. https://doi.org/10.1177/1461444819858278

Zhang, Ziqi and Lei Luo (2019), 'Hate speech detection: A solved problem? The challenging case of long tail on Twitter', *Semantic Web*, 10 (5): 925–45. https://doi.org/10.3233/SW-180338

8

Embodied Wilfulness: #MeToo Girls' Activism, Affects and 'Complaint as Feminist Pedagogy'

Ileana Jiménez

'A complaint: when we let out, spill out, what we are supposed to contain'
(Ahmed 2018)

In the weeks that followed the 6 January 2021 insurrection against the US Capitol, Congresswoman Alexandria Ocasio-Cortez, also known widely by her initials, AOC, posted a video on her Instagram account in which she recounted her experience hiding behind her bathroom door as white supremacists stormed her office chambers. Connecting a national trauma to a past personal trauma, Ocasio-Cortez links the terror of hiding from a mob to her memory of being sexually assaulted: 'I'm a survivor of sexual assault. And I haven't told many people that in my life. But when we go through trauma, trauma compounds on each other' (*The Guardian* 2021: para. 5). She then rightfully asserts that in trying to silence her as well as other Congresswomen of colour, Trump-aligned Republicans were employing the 'tactics of abusers' (*The Guardian* 2021: para. 4).

Invigorated by 'pussy-grabbing' tales in 2016, the nightmare of living under Trump's four-year terror was indeed replete with the 'tactics of abusers' from beginning to end. Ocasio-Cortez reminds us that when we call out violence, tell the truth and make a complaint, there is pushback to the point of insurrection. We complain regardless of the insurrection heading towards us. Indeed, we complain because of it. And like Ocasio-Cortez, we use our bodies while doing so.

This chapter goes back to the start of the school year in 2016, at the height of the Clinton–Trump election cycle and a full year before #MeToo broke as a hashtag in 2017, when a group of girls and I discovered that the New York City high school where I teach and where they learn didn't have a policy to protect them against sexual harassment, abuse and misconduct from either their peers or their teachers. In the midst of news reports about 'pussy-grabbing' and 'nasty women', we made this unexpected discovery during a short rape culture course I led for three days with fellow feminist teacher and scholar-activist, Hanna Retallack, from the UCL Institute of Education in London (Retallack et al. 2016; Ringrose and Retallack 2017). Between the moment of our stunned realization that the school did not have a sexual harassment policy in 2016 and the eventual passing of a new policy in 2018, my students and I launched a series of activist resistances against the school. In what follows, I analyse the ways in which one of my students in the group, Gabi, filed her 'complaint as feminist pedagogy' (Ahmed 2014a, 2017a, 2018, 2021) against the school using not only her own experience with the tactics of abusers but also her embodied wilfulness.

Becoming a Problem in Schools: Wilful Girls Who Complain

Agitating for a new sexual harassment policy, my students activated their understanding of intersectional feminist theory from the courses they had taken with me, assumed oppositional feminist identities (Collins 2009; Combahee River Collective 1986; Crenshaw 1989, 1991; hooks 1984, 1994, 1999; Lorde 1984), and transformed these stances into a praxis of what Sara Ahmed calls 'complaint as feminist pedagogy' or 'complaint activism' (Ahmed 2017a, 2021). Ahmed conceptualized these terms in a series of posts on her research blog, *Feminist Killjoys*; in one particular post, she ponders the notion of 'complaint', which she considers a form of 'disobedience' (Ahmed 2014a). Those who complain are not only disobedient but are also usually those who are most marginalized and thus most susceptible to silencing and surveillance. Ahmed notes that persisting with a complaint is the disobedience itself. Embedded within the complaint is a critique of power and a 'wilfulness' (Ahmed 2014b) that makes the complainer, especially feminist complainers, into 'feminist killjoys' who are not 'happy' with the status quo (2010, 2014a, 2014b). Ahmed explains, 'You are heard as complaining. And maybe you are making a complaint. Or maybe you are making a critique which is heard as a complaint. But to be heard as complaining is also to be heard as speaking in a certain way: as expressing yourself' (Ahmed 2014a).

Enter the wilful girl who is disobedient, the intersectional feminist girl activist with an oppositional mind. Within the course of two years, my students 'expressed' themselves on stage, online and in print raging with complaint about sexual harassment at school. Their wilful strategies were ultimately pedagogical: they taught the school community about the importance of not just having a policy but more importantly about the urgency of creating a culture of consent and of bringing an intersectional lens to the work of addressing sexual harassment and violence in schools. Their two-year activist collective made visible the force of intersectional feminist pedagogy and its ability to travel beyond the classroom into the larger institution, disrupting the status quo of sexism, misogyny and rape culture by relentlessly opening a feminist 'pressure valve' and releasing a range of activisms in response to the post-truth era in which they were growing up (Ahmed 2017b). Converging with Trump's rise, the post-truth era arrived in schools just as much as it had arrived on Capitol Hill. As Ahmed has so often said of those who speak out, we became a problem by naming a problem (2017b). The girls' complaint activism ultimately generated not only pressure against the school but also affective pressures that came from within and without their activist bodies as they pushed hard against the power structures that surrounded them institutionally as well as emotionally.

I am interested in lifting up how my students, and in particular how one student, Gabi, used her body in enacting her own complaint as feminist pedagogy during a school assembly. A light-skinned girl who identifies as both white and Latina, Gabi had spent her years in high school silently enduring various forms of sexual harassment. What might be illuminated about the affective labour of student activism against sexual violence when seen and *felt* through the experience of one girl literally standing up against the tactics of abusers? As a career feminist teacher who also identifies as a queer Latina scholar-activist, I have as much of an investment in exploring not only how my students employ the critical feminist theories and pedagogies they have learned in my classes but also how their activism becomes a felt experience as they enact their own wilful pedagogies. Feminist education scholar Alyssa Niccolini affirms my interest in the felt experience of student activism in schools when she asserts that 'intensities, or affects that traverse bodies in classrooms' indeed do offer 'richly generative, if often overlooked, sites of pedagogical force' that must be examined for what we might learn from them (Niccolini 2016: 232).

By tracing the 'affective intensities' (Ringrose and Renold 2014) of Gabi's experience of lodging her feminist pedagogy of complaint against the school, I hope to show, at least through this one case, how girls' activism against sexual violence generates what I call an *embodied wilfulness* that girls themselves may not even be aware of and yet conveys as much of the force and emotional labour of their resistance as their words do. As Gabi confronts the tactics of her abusers through the recitation of a collective poem that she wrote and delivered with her peers during a school assembly, her body is as much a part of her wilful activism as reading the poem is. By considering these moments of disconcertion or moments that make us pause (MacLure 2013) about Gabi's embodied wilfulness, we may learn how girls' activism is as much an act of the body as it is about acts of speaking out.

Complaint Activism at School: Wilful Girls Speak Out

Within days of discovering the missing sexual harassment policy, the girls staged an assembly that revealed a screenshot from the school's online handbook where the policy should have been. The screenshot laid bare exactly what was 'missing': tucked between 'theft' and 'tobacco use' and other behaviours that the school does not condone, were the words 'sexual harassment'. Where there were clear definitions and repercussions for engaging in behaviours like stealing and smoking, there was no definition or set of consequences that would occur should sexual harassment transpire between students or from a teacher to a student. Placed strategically near the end of the assembly, their screenshot marked a powerful transition to their demands for a new policy. What was even more pressing and impressive about this assembly as complaint activism is that at the dawn of post-truth Trump, these girls demanded accountability at a time when #MeToo was not even yet a hashtag.

Just before they made their reveal, the girls reached the portion of the script where they read a poem they had written about themselves sharing experiences of sexual harassment and assault. Their testimonial poem seamlessly merged their experiences of having been harassed or violated by boys and men either at school and/or in their communities. To protect their identities, most of the girls did not read the lines that revealed their own story. Instead, another girl would read her friend's line. But some girls *did* decide to read lines that were about themselves. One of those girls was Gabi.

Huddled in the form of a Greek chorus, they sat on the steps in front of the stage. The plan was to stand up from within the seated huddle and read one's assigned lines and then sit back down again, allowing for the next girl to stand up alone and read her lines and sit. Up and down, they stood and sat, stood and sat.

Except for Gabi and Helen. They remained standing throughout.
Against the plan. Against the script.
Wilful girls. Disobedient girls. But were they?

Laura: We are going to now share excerpts of stories about harassment and assault that have happened both in and out of school, the presenters are not necessarily the writers of the segments they're sharing. Please be respectful and give your full attention.

Helen: [This school] has been called time and time again a 'safe', 'socially conscious' school.

Gabi: Every male figure that has entered my life has felt the need to express to me how pretty I am.

Selene: I thought nothing of it when I felt something touch me. I assumed that they bumped into me when bending down to tie their shoe...

Saleh: He said he had never been with a 'China girl'.

Gabi: I instinctively adjust my top to cover my exposed shoulder as his words sank into my skin.

Mia: As we continued to hook up, he decided to go ahead and do what I already said wasn't okay.

Selene: I looked down and saw a hand on my ass.

Gabi: I keep my eyes glued down.

Saleh: I have never walked faster in my life.

Selene: I looked him in the eye, speechless.

Gabi: Because it is my job as a young pretty girl to be respectful to men because that is who I am told I need to please in life.

Mia: I told him no, but he kept on asking, even though he knew that I would give him the same response.

Gabi: They are telling me that I'm pretty because I take it, I'm pretty because I won't speak up.

Saleh: We had done nothing to provoke that kind of harassment, but it wouldn't have mattered either way.

Loen: He touched me after I said no, stop, please just stop it.

Selene: He immediately started to blame me and hold me accountable for his actions.

Mia: When he did this to me, my body went numb and it was like I was a robot...

Saleh: I felt nauseated by the whole encounter...

Selene: I began to question whether I had done anything...

Mia: Despite seeing my response, he still continued doing whatever he pleased, until he was done.

Gabi: The pattern continued throughout the year because I had caught his eye and he is my superior.

Loen: I never wanted to say sexual assault and the few times I used these words, I was asked if I 'was sure that's what it was?' I took it back immediately. I was exaggerating. I was being a tease. I never used that term again.

Gabi: Gritting my teeth, I will thank them politely and continue on in silence, entering a stinging reflection.

Helen: These actions are perpetuated at [this school] and beyond.

Embodied Wilfulness: Girls' Standing and Swaying Bodies

Gabi was a senior girl who had been in both my intersectional feminism class and the three-day course on rape culture that Retallack and I had taught. Gabi was also one of the girls who had chosen to read lines that reflected her own experience. Meanwhile, standing in the back of the room was the same administrator who had recently touched her hair in the library while asking her why she didn't visit him anymore in his office. As I watch and re-watch this clip of the assembly, I notice how both Gabi and Helen had stayed standing up to read their lines and never sat down again until the end of the girls' collective reading. The other girls followed the original plan, but Gabi and Helen remained standing. Were they being disobedient to the agreed-upon script? It is obvious that they are not in sync with the other girls. In the video, even their classmate Saleh looks up at them, her face seemingly questioning why her peers are still standing. Thinking back on that day, I also remember feeling agitated at their lack of following the plan. This was partly because it 'ruined' the visual aesthetic we wanted to convey. But this was also because I was scared, especially for Gabi, who had chosen to read about her own experience of sexual harassment from the administrator who was standing in the back of the room.

Now years later, observing Gabi and Helen's standing bodies strikes me differently. When I witnessed the assembly live in 2016, Gabi's standing body made me feel nervous. Knowing that a school administrator had just recently touched her hair in the library and knowing that there had been continued harassment as well as what could be perceived as his stalking of her, I didn't want Gabi to be 'found out' during the assembly. While lines and phrases such as 'every male figure', 'it is my job as a young pretty girl to be respectful to men', and 'I had caught his eye' had been read and approved ahead of time, Gabi and I had gone back and forth on our shared class Google doc removing and putting back the words 'he is my superior'. In the end, these words remained and Gabi said them out loud. I remember feeling concerned that her continued standing would somehow symbolically shout the words 'he is my superior' all the more in the direction of this administrator standing in the back of the auditorium.

Even vaguely accusing a teacher or school leader of sexual harassment during the reading of the poem would have been done entirely without a net to catch us, which was exactly the point of our assembly, to name the missing net. There was no policy to protect the girls at the school, and certainly not the girls on stage. There was no policy that would protect Gabi if the school realized that the 'superior' she mentioned was actually in the room. That was the irony and indeed, the tragedy, of the whole assembly. Nothing could protect these girls if they directly named the boys and men associated with their experiences of harassment and assault at school, whether it had been done at the hands of a student or teacher. What was currently in place at the school was just an abyss of non-action; indeed, it was just a bullet point. At that point in time, student reports were just made verbally to school leaders, which led to minimal investigations of which the processes were inconsistent, leading to more covering up and silencing.

Gabi wanted to lodge her own complaint as feminist pedagogy from within the relatively safe huddle of her peers. She had rightly wanted to call out this school administrator and his sustained sexual harassment of her throughout her school years both publicly to an audience of peers and yet safely within the bodily container of classmates surrounding her. Although she knew she could not say all of the details about her experiences with him, she wanted her own lines in the poem to reveal as much as they could without actually naming names. As much as I was sympathetic and even empathetic to her wilfulness, I did not want her to be placed in a situation that could lead to potential retaliation. Her line in the poem, then, had much more resonance if heard through a knowing ear: 'The pattern continued through the year because I had caught his eye and *he is my superior* [emphasis added].'

I had originally thought that Gabi's continued standing was an act of defiance. I thought that she had remained standing because she wanted to assert her body as a stand-in, as a substitute for a formal complaint that could not yet be made. I thought that she wanted the administrator to know that she was directing her words at him by directing her silent body at him. But watching the video again made me see something new that I had not seen before. For example, I had not remembered that she swayed her body while she read her lines. She kept her eyes down on her script almost throughout the entire section, even when she wasn't reading. She also swayed while she listened to her peers read their lines. Throughout the scene, she never looked out at the audience. She did not even look towards the back of the room where the administrator was standing. Indeed, when she came to the revealing line, she nearly whispered the words 'my superior'.

Remembering Embodied Wilfulness Together

Still baffled by Gabi's silent, swaying body and wondering if it meant defiance and wilfulness or nervousness and anxiety, I decided to speak to Gabi directly. It was winter 2019, and at the time of our meeting, Gabi was now a college junior in New York. We met for breakfast and without much prompting, we immediately reminisced about the rape culture course with Retallack, the revealing assembly delivered just days after Trump was elected and the larger two-year activism that changed both of our lives, not only during that period of time, but into today. She brought her laptop and excitedly showed me a set of slides she was working on for a women's studies course she was taking. In the slides, she described her experience of sexual harassment and the subsequent silencing that had followed her from middle through high school.

I was stunned and proud. Three years on, we were both doing the same research but from different angles: one as the wilful girl and the other as the wilful teacher. Several years after the assembly that changed it all, Gabi was still processing that groundbreaking pre-#MeToo year as much as I was and still am. In fact, she was processing even more than that dark year that we shared together when she was a senior in high school. She had reached back even further into the archive of her own experiences in middle school, naming early moments of not only being harassed and followed by her teachers, but also being ignored, disbelieved and silenced by middle school administrators.

'It was a lot to come across this again', she says about returning to her own digital archive of documents, reflections, memoir pieces and essays that she wrote in my courses from tenth through twelfth grade. As she talks about her own research, she mentions that our classes together, particularly the intersectional feminism course and the three-day rape culture course, were important for the development of her critical feminist consciousness: 'It was empowering to be in spaces that reminded me of consciousness raising groups, and about one person just speaking up and realizing that the personal is political.' She shows me the slides that she had created for her women's studies project, pointing out familiar school photographs of faculty members and colleagues I immediately recognize. Gabi had blocked out these men's eyes in her slideshow, but I knew who they were.

During breakfast, I ask Gabi what she remembers about the assembly from her senior year. She turns to her laptop and finds an old reflection from high school; one she had written in my class just after the assembly. When she reaches the line, 'as I felt their bodies near me, we were together as a collective, we were not victims, we were above everyone else, metaphorically and literally', I smile because I know that here, she is alluding to reading *The Scarlet Letter* in my sophomore English class. Hester Prynne had been placed on the scaffold to be publicly derided and punished for her adultery against her husband who had inexplicably abandoned her in the 'new world'. As she stands on the scaffold in Puritan Boston, Hester is literally above her judging and judgemental community, but the Puritans see her as morally below them for engaging in adultery. But Hester is really the one who stands morally above the hypocrisy of Puritan patriarchy. Likewise, Gabi had believed the same about herself and her peers, that they had been 'above everyone else' morally and politically in their stance on sexual harassment and assault in schools. From Gabi's point of view, they were a cluster of modern-day Hesters defying and revealing school-based hypocrisies. Instead of magistrates, their judges were the school's administrators, and even their teachers and peers. Just like the magistrates, our school administration at that time was all male. Sixteen teenage Hesters filed their joint complaint anyway.

After she finished reading her reflection, Gabi says she remembers Helen standing next to her. It made her feel good that her friend was with her in solidarity. I ask her if she remembered what she felt during that moment. As I listen, I am amazed at how much her perspective has shifted to understanding not only the precarity of that moment for herself and her peers, but also for me. As a high school student, she had been so intent on getting her story heard, but as a young adult in college, she seemed to understand that what we had done that day was not only dangerous for them but also for me too. While we drink our coffee, she turns her head to me and says, 'We were working so hard, we weren't supposed to drop any bombs, or target specific people, or that would be a risk. And that was literally where you worked, it was like you were putting a scarlet letter on your back', she said referring to Hester again. She turns to me again and sighs: 'What I loved was, I wasn't always reading my line, everyone wasn't reading their own line, even though it was different stories and different experiences, it was seamless, it all fit together, it was eerily beautiful even though we were sharing such disturbing stories.' At this point in the conversation, I can tell that Gabi does not entirely remember that she had only read lines about herself, so I ask her to watch the video of the assembly. I watch her as she looks down at the video playing on my phone, at this piece of our shared past. Suddenly she exclaims:

> Why am I standing? Like the reason why it bothers me so much is because it's already such a vulnerable experience and like, I do not have to be standing more than I have to. So literally why am I standing? Everyone else is going up and down like whack-a-moles. And I'm literally standing. Thank god Helen was standing too. Yeah, what the heck... If I'm really being deep, honestly, I guess I was just so in it that I literally... it was the biggest adrenaline, I was at the top of a roller coaster, I was already an anxious enough person, I was so in it mentally. I totally forgot the choreography. I could only see my peripheral vision. I literally have stage fright, like I'm gripping on to my script. I think, honestly, I was scared.

Gabi was scared. That's why she didn't sit down. She forgot to sit down because she felt vulnerable and on the top of a 'roller coaster' of nearly two weeks of sharing stories about her horrible experiences with teachers and students at the school while simultaneously planning a game-changing assembly that was precarious for everyone involved. This was potentially why she didn't look up. This was potentially why she swayed her body from beginning to end while 'gripping' on to her script.

Her own interpretation of her body compels me to ask: Does Gabi's fear embodied in her swaying and standing teach us anything about the nature of activist work with young people? This work is not just about telling inspiring victory stories about teenage girls fighting from atop modern-day scaffolds. MacLure quoting Kathleen Stewart reminds us that we should pay attention to 'the excess and resistance of "the anecdotal, the accidental, the contingent, and the gramentary"' (2013: 170). Gabi's standing, swaying, looking-down body is 'data' that appears 'accidental', something that could be easily overlooked when viewing the assembly video. She was just scared, we could say. She merely forgot the 'choreography' because she was just nervous. But in that 'accident' of forgetfulness, in that 'accident' of nervousness and anxiety, there is something that pulls me in and makes me pause.

This is the affective residue of doing activist work, particularly the activist work of testimony and disclosure, of speaking out one's story of violation. Sharing one's story is at once disruptive and creates interventions on silence, particularly in schools that are invested in a brand of social justice that is shiny and neoliberal, not messy and liberatory. If #MeToo as a 'pedagogical movement represents the power of bearing witness and of bringing individual narratives together toward a communal end' (Clarke-Vivier and Stearns 2019: 71), then we must also begin to bear witness to the emotional, intellectual, and political labour that students and teachers forge in the face of school power structures that would rather these solidarities did not exist.

Public testimony about sexual harassment then is also potentially liberating and healing. In the process of sharing testimony, it may also be frightening, making one forget one's body, even in offering it as evidence of something awful happening to it. The act of forgetting; of being in one's head; of being numb, robotic, nauseated; or just swaying in nervousness is precisely the emotional and political labour that is overlooked. This is precisely what the embodied work of resistance against sexism and misogyny looks like when pressure valves open, when naming problems happen, when sharing one's account occurs (Ahmed 2017b). One's body goes into sway. One's body goes into 'peripheral vision' just to survive the moment. Gabi's swaying body illustrates the 'affective intensities' (Ringrose and Renold 2014) produced when a high school girl places her body in front of a public audience as part of her testimony. In other words, complaint activism against sexual harassment involves not only the language of testimonial but also the language of the silent, swaying body.

Ahmed writes, 'no wonder the arm comes up; it keeps coming up. The arm is a complaint. The arm is complaint made flesh' (2014a). Even though Gabi did not look at the administrator during her reading of her section of the poem, her standing body was her complaint made flesh. Even though she did not 'mean it' or intend it, her nervous, anxious body was still a 'disobedient' body. Though Gabi and Helen continued standing perhaps out of uneasiness or perhaps out of forgetfulness, their bodies still registered powerfully as part of their complaint. Their embodied wilfulness was exactly on cue.

Remaining a Problem: Wilful Futures

In telling this story about Gabi, my mind goes to the girl in the Grimm story who Ahmed describes as 'the willful child: she has a story to tell' (Ahmed 2014b). Gabi noted this herself in our conversation, 'We kind of balanced each other out ... we were able to have that *release of sharing* and [yet] *we took the burden of it off* ourselves by blending [the stories] so well [that] it was harder to pinpoint' whose story belonged to whom (emphasis added). Gabi had and has a story to tell that continues to persist beyond her high school years. For Gabi and for me, this was not only about unexpectedly discovering a missing school policy on a cold New York City day before an important national election. It was not only about our game-changing, screenshot revealing, mic-dropping assembly held during the week that followed Trump's so-called election. And it is not also about the eventual sexual harassment policy that a different group of warrior girls and I wrote a year later. It is about something much larger.

It is about what happens when you become a problem when you name a problem (Ahmed 2017b). It is about the silencing and surveillance that comes when you persist in these efforts for institutional change by relying on individual stories and testimonies on the one hand, and systemic analysis of violence against women and girls on the other. It is about the harrowing solitude that immediately emerges once you start to name a problem. It is immediately noticing that Gabi's harasser, a man who was a senior school administrator, never looked me in the eye again after the assembly. More importantly, he never again bothered Gabi.

Several years after graduating from high school, Gabi's college project is also her persistent complaint that 'keeps coming up' (Ahmed 2014a). She continues in her disobedience. Like Alexandria Ocasio-Cortez, Gabi seems all too aware that trauma compounds upon trauma and that telling these stories in connection with each other across time and space is how we make some kind of sense of the violent chaos it causes within our bodies. Gabi's college project continued her work of embodied wilfulness against the tactics of her abusers from middle through high school. As we spoke to each other that day, I felt confirmed over and again in my belief that feminist pedagogy travels wilfully because my students insist upon living lives that embody these pedagogies (Ahmed 2017b), including their feminist pedagogies of complaint. Gabi and I remain wilful all these years later. We are still becoming a problem.

References

Ahmed, Sara (2010), *The Promise of Happiness*, Durham: Duke University Press.
Ahmed, Sara (2014a), 'Feminist complaint'. Available online: https://feministkilljoys.com/2014/12/05/complaint/
Ahmed, Sara (2014b), *Willful Subjects*, Durham: Duke University Press.

Ahmed, Sara (2017a), 'Cutting yourself off'. Available online: https://feministkilljoys.com/2017/11/03/cutting-yourself-off/

Ahmed, Sara (2017b), *Living a Feminist Life*, Durham, NC: Duke University Press.

Ahmed, Sara (2018), 'The time of complaint'. Available online: https://feministkilljoys.com/2018/05/30/the-time-of-complaint/

Ahmed, Sara (2021), 'Complaint activism'. Available online: https://feministkilljoys.com/2021/04/16/complaint-activism/

Clarke-Vivier, Sara and Clio Stearns (2019), '#MeToo and the problematic valor of truth: Sexual violence, consent, and ambivalence in public pedagogy', *Journal of Curriculum Theorizing*, 34 (3): 55–75.

Collins, Patricia Hill (2009), *Black Feminist Thought: Knowledge, Consciousness, and the Politics of Empowerment*, 2nd ed., New York: Routledge.

Combahee River Collective (1986), *The Combahee River Collective Statement: Feminist Organizing in the Seventies and Eighties*, Albany: Kitchen Table.

Crenshaw, Kimberlé (1989), 'Demarginalizing the intersection of race and sex: A Black feminist critique of antidiscrimination doctrine, feminist theory and antiracist politics', *University of Chicago Legal Forum*, 1 (8): 139–67.

Crenshaw, Kimberlé (1991), 'Mapping the margins: Intersectionality, identity politics, and violence against women of colour', *Stanford Law Review*, 43 (6): 1241–99.

The Guardian (2021), 'Alexandria Ocasio-Cortez says she is a sexual assault survivor', February 1. Available online: https://www.theguardian.com/us-news/2021/feb/01/aoc-alexandria-ocasio-cortez-sexual-assault-survivor-capitol

hooks, bell (1984), *Feminist Theory: From Margin to Center*, Boston: South End Press.

hooks, bell (1994), *Teaching to Transgress: Education as the Practice of Freedom*, New York: Routledge.

hooks, bell (1999), *Talking Back: Thinking Feminist, Thinking Black*, Boston: South End.

Lorde, Audre (1984), *Sister Outsider*, San Francisco: Aunt Lute Books.

MacLure, Maggie (2013), 'Classification or wonder? Coding as an analytic practice in qualitative research', in B. Coleman and J. Ringrose (eds), *Deleuze and Research Methodologies*, 164–83, Edinburgh: Edinburgh University Press.

Niccolini, Alyssa (2016), 'Animate affects: Censorship, reckless pedagogies, and beautiful feelings', *Gender and Education*, 28 (2): 230–49.

Retallack, Hanna, Jessica Ringrose and Emilie Lawrence (2016), '"Fuck Your Body Image": Teen girls' Twitter and Instagram feminism in and around school', in J. Coffey, S. Budgeon and H. Cahill (eds), *Learning Bodies: The Body in Youth and Childhood Studies*, 85–103. Singapore: Springer.

Ringrose, Jessica and Emma Renold (2014), '"F**k rape!": Mapping affective intensities in a feminist research assemblage', *Qualitative Inquiry*, 20 (6): 772–80.

Ringrose, Jessica and Hanna Retallack (2017), 'Sexual harassment at school: What can young people's gender based activism tell us?' Available online: https://ioelondonblog.wordpress.com/2017/12/20/sexual-harassment-at-school-what-can-young-peoples-gender-based-activism-tell-us/

Part Three

Gender Politics beyond the Classroom

9

Populist Politics in a Market-Leninist State: (Re)Thinking Gender in Vietnam

Thanh-Nhã Nguyễn and Matthew McDonald

Introduction

Over the last twenty years Western liberal democracies have experienced a surge of populist post-truth politics in response to economic declines among the working and middle classes. Populist post-truth politics also represents a cultural backlash against progressive social and economic policies such as globalization, environmentalism, same-sex marriage, immigration, secularism and gender equality. Research indicates that the right-wing variant of populism seeks to counter these hard-won progressive gains with its promotion of traditional values and its inclination towards authoritarianism which poses a threat to liberal democratic institutions (Norris and Inglehart 2019; Rodrik 2018; Wodak 2015). A common rhetorical strategy employed by populist parties and leaders is to appeal to people's emotions and beliefs as opposed to objective facts, which has come to be described in the compound noun *post-truth politics*. One of the most dangerous aspects of this style of politics is that it has waged a successful war on epistemology, undermining scientific knowledge and a basis upon which debate and political compromise can take place (Peters 2017).

Much of the existing research on populism and post-truth politics has been conducted in Europe, the United States and Latin America (Anselmi 2018; Mudde and Kaltwasser 2017; Suiter 2016). However, this style of politics has also been featured in Asia (Kenny 2018), yet it remains largely unexplored in comparison. The purpose of this chapter is to analyse how the strategies and techniques of populist style politics have been used to subjugate women to state control in new ways over the last thirty years in the socialist regime of Vietnam. While Vietnam shares several aspects in common with Western liberal democracies when it comes to populist post-truth politics, there are a number of areas where it diverges. As Vietnam is a one-party state, its populist political techniques are sustained through propaganda as opposed to post-truth based.

The chapter begins by charting the Vietnamese government's use of populist politics and propaganda in the early 1990s to counter perceived threats from the encroachment of Western values and lifestyles as the country instituted an open-door policy as a part of its integration into the global economy. As we show, these political strategies have evolved since this time to include a mix of overt manipulation along with implicit forms of influence, foregrounding the complex relationship between Vietnam's competing historical, political and cultural forces. The second part of the chapter moves more specifically to investigate the Vietnamese government's attempts to remake the country's gender order through campaigns designed to reinsert conservative/traditional values as a part of its national socialist agenda. This chapter both makes an argument to extend the notion of post-truth populist politics beyond the context of Western liberal democracies by applying it to Vietnam and shows how the retraditionalization of the gender order is a central part of this project.

Populist Politics in Vietnam

From the Communist revolution to Đổi Mới

Recent research on populism has tended to be positioned within the context of liberal democracies (e.g. Mudde and Kaltwasser 2017; Norris and Inglehart 2019; Speed and Mannion 2017). Nevertheless, this style of politics has also been a feature of autocratic regimes (Anselmi 2018); Vietnam is not an exception. Our analysis of populist politics in Vietnam indicates that it shares several features in common with liberal democracies; however, there are a number of aspects that make it distinctive given the country's one-party rule since 1945 and its tumultuous history. In this section, we situate the shift in Vietnam's modern history in twentieth and twenty-first centuries with a particular focus on how the government has used populism and propaganda to manage the transition from a centrally controlled socialism to what has been described as market-Leninism (London 2009).

The self-proclaimed socialist government of Vietnam and its ruling party, the Communist Party of Vietnam (CPV), emerged from the Indochinese Communist Party[1] (ICP) that grew to prominence in the 1930s. The aim of the ICP was to overthrow French imperialism, Vietnamese feudalism and the bourgeoisie. They officially took power in 1945 in North Vietnam and set about instituting a new and progressive set of policies as the foundation for building a nation that was finally free from foreign control. High on the agenda was the liberation of the peasants in the countryside, the urban working classes, women and children from the capitalist exploitation of the French. However, their declaration of a new nation precipitated a war with the French colonialists who were eventually defeated in 1954.

After the French were defeated, civil war broke out between the Democratic Republic of Vietnam (North Vietnam) backed by China and the Soviet Union, and the Republic of Vietnam (South Vietnam) backed by the United States and its allies. The North eventually prevailed in 1975; however, the country was plunged into poverty, becoming one of the poorest in the world. The collectivization of farms significantly reduced food production, the US trade embargo led to severe shortages and the economy in the south was decimated with the mass exodus and imprisonment in re-education camps of thousands of civil servants, scientists, schoolteachers, medical practitioners, business owners and merchants. Vietnam was also impoverished by its costly 10-year war (1978–1989) against the Khmer Rouge in Cambodia (Goscha 2016; Van Canh 1983).

In the late 1970s and early 1980s, Vietnam had to contend with the cessation of assistance from China (who they fought a border war with in 1979) and the economic demise of the Soviet Union, which had been one of its largest trading partners. This led the Vietnamese government to embark on a reform of their economic policy out of fear that the intensified hunger and poverty would lead to a revolution that might bring down their regime (Goscha 2016). In 1986 the government instituted Đổi Mới (translated as *renovation*), abandoning Stalinist central planning in favour of a socialist-oriented market economy.

The government set about reversing its socialist policies by decollectivizing agricultural production, deregulating state-owned enterprises, allowing the setup of private businesses, promoting foreign direct investment, and in the process opening the economy and society to global forces. As a result, Vietnam experienced rapid economic, social and cultural changes (Nguyen, McDonald, Mate and Taylor 2018; Nguyen, McDonald, Nguyen and McCauley 2020; Nguyen-Vo, 2012; Schwenkel and Leshkowich 2012). Economically, it went from being one of the world's poorest nations to a lower middle-income country now ranked forty-seventh in the world (based on 2019 GDP figures). Since the early 1990s Vietnam has produced strong and stable economic growth averaging five and a half per cent a year, which has translated into an almost four-fold increase in average yearly incomes, lifting millions out of poverty (Brand-Weiner, Francavilla and Olivari 2015; Hansen 2020; World Bank 2019).

Globalization and the Vietnamese Government's Discontents

While the country enjoyed rising living standards, the government had to contend with globalization and its influence on the population, for which it has always maintained moral reservations (Gillen 2011; Hoang 2020; Marr 1996; Nguyen 2016). Compared to Western liberal democracies, Vietnam's integration into the late twentieth-century global economy occurred almost overnight. From a country that had been mired in war and closed to the outside world for many decades, particularly in the North, was rapidly exposed to new cultures and lifestyles, values and social norms primarily from East Asia (South Korea, Japan, Taiwan), Western Europe and North America. The opening of the country once again to foreign media, tourists, goods, information communication technologies and foreign travel (for some) exposed Vietnam to Western and neoliberal values such as individualism, entrepreneurship, competition and consumer culture as well as cultural and political movements such as feminism, secularization, civil society, environmentalism and cosmopolitanism (Miho 2016; Nguyen, Özçaglar-Toulouse and Kjeldgaard 2018; Nguyen 2016; Nguyen et al. 2020; Nguyen-Vo 2012; Scott and Chuyen 2007; Schwenkel and Leshkowich 2012).

The government sought to counter these foreign influences, fearing that they would erode the country's national identity (Pettus 2004) and cede its economic power to the transnational elite (Nguyen-Vo 2012). Fears around the dilution and corruption of national culture by outside forces have been exploited by populist leaders around the world to gain support for their political parties (Norris and Inglehart 2019; Wodak 2015). Since economic liberalization, the Vietnamese government and its 'bureaucracy' has used various means to reassert its authoritarian rule (Dixon and Kilgour 2002; Gillen 2011; Hoang 2020). For example, many of the state's cultural campaigns of the 1990s employed gendered discourses supported by traditional Confucian values to dictate a gender order in the family, the family's position in the nation-state, as well as the individual's position in relation to the state authority (Werner 2009). This represents an about-turn by the VCP that had once repudiated Confucianism, casting it as a feudal form of oppression forced upon the country by Chinese invaders (Eisen 1984).

If we are to understand populist politics as a form of political rhetoric that ignores or offers few policy solutions to many of today's complex problems (Norris and Inglehart 2019), then Vietnam is a good example. The CPV's adoption of a Marxist-Leninist philosophy contains several populist elements, which includes national liberation for 'the common people' (workers and peasants) and a class-based revolution that would see 'corrupt elites' ceding control of the means of production to the workers. The irony, however, is that the CPV uses Marxist-Leninist philosophy to pave the way for its claims to power and administration, yet it in no way adheres to this ideology; nevertheless, this does not mean that a return to Marxist-Leninist principles is possible or desirable. For example, gender liberation is still as far away as it has ever been (Hoang 2020), wealth and income inequality has risen to staggering proportions (Nguyen, Doan and Tran 2020; Nguyen, Nguyen, Nguyen and Nguyen 2020), corruption is rife throughout the public and private sectors (Transparency International 2020), and troublingly, labour activists and members of trade unions are harassed, arrested and imprisoned lest they imperil the country's foreign direct investment (Human Rights Watch, 2009).

Market-Leninism and Populist Politics

Vietnam's current political economic system has been variously described as 'state capitalism' (Keane 2020), 'authoritarian neoliberalism' (Davies 2015) and 'market-Leninism' (London 2009). It is a system in which the government is directly involved in and controls many aspects of business and commercial activity. Instead of giving free reign to the market, the CPV engineers and manages these for their own political ends; it is state-directed coercion designed to insulate against the 'impulses towards greater equality and democratization' (Bruff 2016: 107). As London (2009: 395) puts it, Vietnam retained its authoritarian 'Leninist political institutions' while embracing 'market-based strategies of accumulation'. The system encompasses a mix of political techniques, one of which is populist politics, which is comprised of national liberation and self-determination, socialist idealism and traditional Vietnamese values. These interests are reinforced by the government propaganda through its control of the mass media and the facilitation of a consumer culture (Bui 2016; Leshkowich 2012; London 2009; Ngo and Tarko 2018).

The institution of market-based economic reforms has markedly increased the number of products and services now available for consumption, which is used to seduce the population through appeals to luxury and increased living standards (Keane 2020; Nguyen-Vo 2012). In the post-Đổi Mới era the government has used Vietnamese culture and identity to remoralize wealth and the rise of a petite bourgeoisie (middle class), which it had sought to dismantle during the socialist era (Gillen 2011; Jellema 2005; Leshkowich 2012). Like other countries around the world, the new middle class in Vietnam have come to define themselves through practices of consumption and the lifestyles they confer on personal identity (Earl 2014; Nguyen-Marshall, Drummond and Bélanger 2012). This has been nothing short of a transformation from the austere days of Stalinist central planning to a new era that 'thrives on [...] the hedonism of endless consumption' (Keane 2020: 16).

The Vietnamese government invokes populist political techniques to manage its political economy with 'much media talk of defending "the people" and "the nation" against "domestic subversives" and "foreign enemies"' (Keane 2020: 14). Its primary discourse portrays the nation as an agent of the people and for the people, which has become a commonly used form of propaganda transmitted through the state-controlled mass media and instituted in the national education curriculum. All the while the CPV engages in political patronage with business elites in which it benefits financially (Keane 2020; London 2009).

When we analyse the nature of populism in Vietnam, there are some important distinctions to be made. It does not have a ready source of scapegoats in immigrants and refugees in the same way that right-wing populist political parties do in Europe, Australia and the United States (Mudde and Kaltwasser 2017). Instead, the Vietnamese government blames societal problems on two main sources. Firstly, the lifestyles and products of Westernized culture are blamed for creating 'impure mentalities' and 'illegal behaviour' (Gillen 2011: 276). Secondly, the government finds its scapegoats *internally* where it harasses, arrests and imprisons environmental, democratic and social justice activists, who are delegitimized and branded reactionaries and enemies of the people (Thayer 2014). However, its demonization of these individuals and groups rarely illicit popular support to the same effect that these tactics have achieved in relation to immigrants and refugees in Western countries (Hogan and Haltinner 2015).

Secondly, authors such as Rodrik (2018) link the rise of right-wing populism in the United States and Europe to the economic dislocation wrought by globalization such as wealth and income inequality, the shrinking of the middle classes and the loss of good paying secure work in the manufacturing and industrial sectors. Theories pertaining to economic dislocation are complemented with those that point to a cultural backlash as primary reasons for the electoral success of right-wing populism over the last two decades (Norris and Inglehart 2019). In contrast, Vietnam has experienced economic growth and prosperity, albeit from a very low base, with increases in average yearly incomes and growth in the middle class (Brand-Weiner, Francavilla and Olivari 2015; Hansen 2020; World Bank 2019). However, a growing class disparity due to wealth and income inequality in the country is becoming a problem. Vietnam's brand of populist politics is based on an expedient attitude towards culture, which is used as one of a number of instruments to maintain the government's one-party rule (Gillen 2011).

Lastly, Vietnam has not experienced the same post-truth politics that have 'assailed' Western countries. The United States, for example, has seen attacks on fact-based journalism and the mainstream media who are accused of transmitting fake news, where conspiracy theories (e.g. climate change is paving the way for a socialist takeover) are propagated on social media and accepted as truth by millions, and where scientists, civil servants and politicians are viewed as the elite that 'suppresses free speech and imposes political correctness' (Lockie 2017: 1). In contrast, the government in Vietnam continues to respect (natural) scientists whose advice informs government policy and whose expertise is viewed as contributing to the country's rapidly modernizing agenda. However, the majority of Vietnam's traditional forms of media such as radio, television, newspapers and magazines are owned or partially controlled by the government, and so they are 'subject to regular instructions and direction from the Ministry of Information and Communication and the CPV' (Bui 2016: 104). Like post-truth politics, much of this mass persuasion is misleading, biased, selective and based on lies. However, where it differs from the post-truth politics of the West is that the government's propaganda has become an orthodox discourse where it has been successful to a degree in creating a shared sense of identity, solidarity, respect for the country's history and traditions, and national sovereignty (Thayer 2014).

Populist Propaganda and the Gender Order in Vietnam

Over the last thirty years the Vietnamese government has used populist political techniques and propaganda to cope with globalization. It has done this by using cultural campaigns (e.g. the social evils campaign and poisonous culture, ideas that we discuss below) to manage the transition to a socialist market economy to shore up the country's one-party rule (Gillen 2011). In this section we analyse how the government has mobilized gendered discourses that inform the cultural imaginary of femininity and masculinity; thus, re-educating the public about the gender order, which is a central aspect of the government's populist politics. We analyse this by looking into the state apparatus and the discourses it has used to achieve this.

Since the mid-twentieth century, the gender order in Vietnam has been intimately connected to the struggle for liberation from foreign powers and an independent nation-building agenda. In the forty-year period from 1945 to 1986, which included the establishment of the Democratic Republic of (North) Vietnam, the war with France and then the civil war with South Vietnam, women were recast by the Vietnamese government as warriors and revolutionaries, alongside their roles as mothers, wives, daughters and labourers for the nation, whose prize for their long, hard struggle would be their liberation (Duong 2001; Eisen 1984; Lessard 2006; Turley 1972).

The American-Vietnam War also played an important role in promoting gender equality in North Vietnam. The mobilization of millions of men meant that women served in positions of power in the family, village councils and the fields (Goscha 2016; Turley 1972). Women were also lauded during this period for serving as combat soldiers, truck drivers and for undertaking the extremely dangerous job of keeping open the Đường Trường Sơn (Ho Chi Minh Trail) which came under one of the most intensive bombing campaigns in the history of warfare and for which they paid a heavy price (Turner and Phan 2002). The trail was vital to the success of the North Vietnamese Army (NVA) and the National Liberation Front (Việt Cộng) as it was the primary conduit for supplying them with reinforcements and materiel to fight US forces and the Army of the Republic of Vietnam (South Vietnam) (ARVN).

In the 1960s and 1970s, two of the most prominent Vietnamese scholars of gender – Mai Thị Tú (1972) and Lê Thị Nhâm Tuyết (1975) – attributed the emancipation of Vietnamese women to the country's socialist/national liberation. Advancing gender equality was one of the central tenets of The Communist Party when it came to power.[2] The discourse on gender equality fit the government's modernizing agenda as it sought to separate itself from the country's feudal past and colonial rule (Drummond and Rydström 2004; Turley 1972). 'By wedding the ideals of women's liberation to the people's struggle against colonial rule and a feudal-capitalist class system, the communist party secured women's investment in the goals of national emancipation' (Pettus 2004: 27).

The focus during the socialist era and the American-Vietnam War had been on mass mobilization (Luong 2016). Vietnam's era of communism opened the way for women to enter the public sphere as participants in national liberation and self-determination by transforming themselves into party cadres and warriors in the fight against imperial capitalist domination. Nevertheless, traditional patriarchal values continued to influence society, albeit in a milder form (Chiricosta 2010). Under the new conditions of Đổi Mới, a shift took place with the government linking the economic prosperity of the country to the family, 'with women's work in the household assuming new importance' (Werner 2009: 11). The renewed focus on family and the household became an important location for the government to reassert its authoritarian rule, which has long been a site of women's subjugation and a bastion of patriarchal rule.

In the 1990s, there were various campaigns initiated by the Women's Union and other government-sanctioned mass organizations such as the 'civilized and happy families' (Gia đình văn minh, hạnh phúc) (Pettus 2004). These stemmed from government's fears concerning the erosion of traditional family values in the Đổi Mới era, which it responded to by remoralizing the institution of marriage, heterosexual relations and procreation. Heteronormative families that complied with the state's policies were rewarded with the title of 'cultured family' (Gia đình văn hóa).[3] As well as upholding traditional values, the cultured family campaign was one of several attempts to tie the household more closely to the national development agenda, which stood in contrast to the war-time era when the focus was on class consciousness and national liberation (Goscha 2016). The cultured family and other similar campaigns and movements 'show that the post-Đổi Mới gender regime sought to retraditionalize women despite their increased economic power and professional achievements' (Hoang 2020: 7).

In 1996 the Vietnamese government instituted the 'social evils campaign', which was an 'attempt to fight against decadent and corrupt Western values' as well as to 'reinvent the Vietnamese Communist Party as the gate-keeper of Vietnamese tradition' (Wilcox 2000: 15). The timing of the cultured family and social evils campaign occurred in parallel with several significant globalizing events that took place during the 1990s as well as a conservative political backlash. These include Vietnam's admission to ASEAN (Association of South-East Asian Nations), the normalization of relations with the United States, and, by the early 1990s, the liberalization of the economy and exposure to global culture that had begun to gather pace (Dixon and Kilgour 2002; Wilcox 2000). Đỗ Mười also became General Secretary of the CPV in 1991, whose election represented a conservative backlash against the previous incumbent Nguyễn Văn Linh (1986–1991) who was pushed out of the position because of his progressive policies (London 2009).

The social evils campaign drew on populist political techniques and propaganda to achieve its aims. When the CPV took control in the north of the country prostitution became almost non-existent,[4] being viewed as a form of French imperial capitalist exploitation. However, it remerged in the late 1980s with economic liberalization (Barry 1996). Bars and other similar venues with so-called female entertainment[5] were used predominately by state and foreign entrepreneurs, in particular South Korean, Taiwanese and Japanese men travelling for business to Vietnam to network, access information and establish business relationships (Hoang 2014; Nguyen-Vo 2012). Nevertheless, the government harassed street-level bar girls and sex workers, regarding them as 'fallen sisters' in need of redemption (Nguyen-Vo 2012). If the government was serious about stopping the moral decay that prostitution represented for the country, it would have been more effective to target the state entrepreneurs and foreign businessmen responsible for driving much of its trade.

Another example of this type of social injustice has been the way in which young women were targeted by the social evils campaign as a part of government efforts to manufacture a moral panic. The panic was based on claims that Western values and lifestyles were 'poisoning' (văn hoá độc hại) the Vietnamese culture by promoting promiscuous lifestyles through its magazines, music, films and books. In cases where young heterosexual couples were found to have had sexual relations outside of wedlock, it was young women who were targeted for 'opprobrium as opposed to their male counterparts' (Gammeltoft 2001; Nilan 1999; Rydstrøm 2006). These campaigns and others like it are characteristic of the government's cultural manipulation where they position women as the embodiment of Vietnamese tradition and so are coerced to conform to an ideal that is unrealistic, contradictory and pseudo-emancipatory (Brickell 2015; Pettus 2004; Tran 2012). These characterizations of women have become an integral part of the project of building a modern nation-state. Sinha (2004) argues that such projects have cast different 'modes of belonging' for members based on gender differences. Women, in particular, have been regarded as the essence of the nation, and, therefore, bear more moral responsibilities.

Similar discourses have been observed in other post-socialist countries such as Croatia, Hungary and Poland, which are composed of a mixture of authoritarianism, populism, conservatism and neoliberalism. Like Vietnam, the governments in these countries have instituted a patriarchal familialism where the family, patriarchy and heteronormative framings 'have become something to aspire to' (Stubbs and Lendvai-Bainton 2020: 550). While we do not seek to disregard the advancement of women's rights in the form of greater legal status, access to education and transforming roles (e.g. workforce participation) in the latter part of the twentieth century, we argue that the Vietnamese government uses the legal code of gender equality to deny women's lived experience of inequality and subordination.

One element of the government's discourse of reinstating a patriarchy has been the focus on gender-based roles and responsibilities in the family. Government education campaigns from the 1990s primarily targeted women as they were made responsible for building harmonious, productive and prosperous households (Pettus 2004; Werner 2009). These government dictates have been found to be aligned with Confucian doctrine which 'upholds a womanly virtue as strict adherence to the concept of difference between men and women, masculinity and femininity, [...] guaranteeing harmony and prosperity' (Han and Ling 1998: 65). Issues of gender equality[6] are often muted as topics of debate in Vietnam, as the government and its agencies claim that it has now been achieved as evidenced by women's equal access to education and participation in the workforce, as well as the various laws that have been enacted to protect women's rights. However, the domestic sphere continues to be organized around a patriarchal order, encouraging the wife to pay respect to their husband (Hoang 2020; Werner 2009). The pre-socialist order of the household has come to serve as the basis once again for family values. Under the conditions of Đổi Mới it is a woman's national duty to fulfil their primary roles as a mother, wife, daughter and daughter-in-law (Pettus 2004). This has created a dominant cultural imaginary in which women are expected to maintain traditionally prescribed forms of conduct both inside and outside the home.

These gendered discourses have not only contributed to unequal power relations and workload inside the home; they have also put women at increased risk of violence and oppression. The literature indicates that such discourses have led state actors such as the local people's committees and the Vietnam Women's Union, as well as victims and perpetrators of domestic violence, to perceive violence and coercion as forms of punishment for women who fail to fulfil their roles within the family (GSO 2010; Kwiatkowski 2019; Rydstrøm 2003, 2017). Although the introduction of the Law on Domestic Violence Prevention and Control in 2007 was viewed by the state as an important step forward in addressing domestic violence, the government discourse on women's responsibilities to their families puts them at greater risk as men are led to think that they are entitled to extract these responsibilities from their wife. The implementation of the legal framework has also been undermined by government procedures. Women who are victims of domestic violence when filing for divorce are legally required to go through a reconciliation process with their husband to attempt to resolve their conflicts. This process is hosted by state-supported local reconciliation committees, which often encourage women to remain within the marriage to preserve family unity (Kwiatkowski 2011, 2019).

The Vietnam Women's Union (VWU) has played an instrumental role in the reinstatement of conservative gender order in Vietnamese society in the recent decades (Hoang 2020; Rydstrøm 2016). The VWU, the official state-run organization that represents women's interests, plays a dual role; it is an organization loyal to the Vietnamese government, supporting the implementation of its political strategies and policies related to women, as well as a grassroot movement that promotes women's interests to the state (Rydstrøm 2016). However, the women's interests that the VWU claims to promote must exist within the parameters of the state's discourse on conceptions of the ideal/moral womanhood (Hoang 2020; Pettus 2004; VWU 2020).

The VWU is often complicit in promoting the government's gender-based propaganda. Many of the state-led propaganda stem from the proposition that women and families need to be protected from corrupt Western values and lifestyles lest they fall prey to premarital sex, prostitution, pornography, eschewing marriage, seeking divorce and choosing not to procreate. As previously noted, this false conflation is used as the basis to justify the government's campaign to reinsert a traditional gender order so as to be seen to protect Vietnamese traditions and identity from corrupting forces. Waibel and Gluck (2013: 343) note: 'We found that the VWU fails to challenge traditional gender norms, actually emphasizing women's responsibilities in maintaining a "happy family".'

Conclusion

The purpose of this chapter has been to illustrate that populist politics is not confined to the West only, that governments in Asia such as Vietnam use its strategies and techniques to subjugate women to state control. As Chacko (2020: 204) notes: 'The promotion of conservative gender values has been a feature of the rise of authoritarian populism globally.' Our analysis indicates that the Vietnamese government employs populist techniques to manage and maintain the transition to a market economy, linking economic prosperity to the household and the correct maintenance of family life. In line with this policy, the government has conducted campaigns promoting women's responsibilities for creating a happy and harmonious household, as well as other forms of subjugation which are justified on the basis that foreign (Western) values and lifestyles have the potential to erode the moral fabric of the family and womanhood. The government has undertaken these campaigns to reassert its authoritarian rule by casting itself as the guardian of Vietnamese traditions to revive its flagging support.

Seeking to respond to questions of gender inequality from the perspective of populist politics alerts us to how women figure in the larger project of Vietnam's transition to a market economy. The discourse on women's liberation which emerged along with anti-colonial and national liberation struggles in the early to mid-twentieth century has been co-opted in the interests of the party/state over time. Much of this discourse on equality is moulded within the framework of Confucianism, national sovereignty and a socialism from a bygone era that has little resemblance with contemporary Vietnamese society. There is a need to accept new forms of knowledge production to underpin policy to create a more progressive education system and equitable gender relations. Without it, women and other marginalized groups will continue to be put at risk of discrimination, oppression and limited access to education, work and personal liberty.

Acknowledgements

We would like to thank Emeritus Professor David Marr, Australian National University, for his helpful comments on an earlier draft of this chapter.

Notes

1   The Indochinese Communist Party was renamed the Worker's Party of Vietnam in 1951, then in 1976 the Workers Party of North Vietnam was merged with the Revolutionary Party of South Vietnam to form the now Communist Party of Vietnam (CPV) (Smith 1998).
2   In the first constitution of the Democratic Republic of Vietnam (DRV) (1946), article 9 states that 'Women are equal with men on all aspects'. This was further expanded in the second constitution (1958), in which article 24 states that 'women have equal rights to men in political, economic, cultural, social and domestic sphere, as well as rights to equal pay'. The Law on Marriage and the Family (1959) was passed shortly after giving women the right to own property regardless of their marital status, prohibiting the long historical practice of concubinary and discouraging the mistreatment and abuse of women.
3   The 'cultured family' is defined as one that complies with the state's family planning policy, participates in the workforce, fulfils their obligations as citizens and works

to build harmonious relationships between family members. This policy remains active today and relatively unchanged since it was first written (122/2018/NĐ-CP).
4   The situation was markedly different in the south where the occupation of US military forces fed a thriving sex industry (the Marines first landed in Vietnam in 1965). However, the takeover by the North in 1975 led to a crackdown. Further, the poverty that stalked the country soon after saw the industry almost wither away.
5   The women that work in these establishments are often referred to as 'bar girls' who are employed as waitresses, dancers and prostitutes.
6   See Werner (2009) for an analysis on the conceptualization of gender equality in Vietnam, which is largely understood through an Engelsian lens of emancipation through collective land and labour rights instead of individual equality for women based on their own needs. While there was a shift towards defining equality as relations within the family, it was not in the state's interest to ensure equality between spouses.

References

Anselmi, Manuel (2018), *Populism: An Introduction*, London: Routledge.
Barry, Kathleen (1996), 'Industrialization and economic development: The costs to women', in K. Barry (ed) (2016), *Vietnam's Women in Transition*, 144–158, Basingstoke: Macmillan.
Brand-Weiner, Ian, Francesca Francavilla and Mattia Olivari (2015), 'Globalisation in Viet Nam: An opportunity for social mobility?', *Asia & the Pacific Policy Studies*, 2 (1): 21–33.
Brickell, Katherine (2015), 'Participatory video drama research in transitional Vietnam: Post-production narratives on marriage, parenting and social evils', *Gender, Place & Culture*, 22 (4): 510–25.
Bruff, Ian (2016), 'Neoliberalism and authoritarianism', in S. Springer, K. Birch and J. MacLeavy (eds), *Handbook of Neoliberalism*, 107–17, London: Routledge.
Bui, Thiem Hai (2016), 'The influence of social media in Vietnam's elite politics', *Journal of Current Southeast Asian Affairs*, 35 (2): 89–111.
Chacko, Priya (2020), 'Gender and authoritarian populism: Empowerment, protection, and the politics of resentful aspiration in India', *Critical Asian Studies*, 52 (2): 204–25.
Chiricosta, Alessandra (2010), 'Following the trail of the fairy-bird: The search for a uniquely Vietnamese women's movement', in M. Roces and L. Edwards (eds), *Women's Movements in Asia: Feminisms and Transnational Activism*, 134–53, London: Routledge.
Constitution of the Democratic Republic of Vietnam, Article 9, Congress of Democratic Republic of Vietnam, Section 2, Supplement B (1946).

Constitution of the Democratic Republic of Vietnam, Article 24, Congress of Democratic Republic of Vietnam, Section 3 (1958).
Davies, Nick (2015), 'Vietnam 40 years on: How a communist victory gave way to capitalist corruption', *The Guardian*, April 22. Available online: https://www.theguardian.com/news/2015/apr/22/vietnam-40-years-on-how-communist-victory-gave-way-to-capitalist-corruption
Dixon, Chris and Andrea Kilgour (2002), 'State, capital, and resistance to globalisation in the Vietnamese transitional economy', *Environment and Planning A: Economy and Space*, 34 (4): 599–618.
Drummond, Linda and Helle Rydström (2004), *Gender Practices in Contemporary Vietnam*, Singapore: Singapore University Press.
Duong, Wendy N. (2001), 'Gender equality and women's issues in Vietnam: The Vietnamese woman-warrior and poet', *Pacific Rim Law & Policy Journal*, 10 (2): 191–326.
Earl, Catherine (2014), *Vietnam's New Middle Classes: Gender, Career, City*, Copenhagen: NIAS Press.
Eisen, Arlene (1984), *Women and Revolution in Viet Nam*, London: Zed Books.
Gammeltoft, Tine (2001), 'The irony of sexual agency: Premarital sex in urban Northern Vietnam', in J. Werner and D. Belange (eds), *Gender, Household, State: Doi Moi in Vietnam*, 111–28, New York: Cornell University Press.
Gillen, Jamie (2011), 'A battle worth winning: The service of culture to the Communist Party of Vietnam in the contemporary era', *Political Geography*, 30 (5): 272–81.
Goscha, Christopher (2016), *The Penguin History of Modern Vietnam*, Milton Keynes, UK: Penguin/Random House.
General Statistics Office (GSO) (2010), *Keeping Silent is Dying – Result from National Study on Domestic Violence against Women in Viet Nam*. Available online: https://www.gso.gov.vn/default_en.aspx?tabid=487&ItemID=10693
Han, Jongwoo and L. H. Ling (1998), 'Authoritarianism in the hypermasculinised state: Hybridity, patriarchy, and capitalism in Korea', *International Studies Quarterly*, 42 (1): 53–78.
Hansen, Arve (2020), 'Consumer socialism: Consumption, development and the new middle classes in China and Vietnam', in A. Hansen, J. I. Bekkevold and K. Nordhaug (eds), *The Socialist Market Economy in Asia: Development in China, Vietnam and Loas*, 221–43, Singapore: Palgrave Macmillan.
Hoang, Kimberly Kay (2014), 'Vietnam rising dragon: Contesting dominant western masculinities in Ho Chi Minh City's global sex industry', *International Journal of Politics, Culture, and Society*, 27 (2): 259–71.
Hoang, Lan Anh (2020), 'The Vietnam Women's Union and the contradictions of a socialist gender regime', *Asian Studies Review*, 44 (2): 297–314.
Hogan, Jackie and Kristen Haltinner (2015), 'Floods, invaders, and parasites: Immigration threat narratives and right-wing populism in the USA, UK and Australia', *Journal of Intercultural Studies*, 36 (5): 520–43.

Human Rights Watch, (2009), *Not Yet a Workers' Paradise: Vietnam's Suppression of the Independent Workers' Movement*, Washington, D.C.: Human Rights Watch.

Jellema, Kate (2005), 'Making good on debt: The remoralisation of wealth in post-revolutionary Vietnam', *The Asia Pacific Journal of Anthropology*, 6 (3): 231–48.

Keane, John (2020), *The New Despotism*, Cambridge, MA: Harvard University Press.

Kenny, Paul D. (2018), *Populism in Southeast Asia*, Cambridge: Cambridge University Press.

Kwiatkowski, Lynn (2011), 'Domestic violence and the "happy family" in Northern Vietnam', *Anthropology Now: In the Hopper*, 3 (3): 20–8.

Kwiatkowski, Lynn (2019), 'A "wife's duty" and social suffering: Sexual assault in marital relationships in Vietnam', *Journal of Aggression, Maltreatment & Trauma*, 28 (1): 68–84.

Law on Marriage and Family [Luật Hôn Nhân và Gia Đình] (1959) Chapter 1, Congress of Democratic Republic of Vietnam.

Lê, Thị Nhâm Tuyết (1975), *Phụ nữ Việt Nam qua các thời đại [Vietnamese Women through Different Epochs]*, Hà Nội: Khoa Học Xã Hội.

Leshkowich, Ann Marie (2012), 'Finances, family, fashion, fitness, and… freedom? The changing lives of urban middle-class Vietnamese women', in V. Nguyen-Marshall, L. B. W. Drummond and D. Bélanger (eds), *The Reinvention of Distinction Modernity and the Middle Class in Urban Vietnam*, 95–113, Dordrecht: Springer Netherlands.

Lessard, Marc R. (2006), 'Women's suffrage in Viet Nam', in L. P. Edwards and M. Roces (eds), *Women's Suffrage in Asia: Gender, Nationalism and Democracy*, 121–41, New York, NY: Routledge.

Lockie, Stewart (2017), 'Post-truth politics and the social sciences', *Environmental Sociology*, 3 (1): 1–5.

London, Jonathan (2009), 'Viet Nam and the making of market-Leninism', *The Pacific Review*, 22 (3): 375–99.

Luong, Hy V. (2016), 'Gender relations in Vietnam: Ideologies, kinship practices, and political economy', in A. Kato (ed), *Weaving Women's Spheres in Vietnam: The Agency of Women in Family, Religion and Community*, 23–56, Amsterdam: Brill.

Mai, Thi Tu (1972), *The Vietnamese Woman, Yesterday and Today*, Association of Vietnamese Patriots in Canada.

Marr, David G. (1996), *Vietnamese Youth in the 1990s*, Sydney: School of Economic and Financial Studies, Macquarie University.

Miho, Ito (2016), 'Negotiating with multilayered public norms: Female university students' struggle to survive the Đổi Mới period', in K. Atsufumi (ed), *Weaving Women's Spheres in Vietnam: The Agency of Women in Family, Religion, and Community*, 116–39, Leiden: Brill.

Mudde, Cas and Cristóbal Rovira Kaltwasser (2017), *Populism: A Very Short Introduction*, New York: Oxford University Press.

Nilan, Pam (1999), 'Young people and globalizing trends in Vietnam', *Journal of Youth Studies*, 2 (3): 353–70.

Ngo, Christine and Vlad Tarko (2018), 'Economic development in a rent-seeking society: Socialism, state capitalism and crony capitalism in Vietnam', *Canadian Journal of Development Studies*, 39 (4): 481–99.

Nguyen, Hien, Tinh Doan and Tuyen Quang Tran (2020), 'The effect of various income sources on income inequality: A comparison across ethnic groups in Vietnam', *Environment, Development and Sustainability*, 22 (2): 813–34.

Nguyen, Lan Thi, Matthew McDonald, Susan Mate and Greig Taylor (2018), 'Advancing a cross-cultural narrative approach to career counselling: The case of Vietnam', *Australian Journal of Career Development*, 27 (2): 65–71.

Nguyen, Thanh-Nha, Matthew McDonald, Truc Ha Thanh Nguyen and Brian McCauley (2020), 'Gender relations and social media: A grounded theory inquiry of young Vietnamese women's self-presentations on Facebook', *Gender, Technology and Development*, 24 (2): 174–93.

Nguyen, Thi Quynh Nhu (2016), 'The Vietnamese values system: A blend of oriental, Western and socialist values', *International Education Studies*, 9 (12): 32–40.

Nguyen-Marshall, van, Lisa B. Welch Drummond and Danièle Bélanger (2012), *The Reinvention of Distinction: Modernity and the Middle Class in Urban Vietnam*, Dordrecht: Springer Netherlands.

Nguyen, Nhat Nguyen, Nil Özçaglar-Toulouse and Dannie Kjeldgaard (2018), 'Toward an understanding of young consumers' daily consumption practices in post-Doi Moi Vietnam', *Journal of Business Research*, 86: 490–500.

Nguyen, Thi Thanh Huyen, Thi Thu Hien Nguyen, Thi Le Hang Nguyen and Van Cong Nguyen (2020), 'The impact of international integration on the inequality of income between rural and urban areas in Vietnam', *The Journal of Asian Finance, Economics, and Business*, 7 (3): 277–87.

Nguyen-Vo, Thu-Huong (2012), *The Ironies of Freedom: Sex, Culture, and Neoliberal Governance in Vietnam*, Seattle, WA: University of Washington Press.

Norris, Pippa and Ronald Inglehart (2019), *Cultural Backlash: Trump, Brexit, and Authoritarian Populism*, Cambridge: Cambridge University Press.

Peters, Michael A. (2017), 'Education in a post-truth world', *Educational Philosophy and Theory*, 49 (6): 563–6.

Pettus, Ashely (2004), *Between Sacrifice and Desire: National Identity and the Governing of Femininity in Vietnam*, London: Routledge.

Rodrik, Dani (2018), 'Populism and the economics of globalization', *Journal of International Business Policy*, 1 (1–2): 12–33.

Rydstrøm, Helle (2003), 'Encountering "hot" anger: Domestic violence in contemporary Vietnam', *Violence against Women*, 9 (6): 676–97.

Rydstrøm, Helle (2006), 'Sexual desires and "social evils": Young women in rural Vietnam', *Gender, Place & Culture*, 13 (3): 283–301.

Rydstrøm, Helle (2016), 'Vietnam women's union and the politics of representation: Hegemonic solidarity and a heterosexual family regime', in H. Danielsen, K. Jegerstedt, R. L. Muriaas, and B. Ytre-Arne (ed), *Gendered Citizenship and the Politics of Representation*, 209–34, London: Palgrave Macmillan.

Rydstrøm, Helle (2017), 'A zone of exception: Gendered violences of family "Happiness" in Vietnam', *Gender, Place & Culture*, 24 (7): 1051–70.

Schwenkel, Christina and Ann Marie Leshkowich (2012), 'Guest editors' introduction: How is neoliberalism good to think Vietnam? How is Vietnam good to think neoliberalism?', *Positions: East Asia Cultures Critique*, 20 (2): 379–401.

Scott, Steffanie and Trong Thi Kim Chuyen (2007), 'Gender research in Vietnam: Traditional approaches and emerging trajectories', *Women's Studies International Forum*, 30 (3): 243–53.

Sinha, Mrinalini (2004), 'Gender and Nation', in C. R. McCann and S-K. Kim (eds), *Feminist Theory Reader: Local and Global Perspectives*, 254–72, London: Routledge.

Smith, R. B. (1998), 'The foundation of the Indochinese Communist Party, 1929–1930', *Modern Asian Studies*, 32 (4): 769–805.

Speed, Ewen and Russell Mannion (2017), 'The rise of post-truth populism in pluralist liberal democracies: Challenges for health policy', *International Journal of Health Policy and Management*, 6 (5): 249–51.

Stubbs, Paul and Noémi Lendvai-Bainton (2020), 'Authoritarian neoliberalism, radical conservatism and social policy within the European Union: Croatia, Hungary and Poland', *Development and Change*, 51 (2): 540–60.

Suiter, Jane (2016), 'Post-truth politics', *Political Insight*, 7 (3): 25–7.

Thayer, Carlyle A. (2014), 'The apparatus of authoritarian rule in Vietnam', in J. London (ed), *Politics in Contemporary Vietnam: Party, State, and Authority Relations*, 135–61, London: Palgrave Macmillan.

Tran, Nhung Tuyet (2012), 'Woman as nation: Tradition and modernity narratives in Vietnamese histories' *Gender & History*, 24 (2): 411–30.

Transparency International (2020), *Vietnam*. Available online: https://www.transparency.org/en/countries/vietnam

Turley, William S. (1972), 'Women in the communist revolution in Vietnam', *Asian Survey*, 12 (9): 793–8.

Turner, Karen G and Phan Thanh Hao (2002), '"Vietnam" as a women's war', in M. B. Young and R. Buzzanco (eds), *A companion to the Vietnam War*, 93–112, New York: John Wiley & Sons.

van Canh, Nguyen (1983), *Vietnam under Communism, 1975–1982*, Stanford, CA: Hoover Institution Press.

Vietnam Women's Union (VWU) (2020), *Viet Nam Women's Union Action Plans*. Available online: http://vwu.vn/vwu-action-plans

Waibel, Gabi and Sarah Glück (2013), 'More than 13 million: Mass mobilisation and gender politics in the Vietnam Women's Union', *Gender & Development*, 21 (2): 343–61.

Werner, Jayne (2009), *Gender, Household and State in Post-revolutionary Vietnam*, New York: Routledge.

Wilcox, Wynn (2000), 'In their image: The Vietnamese Communist Party, the "West" and the social evils campaign of 1996', *Bulletin of Concerned Asian Scholars*, 32 (4): 15–24.

Wodak, Ruth (2015), *The Politics of Fear: What Right-wing Populist Discourses Mean*, London: Sage.

World Bank (2019), *Overview – The World Bank in Vietnam*. Available online: https://www.worldbank.org/en/country/vietnam/overview#1

10

Embracing Feral Pedagogies: Queer Feminist Education through Queer Performance

Alyson Campbell, Meta Cohen, Stephen Farrier
and Hannah McCann

Introducing the Feral Queer Camp

This chapter explores how a series of strategies we are calling 'feral pedagogies' can be deployed as a methodology and means of de-domesticating feminist queer knowledges and rewilding the nexus of academic and queer community practice. Here we enlist the definition of feral as 'the domesticated gone wild' to conjure up a way to resist the institutionalization of both queer academics and queer knowledge in the academy and attempt – albeit messily – to take queer ideas back into the streets (Campbell 2018, 2019). In choosing the idea and aspirational practice of going feral we join with a set of communities thinking about ferality and feminism; for example, theorists Kelly Struthers Montford and Chloe Taylor offer the analogy of 'liminal animals':

> Liminal animals are in between the domesticated and the wild; unlike wild animals, they live among humans but, unlike domesticated animals, they are not subordinated to human control, nor are they participating members of human society.
>
> (2016: 5)

We build on this liminal idea of ferality to connect it to queerness' resistance to normative identities. Historically 'queer' has been deployed in a number of ways: it is popularly described – and contested – as an umbrella term (Barker and Scheele 2016); as a mode of affiliation and 'doing' or rethinking kinship (Freeman 2007); as identity (Jakobsen 1998); and as a politics connected to long-held feminist ideas (Marinucci 2010). We use queer rather than the acronym

LGBTIQ+[1] in order to draw on the slippery and boundary-resisting aspects of 'queer' as it has been used in queer theory, where the focus has been on its antinormative potential (McCann and Monaghan 2020).

As both theatre makers and academics, liminally fluctuating between worlds, we set out to make a creative response to this sense of in-betweenness. Rather than making a theatre piece setting out these ideas, we created what we called 'Feral Queer Camp' (FQC): a queer pedagogical enterprise designed, at its most basic level, as a way of gathering together a group of queer people interested in queer theatre/performance simply in order to watch performance and talk about it. Consequently, in parallel with our theoretical understanding, at its heart we use the term queer as determined by the lived experience and positionality of the camp's participants, which has been variously identity-based, feminist, politically inclined and post-(or not!) colonially driven – connected through marginalization in some way or another. Not all campers self-identify as 'queer', and indeed the issue of being 'queer enough' to do the camp arises not infrequently. Part of the work on the FQC is negotiating these concerns.

This chapter provides an overview and analysis of our experiences running the FQC in two locations: for Outburst Queer Arts Festival Belfast in 2019 and Midsumma Festival Melbourne in early 2020. The FQC is designed to sit alongside existing queer arts festivals and in partnership with them, and in each case we put a call out for participants via the festivals and other networks. In our invitation to participants we note its aim is to create a:

> feral cohort who will consider: how we learn (from each other) about what makes performance queer; [...] and, above all, how we might develop a network of queer thinkers who can talk amongst ourselves and to others about queer performance.
>
> (Campbell and Farrier 2020a)

The camp is a way of developing a 'thinking' strand for the festival but, more than this, it sets out to open up a way for queer people excluded from formal education to engage with learning about both performance analysis and queer thinking and their intersections. The conceptual approach of feral pedagogies is particularly significant for the queer community because so many queer-identifying people have been excluded or alienated from mainstream education, and yet have embodied knowledge of queer identity and life. The reasons for this exclusion are well-documented, including poverty, class, racism, transphobia and homophobia, and elitism (see for example Brim 2020a, 2020b; Giroux 2004; Moten and Harney 2004; Schulman 2013). As such, in line with queer and feminist pedagogical aims to cross over the divide between academia and the 'community' (see for example Ahmed 2016; Brim 2020a, 2020b; Halberstam 2003; Muñoz 2005; Schulman 2013), the driving force for the project is to address that exclusion by 'ferrying back and forth' between the two, as Matt Brim puts it (2020a: 412–13). Thus the camp is:

> open to anyone in the community – enthusiasts, developing artists, practitioners: people who have not (yet) had access to, or have been let down by, or have chosen not to enter into, Higher Education but are hungry to encounter a utopian queer curriculum largely of their own devising.
> (Campbell and Farrier 2020b)

However, the FQC is not a one-way exchange. As we explore, the camp is a dialogue between us and the participants while also redeploying the resources of the university, particularly where those resources relate to expertise, access and networking. Our status as academics funded by our university salaries to do the camp work enables our negotiation of partnership with the festivals, including free tickets for performances and networking opportunities to meet artists and organizers. Of course, this immediately draws attention to power imbalances and raises questions about the possibility of a 'feral pedagogy' unfettered by such inequities. In this chapter, then, through a brief contextualizing of the environment we are functioning in – but mostly through our own personal, queerly auto-ethnographic reflections (Holman Jones and Harris 2019) on activities and adventures in the FQC – we suggest that 'going feral' is an aspirational pedagogical practice that can only ever be both flawed and partial, but is nonetheless valuable.

Inclusion/Exclusion: Education in an Age of Populism

The development of the FQC has emerged within a broader context of intensified debates within and beyond the academy around gender and sexuality. On and off campuses, there has been a rise over the last few years in so-called 'gender critical' feminist discourse actively targeting the legitimacy of transgender, genderqueer and non-binary identity and embodiment (Nicholas and Clark 2020). Acting as a rebranded form of radical feminism, these feminists centre biology as a basis for understanding oppression, but in doing so reinforce a strict gender binary/boundaries (ibid.). While historically radical feminism cannot easily be considered 'populist', these 'gender critical' debates dovetail with populist attacks on trans rights. Populist actors continue to stoke 'culture war' debates, with issues around sexuality and gender made a primary target. For example, the 'Sokal Squared' hoax of 2018 involved a group of academics who attempted to publish a series of journal articles based on fabricated gender, race and sexuality studies research, in order to make a mockery of research within these fields (Thompson 2018). Beyond the university, this plays out daily in mass media and popular culture as the circulation of 'fake news', producing another of these messy areas where what is legitimated as 'knowledge' is up for grabs. For example, discourse targeting gender and sexual diversity has been propagated at a state level, with populist characters such as Brazil's Jair Bolsonaro and the United States' Donald Trump implementing transphobic policies and inciting violent action against 'gender ideology'. As scholars have noted, these populist attacks on gender and queer theory/activism have gone hand-in-hand with critiques from 'gender critical' feminists (McCann and Nicholas 2019).

In this context, things appear to have undergone a reversal: the feminist rallying cry of 'biology is not destiny' has shifted in some parts of the discourse to a biological focus as a root of oppression; and freedom of speech, once a watchful energy of the left, has been grasped by the right to render as 'snowflake' the refusal to engage with discourses that deny trans rights. The university as a learning institution sits right in the middle of this wrangle. In the UK much is made in popular media of 'no-platforming' as a process of censoring debate in the very place in our culture it apparently should be allowed. For the queer person with no experience of the university, these debates create a fraught and uninviting terrain.

Certainly at the base of queer as theory is a suspicion of the discursive processes of normalization and from this energy we note that the binaries in much of the discourse about the 'town and the gown', or biology versus social discourse, deserve examining further. This is a pattern reflected elsewhere in the idea of queer on the street and queer in the university – almost as if these were populated by different species. In terms of the FQC, it was clear that this bifurcation does not work in that there are clearly forms of understanding and knowledge commensurate with ideas present in the densest theory (and of course we know that queers in the university take to the streets too – and the university provides little protection from street-level direct or ambient homo/queer/femme/trans-phobia).

Within the broader context of antipathy towards earlier gains made around gender and sexuality activism, we suggest that to advertise and run a 'Feral Queer Camp' utilizing the resources of the university is by its very name a risky venture. Yet the title of the camp, 'Feral Queer', resists domestication of queerness. Indeed, the aim of the camp is to push against normative approaches to gender and sexuality formations within the university space. Penny Jane Burke and Ronelle Carolissen note the gains made by feminist discourses on campus, but argue that 'feminist [and, we would argue, queer] pedagogies do not provide a straightforward solution to the complex power dynamics that circulate around knowledge production and ontological positioning' (2018: 545). FQC works to engage with these feminist issues in its fibre but, crucially, in ways that seek to resist reproducing the inequalities present in university settings (though clearly we are not always successful at this). Brim and Burke and Carolissen are focused on universities in their important work, where pedagogic practices tend to self-replicate; however, we have tried to stretch the reach of the university and what counts for us as pedagogy.

The Messy University

In the context of a discussion about the relation of the university to queer work, then, we must note that the boundaries between them are more porous than they first might appear, more messy and commingled. Though, of course, we do not deny inherent power differentials in the discussion: we have to concede that the university is not as open or accessible as this porosity implies, and mostly it is one way, as is the case with power inequalities. The university makes gestures towards engaging with queernesses and their relation to minoritarian knowledge gained and embodied through non-normative experiences. However, as Muñoz notes, often these knowledges are not enfolded into widespread or appreciated understanding: 'I understand the theory I teach, the pedagogy I perform, as a contribution to minoritarian knowledge. Yet [...] within majoritarian institutions the production of minoritarian knowledge is a project set up to fail' (2005: 120). Although we would not wish to disengage with the project of building minoritarian knowledge within the majoritarian framework of the academy, we do not think this is the only way in which we might deal with the university's civic responsibilities. In our feral endeavour, we are committed to the ideal of the civic duty of the university and our place within it in order to operationalize disruptive pedagogies. We attempt this not only by engaging with discourses within institutions, but by working with them out in the world. This is a less organized and scheduled context, which brings different issues, including challenging our domestication into a world of timetables and room bookings.

Reflection 1: Looking to Camp

Although discourses of queer rewilding are growing in queer thought (Halberstam and Nyong'o 2018), the experience of the FQC in Belfast gives us pause to think, as ever, about those never really domesticated in the way that *re*wilding might imply. An emblematic moment of the camp's positioning 'outside' the main programme of the Outburst Queer Festival is when we searched for a venue to hold a discussion with some of the queer performers at the festival.

> It is November in Belfast, that means it is raining. We make our way to a well-known queer venue to meet with some international queer performers and members of the Feral Queer Camp (the campers or feralers, we named ourselves). We hug building-sides as we make our way through a torrential downpour (heavy, even for November in Belfast) and hurry to the safety of the venue. We arrive. It's closed. We call. No answer. We wait, damper by the second.
>
> We formulate a Plan B – nothing new here for the camp, it keeps us on our toes – and I head off to the local theatre, where there is public space in which we can meet. Alyson and Meta stay huddled under an umbrella to direct the artists and the campers to me. I make my way into the theatre and find a nook, a spot in which the theatre has collected a number of books relating to performance, art and film. I wait.
>
> As I wait I scan the books, as my eye always does when it sees a bookshelf, and note that despite these books being laid out for the public to look at, very few of them look well thumbed. The theatre as a civic space is gestured here, but in some way its tone is slightly off, these are books that presuppose something about the public who will look at them.
>
> Alyson, some feralers and the artists arrive, and we begin talking. Part of the meeting is given over to interviewing the artists (Dima Matta and Ana Beatriz Martínez) and we want to record them. The building with its clean walls resists, the sound reverberates, and I find it hard to hear and record the meeting. After interviewing the artists, we hang out with the feralers to carry on the conversation. The discussion turns to the interviews and other works we have seen so far in the festival; the insights the campers bring to the discussion are, as ever, enlightening and sharply perceptive – in particular in this iteration of the camp, in the context of the North of Ireland, the discussion around race, postcolonialism and representation are uppermost in the group's mind. I find the interaction and the discussion energising.

Through reflecting on this small and pretty normal moment in the camp in relation to how queer performance situations might engage with pedagogy, or andragogy (though the gendered etymology of that term sits awkwardly) it becomes acutely clear, that the (default?) domesticated structures of the camp are reflected in the expectations of how it is organized. The sense of rising anxiety when there is no space can mirror the sensation we have when there is a double-booked lecture hall. When the feralers arrived at the theatre, this sense of being responsible continued – like a teacher worrying about behaviour, doing the right things in the right buildings and, likewise, about the emotional impact of performance or discussions on 'our' campers.

This moment serves as a reminder of the impacts of choosing to be 'outside' the festival as much as possible and therefore the relative importance given it. For us it also meant closely thinking through how the structures of organizing are themselves enmeshed in colonizing energies. Things that are germane to our institutional expectations (planning, availability to come to sessions, being on time etc.) had set our initial understanding of how the camp might run. We have learned from this! Our structures set up under-articulated and unrealistic expectations around how learning happens and how access to space, time and resources (particularly for some feralers who live hand-to-mouth or have caring responsibilities) have an impact on the way the camp progresses. Importantly, the camp offered us, the Camp Captains, direction for how we might rethink future iterations.

Such rethinking provided an opportunity to dig deep in order to understand, at a material level, the granularity of those expectations, which are felt most keenly by those they exclude. From the moment we began cooking up the camp we understood that access to information is paywalled by institutional structures; this is plain to see. In our impulse to address this by redirecting some of these institutional resources, we perhaps did not adequately consider the reality of the extent to which we too are inculcated/implicated as a resource. This is not to say that we are passive commodities in a market – we are privileged enough to openly exercise resistance – but still, like the structures that set not only an agenda but the languages with which an agenda can be recognizably expressed, the foundational normalizing impulses of structuring learning in the queer wild needs minding. Such normalizing impulses too are wily, mobile and horizon-narrowing at a very subtle, deep and profound level. Following Muñoz (2005), the process of thinking of the camp in terms of minoritarian knowledge already situates it in relation to a dominant knowledge form, which in some ways the Camp Captains recirculated in how we organized ourselves and the activity. There is, however, a requirement for this kind of radical pedagogy to embody, as much as we can, a different kind of learning exchange.

Nor perhaps did we fully perceive these institutional structures to be in service of forms of control that resist ferality. The next time we are waiting in the rain for a group, and a room, we'll remind ourselves to take a breath and examine the urge to structure and control and remember there are no validated and tested 'learning objectives' here, just the opportunity for exchange and refuelling.

Pedagogy towards Alternative Kinship or Queer Kinship towards Pedagogy

As established above, one of the key aspects of the FQC is that it offers a porous space between worlds: of the academy and the broader queer community, blurring these distinctions. Unlike the academy, to belong to the group one need not be studying, or an already established scholar, and, likewise, one need not have to specify their relation to 'queer' identity in order to belong – although some participants did feel they needed to articulate their position. The space is, however, curated – it is not accidental and does not emerge organically from work or friendship networks (though it may have subsequently stimulated these kinds of belonging). Given these aspects, the FQC provides a unique example of kinship, that is, sexual citizenship, or belonging around queer identity.

Butting up against traditional identity politics are notions of queer belonging, and the FQC offers a way of envisioning queer kinship that is directed explicitly towards queer community activities (in this case, theatre) rather than one's personal identification. This shift of focus as the mode of connection does not, however, sideline identity. Gender identity and sexual identity and experience is a key focus of discussion, yet this is usually directed towards analysing the shows in question rather than one's own identity credentials. Here the anxiety of 'queer enough' can be displaced onto the theatre shows themselves to ask if these performances are 'queer enough'. In doing so the political mode is shifted from the individual as the source of politics, to holding the artist/s accountable as political or cultural workers.

During the Melbourne FQC we met with each other on a routine basis for discussions and catch ups that were more often than not social rather than obviously 'educational'. In this way – echoing the queer trope of the 'chosen family' – the rituals of the FQC came to feel like family gatherings. The concept of 'kinship' has a difficult history in terms of its anthropological uses in service of colonialism, heteronormativity, and in terms of the way that biological family structures may be abusive, or dysfunctional. That is to say, kinship is not necessarily a 'good' thing, but queer theorists have raised the question of how queer communities 'do' kinship differently, in ways that resist harmful normative structures of belonging that are based on 'blood' and nuclear arrangements. FQC was a way for us to curate an alternative space of belonging, and to appropriate the funds of the university to a queer(er) end. The campers varied widely in age, academic and theatrical experience, coming some way towards meeting Halberstam's assertion that queer pedagogy must entail breaking down 'intergenerational conflict' and hierarchies of the normative family unit (2003: 363).

Yet, while the camp provided an alternative kinship network, it *was* also about pedagogy. A key focus was learning from one another's insights, reflections and experiences, rather than the convenors of the group acting as 'the' source of knowledge, though this hierarchy was inevitable as we planned and led workshops.

Reflection 2: Who Is a Queer Theorist?

The Melbourne FQC included a session called 'Introduction to Queer Theory'. After all, with 'queer' in our camp title it seemed vital to discuss 'queer theory' and how it might be relevant to the camper experience (or not!). As Lauren Berlant and Michael Warner lamented in the 1990s (1995), the absorption of 'queer' into the academy risked alienating and separating off from the very queer activism from which it had sprung. How were feral campers thinking about 'theory' in relation to queerness, if at all? This was an opportunity for a pedagogical moment not just for the campers – but for us in the academy, to be reminded of the relation between theory and queer lived experiences beyond views from what is often popularly described as the 'ivory tower'. The queer on the street *is* the expert when it comes to negotiating their life complexities so that they can see and talk about queer performance work.

People were enthusiastic but cautious about the queer theory session. 'Theory' seemed a daunting prospect for many, and there was a reticence to think of 'queer' identity and 'queer' theory as related. For some, the identity of 'queer' was more often expressed in terms of 'LGBTQIA+' identities, while others resisted the default to 'queer' as an umbrella term. When we talked about people's first memories of coming across the term 'queer', it wasn't always as a positive thing. Some participants could – as Heather Love notes of the term – still 'hear the hurt in it' (2007: 2).

I handed out post-it notes and colourful pens, and asked people to jot down words that they associate with 'queer', without yet thinking of that daunting thing, 'theory'. When people had come up with a few words each, I then stuck a post-it note in the centre of the table that said, 'QUEER SEEING/FEELING', with a drawing of pink triangular-shaped glasses. I asked people to put things that they felt were 'very' close to 'queer seeing/feeling' near the glasses, and 'less' queer 'seeing/feeling' further away. Close to the centre people put a flurry of notes such as 'messiness', 'angry', 'communes', 'subversive', 'margins', 'disruption', 'taboo', 'pleasure'.

I talked with the campers about how part of the point of the exercise was simply to 'centre' queerness – something that is so often pushed to the margins. Here, in this room, we had created a space where the 'margins' were at the centre. This was, as José Esteban Muñoz describes, teaching as 'a "putting into action" of theory' (2005: 118). When I suggested this, one of the campers appeared to have tears in her eyes – feeling moved by the reconfiguration of 'normal' offered in this space. I was suddenly aware of my years of teaching gender studies classes, where this reconfiguration is a classroom norm – something that I often take for granted in the university setting.

In this group setting we talked about the history of the term queer, and the influence of HIV activism in the 1980s and 1990s on the emergence of activism calling itself 'queer', and then subsequently 'queer theory' in the academy. These activities and discussion points were designed to get back to the 'roots' of queer theory to ask – what is the point of queer 'theory'? What can queer theory do? What do we want queer theory to do and to be? In other words, to think through how queer experience has historically, and should continue to, inform the basis of 'theory'. In this way this workshop addressed Aideen Quilty's point that pedagogy can be activism, that 'education is not a neutral process, it can be used to establish and maintain conformity or be part of a process of liberation and social change' (2017: 116). Coming from this 'ground up' angle allowed campers to see that they are all already doing queer theory if they deploy the rubric of 'queer seeing/feeling' that they had set up earlier in the session.

However, during the session a post-it near the 'queer' centre was read out; it said 'stupid lesbians'. While no one felt confident enough to speak up in the moment, this had reverberations in the room and beyond. It became clear that brushing lightly over this term (read as ironic, perhaps?) had left several of the campers who identified as lesbian uncomfortable and distressed. This had much to do with a lived/deeply-felt sense of erasure as a lesbian, particularly in the context unpacked above, in which to claim identity as a lesbian is sometimes to risk equation with that trans-exclusionary radical feminist extreme. The issue was discussed at the next camper catch up, but it was never fully resolved. It is a jarring reminder of the difficulties of talking about identity in ways that feel safe and that make space for everyone. This incident hints at the troubles and difficulties of belonging that are so often faced in queer spaces – and how conversations about 'queer' can never really be contained: there is not a neat pedagogical map that we can simply adhere to.

Going Wild (or Not)

For all the camps we do, we structure a final get together with the feralers at which we talk through what we have done, how we feel about it, what we might do differently and how we can stay in touch. As almost the last event of a very full three-week FQC programme across the Midsumma Festival in Melbourne, we held a Picnic in the Park – and this time the event was open to both campers and the wider public (who would be consulting the Midsumma guide, so a queer public perhaps/ideally, or something allied) (Campbell and Farrier 2020c). Structuring an event like this requires the sort of scheduling and planning required by universities (as noted above) but also festivals, with their guides published months beforehand. Despite our notions of queer ferality, this pushes us back into the sort of territory that Freeman defines as the 'chrononormative', or 'the use of time to organize individual human bodies toward maximum productivity' (2010: 3).

The picnic was structured around the idea of bar-hopping, which was reconfigured as 'picnic rug-hopping', and the informal gatherings which have so often – and often unhelpfully – been structured around alcohol in LGBTQI+ communities, were now organized instead around hummus and licorice allsorts. We planned for three to four rugs, each rug holding a temporary community that would gather round a question and eat their way through chats in their own 'world' of a square piece of material.[2]

The focus for the picnic was very much around queer performance and its place in our lives. As we have noted, there is a stated – and felt – resistance to hierarchy in anything queer worthy of the name. This plays out also in response to putting highly structured activities into an FQC event. In truth, it is all structured, but perhaps sometimes less overtly so, in that in some contexts conversations and plans go out in all sorts of directions. But in this case, I think because of our concerns about how to 'control' (sic) the unpredictability and 'wildness' (sic) of the situation (manicured gardens), we had structured for a range of contingencies and prepared a set of questions/tasks we were keen to tackle, drawing on the campers' and wider queer performance-going community's collective knowledge.

As it turned out, we made and ended up staying in three rug groups and didn't actually rug-hop in the end. Perhaps because of the extremely hot day, or because there was a lot of food to share. And, perhaps, the sun and food lifted our mood away from 'all that's wrong' to what we could change, so that questions about what we could do, curate and make were a vital activating cue. Of all the FQC events, perhaps this was the most utopian-leaning, dreaming of futures collaboratively.

Reflection 3: Gazebos and Rugs, Circles and Squares

Our discussions revealed that, in this collective, we did not seem to have a strong, shared history of queer performance – but that we had each experienced performance that made a difference to us and wanted to experience more. The rug discussions, among people who had allied themselves with the idea of the 'feral', unsurprisingly showed stronger leanings towards the nonbinary and the crip in queer performance.[3] The discussion was not only fixed on critiquing the present programme (such as the abundance of white, gay, cisgender men) but also on what we might do, redesign, rearticulate, reform. One rug group decided to enact their dream performance in a pair of still images that picked up on the circular shape of the gazebo we had gathered in for the picnic to form a circular playing space; and there was something about the relationship with the sky as it was framed by the architecture of the gazebo that filtered in to this communitarian scenography. Such a simple exercise, but suddenly the bodies were speaking too, performance was invoked in the air and on the grass, and the potential of new collaborations emerging out of the camp felt possible.

What was it about this event that worked? How could we learn from it as we wrangle with all the questions about our compromised queerness, being within and from the academy, and our dilemmas about what makes the feral queer camp often neither queer nor feral? We reflected on the day's activities and have come to a series of potential answers:

1. Perhaps it was going back to focus more specifically on performance and what it might do.
2. The blue sky that literally worked its way into our collective dreaming.
3. Definitely the sharing of food. In both Belfast and Melbourne, we have experienced the most satisfying events as based around food.

4. Could it be that it was the closest we got to actual 'camping'? In the sense that we were outdoors, in the (relative) wild. The constraints emanating from the shape of a traditional classroom (the institutional four walls, like those in which we had some meetings) seemed not to be as fully present.

We learn, we keep on learning, from our feral campers and these attempts we make – and this two-way traffic seems a vital pre-requisite for a feral pedagogical undertaking.

[In]Conclusion: Feral Potentials in Pedagogy

The practice of *doing* feral, queer camping throws our theories and aspirations into stark relief. Our notions of ourselves as academics 'going feral' is, in reality, still overwhelmingly circumscribed by our domestication and institutionalizing into the academy (Campbell 2019, 2020). As Brim reminds: 'We are our institutions. We are not our institutions. But in important ways we are of our institutions' (2020a: 412). But rather than give up because it is messy and 'not queer enough', here it is the queer theorists who acknowledge the contradictions, but urge action anyway, that keep us going. In his concept of 'poor queer theory' Brim draws on his Staten Island Ferry commute to his institution to call for 'structural crossing over or "queer-class ferrying" between high-status institutions [...] and low-status worksites of poor queer studies' (2020a: 398).

This theme of 'in but not in, in but not of', is continued/exemplified in la paperson's figure of the 'scyborg', which they dream up as 'the agentive body within the institutional machinery' – it 'subverts machinery against the master code of its makers; it rewires machinery to its own intentions' (2017: Chap. 4). By exploiting the resources of the elite institutions we work in (stealing what we can) for FQC we explore this messy, tenuous, liminal position. We have chosen the idea and aspirational practice of going feral; much like the scyborg or the liminal animal, the feral academic inhabits this twilight world of in/of/not of. Halberstam might call it/us 'public intellectuals', who are 'people who refuse the boundaries between community and campus, activism and theory, classroom and club' (2003: 363). What chimes between Brim, la paperson and FQCs is that we all work to continue to blur these edges, and perhaps in that blurring do our roles wrong, mess up our timelines a bit, tread a sticky line involving being, and simultaneously resisting being, maximally productive, and focused instead on how in and through pedagogy we come together, how we exchange and challenge our relative privileges. The FQC thus tussles with this complexity around in/of/not of, while also pulling on feminist materialist strategies, such as Judy Rohrer's, that focus on who is actually 'in the room' (2018: 567).

We understand through the choice to explore moments of learning about our pedagogy that we are almost always in a bind in this kind of project. We understand too that although we feel we are working to resist the structures that reproduce privilege, we are also relying on some of those very structures to facilitate the project and enable our conversations. We are OK to varying degrees with the uncomfortableness this brings. However, we draw strength from some ideas that circulate in queer and feminist discourses that help us come to (some kind of) terms with privilege and how we might wield it resistively while also understanding and feeling that we are subject to it. We are drawn to Ahmed's 'affinity of hammers' as a way of 'chipping away at structures' (2016). Like Brim, riffing off a special edition of *Gay and Lesbian Quarterly*, we also see the power of the middle, the regional, compromise as a process of resisting the demands of the 'metronormative' so prevalent in discourses of queerness (2020b: 24).

What we can take from the camps as we have experienced them is that they sit well with the resistance queerness has to normativity and upending binaries – so although feral might imply the 'abnormal' in this context, the work in the camps renders the university's processes and procedures bizarre. Working with those outside the university brings into sharp relief the strangeness of the forms of knowledge and cultural behaviours prevalent in the university. In so doing, the 'street level' embodied material experience with which we engage also helps us question the sanitizing boundaries of the university and how its disciplines and spaces are policed (why can't we be loud in a theatre building?).

Critically the experience of the camp teaches us to continue to work on de-teachifying ourselves, to un-do the processes of learning the structures and patterns that we use in seminars, which are disrupted when they are taken into other spaces, and likewise our teaching spaces disrupted when the feralers enter into them.

Acknowledgements

The authors would like to acknowledge the generous support for the Feral Queer Camps from Midsumma Festival, Melbourne; Outburst Queer Arts Festival, Belfast; Victorian College of the Arts, The University of Melbourne; the Creativity and Wellbeing Research Initiative (CAWRI), The University of Melbourne; The Royal Central School of Speech and Drama; and, most of all, our several cohorts of feral campers.

Notes

1 Refers to Lesbian, Gay, Bisexual, Transgender, Intersex, Queer and other.
2 The rug exercises included: #1: collect up a list of queer performance you've seen/experienced that left some mark, however weak or strong; #2: what would you programme in your ideal queer arts festival?; #3: dream up a new queer performance that you would like to see or *make*.
3 See Robert McRuer, *Crip Theory: Cultural Signs of Queerness and Disability* (New York: New York University Press, 2006).

References

Ahmed, Sara (2016), 'An affinity of hammers', *TSQ: Transgender Studies Quarterly*, 3 (12): 22–34. https://doi.org/10.1215/23289252-3334151

Ahmed, Sara (2017), *Living a Feminist Life*, Durham: Duke University Press.

Barker, Meg-John and Julia Scheele (2016), *Queer: A Graphic History*, London: Icon.

Berlant, Lauren and Michael Warner (1995), 'Guest column: What does queer theory teach us about X?', *PMLA*, 110 (3): 343–9.

Bousquet, Marc (2008), *How the University Works: Higher Education and the Low-Wage Nation*, New York: New York University Press.

Brim, Matt (2020a), 'Poor queer studies: Class, race, and the field', *Journal of Homosexuality*, 63 (3): 398–416. https://doi.org/10.1080/00918369.2018.1534410

Brim, Matt (2020b), *Poor Queer Studies: Confronting Elitism in the University*, Durham: Duke University Press.

Burke, Penny Jane and Ronelle Carolissen (2018), 'Gender, post-truth populism and higher education pedagogies', *Teaching in Higher Education*, 23 (5): 543–7. https://doi.org/10.1080/13562517.2018.1467160

Campbell, Alyson (2018), 'GL RY: A (W)hole lot of woman trouble. HIV dramaturgies and feral pedagogies', in Alyson Campbell and Dirk Gindt (eds), *Viral Dramaturgies: HIV and AIDS in Performance in the Twenty-First Century*, 49–67, London: Palgrave Macmillan.

Campbell, Alyson (2019), 'Going feral. Queerly de-domesticating the institution (and Running Wild)', in Peter Eckersall and Helena Grehan (eds), *The Routledge Companion to Theatre and Politics*, 177–80, Abingdon and New York: Routledge.

Campbell, Alyson (2020), 'Queering pedagogies', *Theatre Topics*, 30 (2): 117–24. https://doi.org/10.1353/tt.2020.0018.

Campbell, Alyson and Stephen Farrier (2020a), 'Feral Queer Camp: Home,' Feral Queer Camp. Available online: https://feralqueercamp.com/ (accessed 22 December 2021).

Campbell, Alyson and Stephen Farrier (2020b), 'Feral Queer Camp: About,' Feral Queer Camp. Available online: https://feralqueercamp.com/about-feral-queer-camp/ (accessed 22 December 2021).

Campbell, Alyson, and Stephen Farrier (2020c), 'Feral queer camp: Picnic in the park', Midsumma Festival. Available online: https://www.midsumma.org.au/whats-on/events/feral-queer-camp-picnic-in-the-park/ (accessed 15 October 2020).

Dahl, Ulrika (2014), 'Not gay as in happy, but queer as in fuck you: Notes on love and failure in queer(ing) Kinship', *Lambda Nordica*, 19 (3–4): 143–68.

Freeman, Elizabeth (2007), 'Queer belongings: Kinship theory and queer theory', in George E. Haggerty and Molly McGarry (eds), *A Companion to Lesbian, Gay, Bisexual, Transgender, and Queer Studies*, 295–314, Malden: Blackwell.

Freeman, Elizabeth (2010), *Time Binds: Queer Temporalities, Queer Histories*, Durham and London: Duke University Press.

Giroux, Henry (2004), 'Cultural studies, public pedagogy, and the responsibility of intellectuals', *Communication and Critical/Cultural Studies*, 1 (1): 59–79. https://doi.org/10.1080/1479142042000180926

Halberstam, Jack and Tavia Nyong'o (2018), 'Introduction: Theory in the wild', *South Atlantic Quarterly*, 117 (3): 453–64. https://doi.org/10.1215/00382876-6942081

Halberstam, Judith (2003), 'Reflections on queer studies and queer pedagogy', *Journal of Homosexuality*, 45 (2–4): 361–4. https://doi.org/10.1300/J082v45n02_22

Holman Jones, Stacy and Anne M. Harris (2019), *Queering Autoethnography*, New York: Routledge.

Jakobsen, Janet R. (1998), 'Queer Is? Queer Does? Normativity and the Problem of Resistance', *GLQ: A Journal of Lesbian and Gay Studies*, 4 (4): 511–36. https://doi.org/10.1215/10642684-4-4-511

Love, Heather (2007), *Feeling Backward: Loss and the Politics of Queer History*, Cambridge: Harvard University Press.

Marinucci, Mimi (2010), *Feminism Is Queer: The Intimate Connection between Queer and Feminist Theory*, London and New York: Zed Books.

McCann, Hannah and Lucy Nicholas (2019), 'Gender troubles', *Inside Story*, 18 February. Available online: https://insidestory.org.au/gender-troubles/

McCann, Hannah and Whitney Monaghan (2020), *Queer Theory Now: From Foundations to Futures*, London: Red Globe Press.

McRuer, Robert (2006), *Crip Theory: Cultural Signs of Queerness and Disability*, Cultural Front, New York: New York University Press.

Montford, Kelly Struthers and Chloë Taylor (2016), 'Feral theory: Editors' introduction', *Feral Feminisms*, 6: 5–17. (Open Access.)

Moten, Fred and Stefano Harney (2004), 'The University and the undercommons: Seven theses', *Social Text*, 22 (2): 101–15.

Muñoz, José Esteban (2005), 'Teaching, minoritarian knowledge, and love', *Women & Performance: A Journal of Feminist Theory*, 14 (2): 117–21. https://doi.org/10.1080/07407700508571480

Nicholas, Lucy and Sal Clark (2020), 'Leave those kids alone: On the uses and abuses and feminist queer potential of non-binary and genderqueer', *Journal of the International Network for Sexual Ethics & Politics*, 8 (Special Issue): 36–55. https://doi.org/10.3224/insep.si2020.03

Paperson, la (2017), *A Third University Is Possible*, Minneapolis: University of Minnesota Press.
Quilty, Aideen (2017), 'Queer provocations! exploring queerly informed disruptive pedagogies within feminist community-higher-education landscapes', *Irish Educational Studies*, 36 (1): 107–23. https://doi.org/10.1080/03323315.2017.1289704
Rohrer, Judy (2018), '"It's in the Room": Reinvigorating feminist pedagogy, contesting neoliberalism, and trumping post-truth populism', *Teaching in Higher Education*, 23 (5): 576–92. https://doi.org/10.1080/13562517.2018.1455656
Schulman, Sarah (2013), *The Gentrification of the Mind: Witness to a Lost Imagination*, California: University of California Press.
Thompson, Jay Daniel (2018), '"Sokal squared" and the absence of academic time', *Overland*, 8 November. Available online: https://overland.org.au/2018/11/sokal-squared-and-the-absence-of-academic-time/

11

Fight the Patriarchy: Digital Feminist Public Pedagogy and Post-feminist Media Culture in Indonesia

Annisa R. Beta

Using social media platforms, young feminist activists have earned a prominent position as they actively renew popular interest in feminism. With the help of celebrities and corporations, feminism becomes 'cool' for girls and young women. Organizations that started online like Hollaback! and hashtags like #MeToo have made significant contributions to the progress of women's rights, especially in uncovering stories of sexual assaults and rape culture. These platforms have enabled more girls and young women to learn about the dangers of misogynistic and patriarchal cultures. Nevertheless, most scholarship on digital feminist activism and popular feminism often reference case studies from the United States, Britain and other Global North countries. Does this mean the young people in the Global South are not participating in making feminism accessible to the masses, or are their efforts just not being recognized by scholarship which prioritizes the voices and examples from the Global North? Are girls and young women in developing countries 'out of space' and 'out of time' (Saraswati and Beta 2021) with regard to the rise of digital feminist activism?

In response to those questions, this chapter looks into how young feminists in Indonesia have actively deployed Instagram as a platform of 'digital feminist public pedagogy' (Mendes et al. 2019; Retallack et al. 2016). It suggests the necessity of interrogating the historical and political settings within which the digital feminist public pedagogy platform is located to understand feminism as it is practiced by young people beyond the Western-centric narratives of post-feminist media culture (Gill 2007, 2017; McRobbie 2009). In the following sections, I will detail what I mean by digital feminist public pedagogy and transnational post-feminist approach before moving on to a brief political history of feminism and women's movement in Indonesia. I point to the erasure of progressive women's history in educational institutions and the non-existent sex education for Indonesian young people. The chapter focuses on a popular young feminist Instagram account called Lawan Patriarki (@lawanpatriarki) to demonstrate the emergence of online feminist groups led by young women. I conclude by making the case of the deferring generalizing the label 'post-feminist' to the young feminist social media accounts for their often ambivalent, and lack of coherence, in feminist narratives. Instead, we have to look into how cultural, historical and socio-political settings condition how they *do* feminism.

Digital Feminist Public Pedagogy

By public pedagogy, I refer to the 'forms, processes, and sites of education and learning occurring beyond formal schooling and is distinct from hidden and explicit curricula operating within and through school sites' (Sandlin et al. 2011: 338–9). A feminist public pedagogy emphasizes participatory learning, personal experience and critical thinking skills (Creasap 2014: 156). Practices of feminist public pedagogy gone digital, thus, make use of the platforms and tools available to many today. Social media platforms like Twitter, Instagram, Facebook or TikTok could be mobilized by users, many of whom are young people, 'to connect, educate, and visibly engage with a range of feminist issues' (Mendes et al. 2019: 100). The platforms open the access to participation and engagement on everyday politics, validation to personal experience, and information and knowledge about what critical thinking entails in relation to feminism and gendered power relations with fewer constraints or the limitations that formal education institutions often impose.

On the one hand, the use of social media by girls and young women for knowledge-sharing challenges concerns about post-feminist media culture. On the other hand, popular online feminism has been claimed to chart the path towards a 'fourth wave feminism' (Retallack et al. 2016). While more scholars are welcoming the possibility of feminism moving towards its fourth wave, this chapter opts out from the simplification of feminist histories and progress (Hemmings 2011; Lusty 2017). Instead, I propose a reconsideration in the ways in which post-feminism can be considered transnationally, especially in relation to digital feminist public pedagogy. What is post-feminism? In her germinal work, Angela McRobbie (2009) warned us of the emergence of post-feminism, an anti-feminist sentiment that promotes the discourse of choice and consumerism that seems to celebrate gender empowerment but is actually an instrumentalization of feminism. Extending McRobbie, Rosalind Gill proposes that post-feminism should be seen as a sensibility that needs to be studied as a critical object in itself, not requiring 'a static notion of one single authentic feminism as a comparison point' (2007: 148). This sensibility includes the assumption that femininity is inscribed in the body, the emphasis on subjectification and disciplining the self, the focus on individualism and choice, the popularity of makeover discourse, the re-emergence of the discourse of natural sexual difference, cultural sexualization, the focus on consumerism and commodification of identity politics, and social inequality and exclusions based on race, ethnicity, class, age, sexuality, disability and other forms of discriminations (Gill 2007). In most Western settings, post-feminism has become hegemonic, by celebrating women's individual achievements, consumerism and confidence (Gill 2017).

Simidele Dosekun (2015) significantly contributes to the post-feminist literature by pointing to the transnational implication of post-feminist culture and sensibility in the Global South. Thinking about post-feminism transnationally facilitates a critical lens for feminist scholars when examining contemporary feminist cultures outside the Anglo–American or European contexts. This lens avoids perpetuating the idea that feminism is a 'transfer' from the West to the rest, and it helps us to think about post-feminism as 'an entanglement of meanings, representations, practices, and commodities' that moves across borders (Dosekun 2015: 965). A transnational post-feminist approach can help us understand how post-feminist individualism and celebration of the 'body' as the site through which femininity is spectacularized have been deployed by young feminists living in more collectivist, and to some extent conservative, societies like Indonesia to challenge the dominating discursive formations of gender, sexuality and the roles of women in public life. This is not a justification of post-feminism, but rather a call for an examination of transnational post-feminist culture that may be messy, ambivalent and contradictory. As the research materials introduced below will show, it is important for us, feminist scholars, to pause for a moment and reconsider how post-feminist dynamics may play out in different settings before we do a moral assessment of post-feminist sensibility.

This chapter explores how young feminists actually *do* feminism and how they have encouraged the emergence of feminist public pedagogy on social media. One critical role of public pedagogy is to create an emerging part of the publics whose existence could challenge the dominant public discourse; in other words, public pedagogy helps create counterpublics. Counterpublics are 'parallel discursive arenas where members of subordinated social groups invent and circulate counterdiscourses', expanding the discursive space in stratified societies (Fraser 1990: 67). The relations between dominant publics and counterpublics, nevertheless, may look different in post-authoritarian societies like Indonesia. The convergence of digital media and the opening and liberalization of media and political landscape have produced 'complexly mediated public spheres' which are 'public spheres that are at once more participatory and more fractured and convulsive than ever before' (Strassler 2020: 11–12). The following section explains how shifts in Indonesia's political and social history can help us understand the opportunities and challenges in the ways in which young feminists learn about and discuss feminism online.

Feminism and Women's Movements in Indonesia

Feminist ideals championing women's rights and equality are not new in Indonesia. Diverse women's organizations and movements, from religious ones to those that could be categorized as more modern and secular, which champion women's rights to education and participation in public have been present at least since the anti-colonial movement which started in early 1900s. Susan Blackburn (2004) traces the significance of access to education during the colonial era to the birth of modern women's organizations which led to the creation of the national women's federation in 1928. After Indonesia's independence in 1945, women's organizations flourished and played a key role in supporting nation-building processes. However, between 1965 and 1966, when in some parts of the world feminism moved on to new 'waves', in Indonesia feminist and women's groups were annihilated. Saskia Wieringa (2002) highlights the significance of the violent obliteration of the Indonesian Communist Party (PKI) and its women's organization, Gerwani (*Gerakan Wanita Indonesia* or Indonesian Women's Movement), to women's political consciousness and the subsequent rise of the New Order authoritarian regime under Suharto (1966–1998). The regime systematically reshaped ideals of femininity and actively reproduced the myth that women's involvement in politics was equal to perversion and sexual disorder. Good women were supposed to be domesticated and docile. Structurally, this also meant that women no longer had the same liberty to organize formally. The regime, instead, controlled existing women's organizations and created state-backed organizations called Dharma Wanita and PKK which actively created programmes to re-subordinate women's roles in the society by teaching wife 'duties' such as cooking, taking care of children and doing house chores (Wieringa 2002: 318).

Feminist movements and organizations in post-authoritarian Indonesia have mushroomed since the downfall of the authoritarian regime in 1998. They are often driven by educated women whose activism plays a key role in increasing the number of women politicians and legislators, as well as creating programmes with grassroots and non-government organizations (NGOs) to improve women's conditions. However, for most girls and young women, knowledge about feminism has until recently been largely inaccessible – unless they have received a university education with a focus on social issues and/or have actively participated in activist organizations or NGOs. Post-Suharto Indonesia has also undergone a 'conservative' turn (van Bruinessen 2013), which means more conservative Islamic values have encroached on more moderate Muslim ones and have consequently shifted how gendered roles are discursively and publicly performed. Saskia Wieringa (2015) argues that the spectre of the New Order's patrilineal and heteronormative gender politics has re-entered Indonesia's political and social lives as state officials now promote conservative religious values via a 'gender harmony' discourse and the idealization of a 'happy Muslim family.' Furthermore, in most schools in Indonesia, the history of Indonesia's women's movements is never discussed in detail. The account of the involvement and complexity of different women's organizations throughout the twentieth century is often subsumed under 'controversial' topics, avoided by school curriculums and by the school teachers (Ahmad 2016). When it is discussed, the discourse of women's empowerment is reduced to the heroic figure of Kartini, a Javanese elite who in the 1920s started a school for girls. Furthermore, sex education in schools also resorts to youth sexuality being suppressed with abstinence a popular solution (Dzulfikar 2019; Tsuda et al. 2017). Meanwhile, it has been reported that more than half of Indonesia's adolescents have experienced sexual harassment (Cahya 2019). Parents also rarely converse with their children about sexual and reproductive health (Nurachmah et al. 2018). In short, although the first decade of post-authoritarian Indonesia witnessed the growth of the progressive women's movement, feminist and gender empowerment ideas are challenged by the encroaching conservatism[1] and rarely reach most young people.

Access to the internet and social media platforms has since increased in post-1998 Indonesia, and it has opened new ways to gain, produce and circulate information and knowledge. Instagram, in particular, is popular among Indonesian youth (Ganesha 2017; Statista 2020) to not only share about their personal lives but also participate in online groups. Therefore, the emergence of online young feminist groups on social media platforms like Instagram signals an important shift in the discourse around gender and sexuality, at least among young Indonesians. Formal feminist organizations usually driven by more senior feminist activists focus on structural intervention in order to create larger change. Popular young feminist social media accounts, on the other hand, are more interested in the smaller details, defining terms, explaining in plain language why some legislations are important for young people, creating inspirational posts and encouraging their followers to live in more equitable and non-misogynistic environments. While the Indonesian Electronic Information and Transactions Law (UU ITE) has limited online expressions and debates, the young feminist accounts I observed have been able to navigate the social media platform to serve their objectives of critical knowledge sharing. The following section sketches the everyday and mundane attempts to make feminism popular and accessible to young Indonesians via social media. By discussing the types and regular themes as well as sharing some examples, I hope to begin the initial steps to understand how digital feminist public pedagogy can play an important role outside Western settings.

Fight the Patriarchy!

The analysis presented here is based on one year of Instagram posts of a popular online young feminist group, Lawan Patriarki (fight the patriarchy) or LP. The group was founded by a young woman named Ara (pseudonym). After graduating from the university, Ara learned about feminism and gender equality by herself through her travels in Indonesia and reading books and materials online and decided to create an Instagram account to share her knowledge about feminism. This account attracted thousands of new followers, volunteer administrators, and today has uploaded thousands of Instagram posts educating its young followers about feminism and agitating them to demand better manifestations of gender equality by the government as well as in everyday life. I started to do digital ethnographic work following their Instagram feed and participating in their group chats in October 2018, less than a month after the account was created in September 2018. In late 2018, the number of followers of LP's Instagram accounts was around ten thousand. It quickly grew in late 2019 following Indonesia's student-led protest (which I will briefly discuss below), and by January 2021, the account's followers numbered more than 200,000.[2] Not only did the number of followers increase quite dramatically, the number of chat groups they administer on WhatsApp and Line messaging applications also grew. They now have tens of group chat rooms where their followers can share interesting articles and books on gender, sexuality and feminism. The chat room participants also frequently ask one another for advice related to not only social and political issues but also personal issues.

The group represents a shift in the direction of feminist organizing and consciousness raising by young women in contemporary Indonesia. It was neither started by feminist activists familiar with NGO or government circles, nor was it founded by those formally educated in gender studies or other related fields. LP is part of the mushrooming of social media accounts founded by young women who felt uneasy about the gender-based inequalities in Indonesia. Similar accounts emerged around the same time on Instagram in 2018–2019, including Feminis Surabaya (@arekfeminis), Feminis Yogyakarta (@feminisyogya), Perempuan Tagar Tegar (@perempuantagartegar) and many others. Most of these accounts were founded by young women still studying at university, or like Ara, just recently graduated. Some of these accounts, however, are not as active as LP nor do they have a similar following. Nevertheless, the growing number of social media accounts founded by young women outside the usual feminist activist circles, like Hollaback! Jakarta (@hollaback_jkt), Indonesia Feminist (@indonesiafeminis) or Perkumpulan Lintas Feminis Jakarta (@jakartafeminist), demonstrates the popularity of and the increasing interest in feminism among Indonesian youth. Although one could argue that the popularity of young feminist groups on social media in Indonesia is consistent with the rise of popular feminism in the West (Banet-Weiser 2018), using a transnational, post-feminist approach allows me to de-centre the West and, instead, to 'see, trace, and try to make sense of the lines of complex connection and disjuncture between new and quite particular logics of femininity across transnational contexts' (Dosekun 2015: 972).

LP and other online young feminist groups' grassroots beginnings also suggest a form of public pedagogy that has successfully distributed interests on and knowledge about feminism and gender equality among young Indonesians, the reason why this chapter found it urgent to understand how social media facilitated its teaching and learning processes among Indonesian youth. Further, with the lack of information on the history of Indonesia's women's movement, only through informal sharing and, arguably, digital public pedagogy could the young feminists learn from one another and address their concerns about gender inequalities.

LP's Instagram feed is filled with discussions that address gender inequality, issues on sex and sexuality, and including more serious discussions like sexual violence and Indonesian laws and political issues related to gender. They actively post explainers of current issues as well as foundational definitions related to gender, sexuality and feminism to educate their followers. They address microaggressions that young women everywhere have experienced in language, tone and visual representation that is accessible and relevant. They encourage self-love and the capacity to subvert gendered social expectations. They discuss gender rights and women's rights in accessible ways, in language that can be understood by many, including a series of very useful explainers about Indonesian laws, such as the Anti-Sexual Violence Bill (RUU PKS), the Criminal Code (RKUHP) and the Family Resilience Bill. Clearly, more research has to be done to understand how the founders, administrators and followers of feminist social media accounts like LP imagine their roles in public. However, my point here is to illustrate the key topics considered urgent by the young women and popular among the readers. Below, I share the typologies of LP's Instagram account drawn from themes and categories emergent from grounded theory analysis (Charmaz 2014). These posts offer insights into the possibilities of 'doing feminism online' and how young feminists negotiate activism in post-authoritarian Indonesia. The aim is to understand how the digital labour done by popular young feminist groups like LP could give us an initial sketch on the ways in which young women respond to the increasing popularity of feminism online and their grounded realities in Indonesia.

Key Themes

There are at least five types of posts regularly uploaded by LP: explainer posts, confessional accounts, call out posts, inspirational posts and posts of protests and demonstrations. Explainer posts usually provide a general description of a topic or definitions of concepts usually reserved for specialists. They are inherently pedagogical in the ways in which they aim to distribute knowledge about a particular topic or concept to the general audience. Confessional accounts of assault and *'Cerita Perempuan'* (women's story) is the second kind of post regularly uploaded to LP. It is a series of confessional accounts sent by LP's followers via the direct messaging feature of Instagram. The confessions would usually be about the sender's experience and trauma related to sexual violence or traumatic experiences. LP then, with the consent of the sender, would screenshot their messages and post the story anonymously. The third type is the 'call out' posts. 'Call out' posts are usually meant to record social media users, news items, videos, photos or claims that are sexist, misogynist, homophobic, racist and generally anti-feminist. These posts are usually of screenshots that are treated as 'evidence' showing the problematic claims. Lisa Nakamura (2015) points out how this 'call out' culture is important in educating the public about problematic claims but it relies on unpaid digital labour done by marginalized groups. As a form of digital labour, call out posts require one to manage records of claims that could be dangerous for the marginalized groups, and later are shared for free on social media, giving free 'education' to usually the dominant group. The fourth type is inspirational posts. These are the posts made specifically to respond to the general patriarchal discourse young women are socialized with. The response would usually use quotes and images that could inspire and encourage the followers to be strong, confident, independent. This type of post is common in popular feminist discourses (Banet-Weiser 2018). The fifth type includes posts of protests and demonstrations. These posts would usually show images or videos of protestors holding a banner or poster. LP would thank them and encourage their followers to participate or support the protests.

The variety of topics discussed in LP's Instagram feed encourages a shift in the ways in which the followers think about gender and sexuality, particularly as a way to encourage critical consciousness among its followers about equality, feminism, women's rights and the public participation of young women. There are five most-posted themes: women and gender empowerment, self and body, sexual assault, laws and protests and relationships. LP rarely relies on coherent narratives of a particular feminist category, and as demonstrated by the extensive range of themes the account has discussed, it refutes the need to stabilize what feminism should mean for its followers. Rather, it is more interested in sparking the interests of young Indonesians in feminism, sexuality and gender empowerment. It will be apparent too in the posts discussed below that LP's Instagram posts allude to that of Riot Grrrl zine-making practices: the posts are usually creatively made by the administrators or sourced from their followers and other online accounts, and they are unapologetic (Comstock 2001; Goulding 2015), even though Ara, the founder of LP, was not familiar with Riot Grrrl (author's personal communication 2020). In other words, young feminist social media accounts like LP offer a new challenge in rethinking post-feminist media cultures outside the dominant Anglo–American model. They are not simply 'a tame, derivative copy of its putative Western original' (Dosekun 2015: 963). Below, I discuss the key themes emerging in LP's posts.

Challenging Misogyny

In an 'inspirational' post liked by more than 1,400 followers, LP uploaded an illustration of a woman with a crown and a quote: 'What is a queen without her king? A queen.' The caption, written in English, states: 'Wear what you want. Cause it's all about having the confidence. Proud to be women empowerment [*sic*]. So, be a queen better dream [*sic*], in the scene, make it big on the screen. Do you see I made my dream reallity [*sic*]' (Lawan Patriarki 2019e). In another post that was similarly popular, LP uploaded an image that screenshots a message from a user calling out a misogynistic meme. The meme shows a man doing house chores and claims that 'If your man touches these, you have failed as a wife'. The user's message claims (translated from Bahasa Indonesia): 'I'm like: You stupid! What's wrong with men doing house chores? I actually want a husband that does house chores so we can work together well.' The caption of the image reads 'Yes. An equal household' (Lawan Patriarki 2019f). Women's independence, in the two posts, is understood as a given. They were centred around young women's choice and individuality, which could be assumed as celebrating some type of post-feminist sensibility. Independence, choice and individuality have been part and parcel of what Rosalind Gill and Shani Orgad call the 'cult(ure) of confidence' (2015). Girls and young women in the Global North have been treated and hailed as the group that represent empowerment best and are thus in need of confidence boosting in a variety of contexts (Gill and Orgad 2015: 328). However, ideas of self-determination as represented by the posts, I contend, provide a counterdiscursive narrative for young women in Indonesia to rethink their independence and future. The celebration of women's self-reliance (as a 'queen') and demands for equality in a household should be seen as a response to the dominating neo-traditionalist forces in Indonesia that re-idealizes women's domestication (Wieringa 2015: 37).

Body Autonomy and Body Image

LP also celebrates women's autonomy of their body. Topics like self-love, body positivity, mental health and ways to deal with body shaming are regularly discussed to challenge patriarchal social norms that often corner young women and their confidence of their body. For instance, in a post uploaded with an image of the American comedian, Amy Schumer, the caption reads:

> 10 Facts Every Woman Should Know: 1. Everyone has rolls when they bend over. 2. When someone tells you that you're beautiful, believe them. They aren't lying. 3. Sometimes we all wake up with breath that could kill a goat. 4. For every woman unhappy with her stretch marks is another woman who wishes she had them. 5. You should definitely have more confidence. And if you saw yourself the way others see you, you would. (Cause you are absolutely beautiful and nobody should tell you otherwise!). 6. Don't look for a man to save you. Be able to save yourself. 7. It's okay to not love every part of your body.... .but you should. 8. We all have that one friend who seems to have it all together. That woman with the seemingly perfect life. Well, you might be that woman to someone else. 9. You should be a priority. Not an option, a last resort, or a backup plan. 10. You're a woman. That alone makes you pretty damn remarkable. -Austin Blood (Lawan Patriarki 2019a)

The image of Schumer, often seen as one of the popular figures of white feminism in the United States (Colpean and Tully 2019), is repurposed by LP here to speak about the impossible beauty standards young women often have to deal with. A reference to Schumer could be seen as reference to the kind of feminism that celebrates individualism and thus reprivatizes concerns about the body. But, as I contend above, young feminist media accounts like LP do not see any contradiction in making such reference as they are more interested in challenging dominant discourse about ideal womanhood. Another example of this is a make-up video made by user @blackxugar posted by LP with the caption 'Indonesian beauty standard is invalid because I am pretty and beautiful and gorgeous and sweet and you too❤ Who the hell are you telling me and other *item-pesek* [dark skinned, flat nose] fellas ugly? We are beautiful, darling'❤ (Lawan Patriarki 2019c). The focus on women's face and body as the representative of one's femininity could be understood as a form of post-feminist sensibility. Nevertheless, we should consider how rare a celebration of 'dark skinned and flat nose' facial features happens in postcolonial societies like Indonesia, where fair-skin, and to some extent whiteness, is usually seen as desirable (Saraswati 2013). In other words, we cannot take for granted this redefinition of beauty and the body by the young feminists that goes beyond the white and Western ideals and thus extends beyond how post-feminist sensibilities are usually framed.

Sexual Violence

Another theme often discussed by LP and which has captured much of its followers' attention is one related to sexual violence. Indonesia's National Commission on Violence Against Women (Komnas Perempuan) reported that sexual violence cases have increased almost eightfold between 2007 and 2019, to 331,471 reported cases (Sen and Kazi 2020). Using different techniques, including storytelling, young feminist groups like LP play an important role in educating the public, particularly young women, on what sexual violence may entail. For LP, its *Cerita Perempuan* (women's story) series has been effective in sharing the urgency of understanding and dealing with sexual violence for its young followers. LP would share screenshots of messages from their followers telling painful and traumatic stories of how they were assaulted by the people closest to them. For example, in December 2018, LP uploaded a series of images screenshotting a story from their followers about how the person she was dating, who she assumed was a good and religious person, was touching her inappropriately, often without her consent. Encouraging the followers to read carefully, this post was captioned (translated from Bahasa Indonesia) 'LET'S READ. [Some men] pretend that they want to protect women but they actually want to ruin us. We don't believe you. It's good that we women are the strongest group of humans in the world, willing to educate ourselves, to protect ourselves, to heal ourselves until today' (Lawan Patriarki 2018). Posts uploaded under the theme of relationship also often call out behaviours that are misogynistic and sometimes abusive that are usually assumed as 'romantic'. For instance, one post was based on screenshots of a Twitter thread sharing a user's reflection from witnessing her friend in an abusive relationship. After recounting the story, the user suggests 'From my friend's experience, I realize how obsessive, possessive, and manipulative her partner was even though his behaviours were often interpreted as sweet and romantic' (Lawan Patriarki 2019b). LP also regularly uploads explainer posts defining different types of sexual violence. These posts could be simple explainers uploaded as a slider post (which includes multiple images in one post). In one of their uploads, for instance, LP made a list of different types of sexual violence, encouraging their followers to distribute it further 'so that those who do not know or understand do not need to be victims of sexual violence in order to fight for the Anti-Sexual Violence Bill' (Lawan Patriarki 2019g). The three examples illustrate how young feminists in Indonesia like LP are joining the global force of feminist accounts and hashtags making use of social media as platforms for storytelling to articulate individual experiences of sexual assaults, toxic relationships and rape culture (Mendes et al. 2019). LP attracts the followers' attention by focusing on the individual stories and making sure that learning about different types of sexual violence is seen as accessible and urgent. This urgency then helps LP in campaigning for a legislation.

Laws and Protests

While some of the account's posts focus on individual empowerment, LP also openly encourages their followers to actively support certain bills or legal cases and – when necessary – encourages them to join protests. The most prominent one is that of the Anti-Sexual Violence Bill, more popularly known as RUU PKS. The bill was put forward by the National Commission on Violence Against Women with the support of feminist and gender empowerment non-profit organizations since 2012. However, the Indonesian government, including the House of Representatives, has been delaying the bill due to mounting pressure from more conservative groups. While formal organizations continue to negotiate with the government, feminist social media accounts like LP actively communicate the urgency of the bill and the content of the bill to their followers, and, like the example I mentioned above, how the bill could personally help women's lives, especially of those who are the victims of social violence. I contend that the online campaigns of LP and other young feminist accounts, along with NGOs and the National Commission, have successfully influenced Indonesian young people in being more critical and vocal about legislative and executive processes in the country. In fact, the biggest student-led protest after Reformasi in 1998 was organized in September 2019 in response to the government's constant delay of discussing RUU PKS as well as the plan to prioritize the revision of the Indonesian criminal code. LP actively records the activities of students participating in the protests, thanking them for going to the streets. In a post with more than 270,000 likes uploaded on 24 September 2019, LP uploaded a series of images with protestors holding up signs critiquing the government. The caption reads (translated from Bahasa Indonesia): 'Thank you to all of you friends from all over Indonesia who have gone to the streets today...' (Lawan Patriarki 2019d). While it is difficult to pin down a particular kind of feminism supported by LP, it is nonetheless clear that it provides pedagogical opportunities and affective spaces for sharing individual stories and, at the same time, extend the stories and personalized narratives to encourage more young people to take active roles in public concerns. The posts LP uploads are less about a consistent feminist discourse and more about a remix of references as well as audio, visual and textual materials that could be useful to encourage a counterdiscourse about gender and sexuality in contemporary Indonesia.

Conclusion

In this chapter, I have demonstrated that social media and feminist groups like LP and many others represent a powerful platform for digital feminist public pedagogy. Feminist social media accounts open access to education, especially among young women, to learn from each other in non-formal conditions outside schools and universities, allowing, in other words, a form of a public pedagogy. A public pedagogy is indispensable in a post-authoritarian society like Indonesia because it does not necessarily have to follow a model of normative or moralistic education. Rather, a pedagogy that is public in itself relies on a heterogenous understanding of what is important, what is worth sharing, what is socially and culturally urgent to be understood – rather than following rigid sets of curricula. The presence of public pedagogy is important especially in times when the boundaries of public and private spaces are reconfigured by digital media.

This type of digital feminist public pedagogy, I argue, is particularly significant in Indonesia for several reasons. First, it emerges from a lack of access to progressive histories of feminist and women's movements in Indonesia in formal education. Second, there is a literal lack of space for young women and youth in general to have meaningful discussions and debates about feminism, gender and sexuality, but also because of the general public perception that young women, and youth in general, cannot be taken seriously. Third is the unfortunate social and cultural stigma that is often attached to terms such as feminism or gender empowerment, but more importantly to victims of sexual abuse or violence.

While it is notable that there is no coherent narrative of feminism championed by popular young feminist accounts like LP, it is important to consider how the 'messiness' does not detract from the impacts of the message – this 'messiness' perhaps represents their grassroots vitality and passion which made accounts like LP attractive to its young followers. By looking into how feminism is practiced by young people in an increasingly conservative and post-authoritarian society, this chapter encourages a deferral in generalizing the label of 'post-feminism' and de-centring Western feminism in analyses of feminist practices and activism in 'the Global South'. The seemingly ambivalent and contradictory references deployed by the young feminists reveal the historical, social, political and cultural specificities by which feminism is practiced, enabled by digital media cultures.

Acknowledgements

I would like to thank Mursyidatul Umamah for her assistance.

Notes

1 By conservatism here, I am referring to the tendency to champion heteronormative, sexist and misogynist perspectives that somewhat assumed to be the way of the past or related to 'traditions'. While conservatism in Indonesia is closely tied to the global Islamic revival, I am not claiming that Islam is the cause for its rise. Indonesia has had progressive and moderate Muslim organizations pushing for anti-colonial movements and women's empowerment for at least a century now.

2 In February 2021 and up to the final phases of me writing this chapter, however, LP had to temporarily suspend its Instagram accounts because of an ongoing defamation case (WS & Co 2021).

References

Ahmadise, T. A. (2016), *Sejarah Kontroversial Di Indonesia: Perspektif Pendidikan*, Jakarta: Yayasan Pustaka Obor Indonesia.

Banet-Weiser, Sarah (2018), *Empowered: Popular Feminism and Popular Misogyny*, Durham: Duke University Press.

Blackburn, Susan (2004), *Women and the State in Modern Indonesia*, Cambridge: Cambridge University Press.

Cahya, Gemma Holliani (2019), 'Sexual harassment in public spaces rampant among minors: Survey', *The Jakarta Post*, 17 July. Available online: https://www.thejakartapost.com/news/2019/07/16/sexual-harassment-in-public-spaces-rampant-among-minors-survey.html

Charmaz, Kathy (2014), *Constructing Grounded Theory*, 2nd ed., London, Thousand Oaks, New Delhi, Singapore, & Washington DC: Sage.

Colpean, Michelle and Meg Tully (2019), 'Not Just a Joke: Tina Fey, Amy Schumer, and the Weak Reflexivity of White Feminist Comedy', *Women's Studies in Communication*, 42 (2): 161–80. https://doi.org/10.1080/07491409.2019.1610924

Comstock, Michelle (2001), 'Grrrl zine networks: Re-composing spaces of authority, gender, and culture', *JSTOR JAC*, 21 (2): 383–409.

Creasap, Kimberly (2014), 'Zine-Making as Feminist Pedagogy', *Feminist Teacher*, 24 (3): 155–68. https://doi.org/10.5406/femteacher.24.3.0155

Dosekun, Simidele (2015), 'For western girls only? Post-feminism as transnational culture', *Feminist Media Studies*, 15 (6): 960–75.

Dzulfikar Luthfi, T. (2019), 'How to teach sex education in Indonesia: Academics weigh in', *The Conversation*, August 29. Available online: http://theconversation.com/how-to-teach-sex-education-in-indonesia-academics-weigh-in-122400.

Fraser, Nancy (1990), 'Rethinking the public sphere: A contribution to the critique of actually existing democracy', *Social Text* 25/26: 56–80.

Ganesha, Amal (2017), 'Instagram has 45 million users in Indonesia, the largest in Asia Pacific', *Jakarta Globe*, 27 July. Available online: http://jakartaglobe.id/news/instagram-45-million-users-indonesia-largest-asia-pacific/ (accessed 11 June 2018).

Gill, Rosalind (2007), 'Postfeminist media culture: Elements of a sensibility', *European Journal of Cultural Studies*, 10 (2): 147–66.

Gill, Rosalind (2017), 'The affective, cultural and psychic life of postfeminism: A postfeminist sensibility 10 years on', *European Journal of Cultural Studies*, 20 (6): 606–26.

Gill, Rosalind and Shani Orgad (2015), 'The Confidence Cult(ure)', *Australian Feminist Studies*, 30 (86): 324–44. https://doi.org/10.1080/08164649.2016.1148001

Goulding, Cathlin (2015), 'The spaces in which we appear to each other: The pedagogy of resistance stories in Zines by Asian American Riot Grrrls', *Journal of Cultural Research in Art Education*, 32: 161–189.

Hemmings, Clare (2011), *Why Stories Matter: The Political Grammar of Feminist Theory*, Durham: Duke University Press.

Lawan Patriarki (2018), NYOH BACA Kedok melindungi perempuan padahal bermaksud merusak [Instagram image]. Available online: https://www.instagram.com/p/Br9WAOMAb-U/

Lawan Patriarki (2019a), 10 facts every woman should know [Instagram image]. Available online: https://www.instagram.com/p/B06MEODgf9T/

Lawan Patriarki (2019b), Ihhh pacarrr aqutuuu so sweeet bangeddddhhh [Instagram image]. Available online: https://www.instagram.com/p/B0-34tIgdTd/

Lawan Patriarki (2019c), Indonesian beauty standard is invalid [Instagram video]. Available online: https://www.instagram.com/p/Bt-4B-6FME_/

Lawan Patriarki (2019d), Terimakasih kepada teman-teman di seluruh Indonesia [Instagram image]. Available online: https://www.instagram.com/p/B2wmcNDALo5/

Lawan Patriarki (2019e), Wear what you want [Instagram image]. Available online: https://www.instagram.com/p/BswjjWMAHvG/.

Lawan Patriarki (2019f), Yap. Rumah tangga yang setara [Instagram image]. Available online: https://www.instagram.com/p/BsVDpL5AIqp/

Lawan Patriarki (2019g), Yuk kenali apa saja bentuk-bentuk kekerasan seksual dan dampaknya bagi korban [Instagram image]. Available online: https://www.instagram.com/p/BtQZsQeAEMA/

Lusty, Natalya (2017), 'Riot Grrrl manifestos and radical vernacular feminism', *Australian Feminist Studies*, 32 (93): 219–39.

McRobbie, Angela (2009), *The Aftermath of Feminism: Gender, Culture and Social Change*, London: SAGE.

Mendes Kaitlynn, Jessica Ringrose and Jessalyn Keller (2019), *Digital Feminist Activism: Girls and Women Fight Back against Rape Culture*, Oxford: Oxford University Press.

Nakamura, Lisa (2015), 'The unwanted labour of social media: Women of colour call out culture as venture community management', *New Formations* (86): 106–12. https://doi.org/10.3898/NEWF.86.06.2015

Nurachmah Elly, Yati Afiyanti, Sri Yona, Rita Ismael, John Toding Padang, I Ketut Suardana, Yulia Irwin Dewit, Kelana Kusuma Dharma (2018), 'Mother-daughter communication about sexual and reproductive health issues in Singkawang, West Kalimantan, Indonesia', *Enfermería Clínica*, 28 r: 172–5. https://doi.org/10.1016/S1130-8621(18)30061-5

Retallack, Hanna, Jessica Ringrose and Emilie Lawrence (2016), '"Fuck your body image": Teen girls' Twitter and Instagram feminism in and around school', in Julia Coffey, Shelley Budgeon and Helen Cahill (eds), *Learning Bodies*, 85–103, Singapore: Springer.

Sandlin, Jennifer A., Michael P. O'Malley and Jake Burdick (2011), 'Mapping the complexity of public pedagogy scholarship: 1894–2010', *Review of Educational Research*, 81 (3): 338–75.

Saraswati, Ayu, L. (2013), *Seeing Beauty, Sensing Race in Transnational Indonesia*, Honolulu: University of Hawaii Press.

Saraswati, Marissa & Annisa R. Beta (2021), 'Knowing responsibly: Decolonizing knowledge production of Indonesian girlhood', *Feminist Media Studies*, 21(5): 758–74, DOI: 10.1080/14680777.2020.1763418.

Sen, Anjali and M. Kazi Jamshed (2020), 'Will we ever end violence against women?', *The Jakarta Post*, October 7. Available online: https://www.thejakartapost.com/academia/2020/10/07/will-we-ever-end-violence-against-women.html

Statista (2020), Indonesia: Share of Instagram users by age 2020. Available online: https://www-statista-com.eu1.proxy.openathens.net/statistics/1078350/share-of-instagram-users-by-age-indonesia/ (accessed 20 January 2021).

Strassler, Karen (2020), *Demanding Images: Democracy, Mediation, and the Image-Event in Indonesia*, Durham: Duke University Press.

Tsuda, Satoko, Sri Hartini S, Elsi Di Hapsari and Satoshi Takada (2017), 'Sex education in children and adolescents with disabilities in Yogyakarta, Indonesia from a teachers' gender perspective', *Asia Pacific Journal of Public Health*, 29 (4): 328–38. https://doi.org/10.1177/1010539517702716

van Bruinessen, Martin (2013), 'Introduction: Contemporary developments in Indonesian Islam and the "Conservative Turn" of the early twenty-first century', in M. van Bruinessen (ed), *Contemporary Developments in Indonesian Islam: Explaining the 'Conservative Turn'*, 1–20, Singapore: Institute of Southeast Asian Studies.

Wieringa, Saskia (2002), *Sexual Politics in Indonesia*, London: Palgrave Macmillan UK. https://doi.org/10.1057/9781403919922

Wieringa, Saskia (2015), 'Gender harmony and the happy family: Islam, gender and sexuality in post-reformasi Indonesia', *South East Asia Research*, 23 (1): 27–44.

WS & Co (2021), Kami selaku kuasa hukum dari klien kami, bersama ini menghimbau [Instagram image]. Available online: https://www.instagram.com/p/CLi8pJKhK8D

Conclusion

Beyond True and False: Reflecting and Rebuilding towards Feminist Pedagogies of Care

Akane Kanai, Julia Coffey, Penny Jane Burke and Rosalind Gill

This collection was written across a period of time that was profoundly affecting for us. Even from a position of relative privilege and security, this time felt acutely unstable and unsafe. The formation of this collection was spurred, in significant part, by our reaction as Western feminist scholars to a state of affairs signalling a concerted rollback of cultural gains that were hard won. In 2017, we had seen the triumph of Brexit and Trump was at the beginning of what would become his single-term Presidency. We watched in horror as attempts to hold former President Trump to account in the established and independent media such as CNN, and by the courts, were sidestepped or denounced by him as 'fake news'. We sensed then that these diversionary tactics were explicit attempts to cast doubts over independent, rigorous reporting; to take advantage of the increasingly marketized, individualized and consumer-oriented production of news; and indeed, to lay the groundwork for blatant mistruths to be seen as legitimate alternatives to the knowledge produced by 'corrupt elites' in institutions such as universities and government. There seemed to be so many policies being wound back and new ones proposed, it felt almost impossible to keep track. Reneging on the United States' commitment to address climate change by pulling out of the Paris Agreement, forcibly removing children from their parents, the construction of a wall to keep out those from Mexico and other parts of Latin America, the instigation of an unprecedented travel ban on all coming from majority-Muslim countries, attacks on women's rights to abortion and transgender support services, hard-fought wins for environment, feminist and social justice issues – all seemed to be unravelling at a frightening pace, with unimaginable consequences for future generations across the globe. Black Lives Matter protests shone a light on the embodied racialized politics of inequality and its structural, carceral consequences for African-American people. Yet Black resistance has consistently been met with articulations of white supremacy. The homicidal riots on Capitol Hill in early 2021 marked the end of Trump's first chaotic and catastrophic term in office. Trump's ultimate lies about having won the 2020 election culminated in the deadly riots on the Capitol building, in which white supremacists enacted a highly gendered and racialized violation of this institutionalized space of democracy, as Ileana Jiménez has noted in this collection. All the while, new variants of COVID-19 continued to rage across the globe, with millions dead, and existing gendered, racialized and economic inequalities sharpening. As feminist scholars of sociology, education and cultural studies, we wondered what future for feminism and the planet could exist in such an uninhabitable political and environmental climate.

There have been significant changes since then, and yet the sharp inequalities and violence of austerity politics combined with authoritarian neoliberalism (Tansel 2017) and populism have deepened their effects. We note Twitter's move to permanently 'deplatform' Trump initially showed some impact in reducing the volume of disinformation circulating on social media. Media Matters, the liberal-leaning media advocacy group, found that interactions with right-leaning pages dropped in the aftermath of Twitter's ban (Zudjik and Wagner 2021). Right- and left-leaning posts drew roughly equal amounts of engagement after the ban, the group found, reversing a long trend of right-wing content outperforming other political content (Zudjik and Wagner 2021). Yet, these attempts to set clear parameters of civil speech on mainstream social media platforms, however, has meant new spaces for right-wing politics have arisen. When Parler, the primary destination for right-wing and QAnon users alienated by Facebook and Twitter, was suspended in Apple and Google's App stores, other apps including Gab and Telegram emerged as the alternative platforms for the right. Commentators have suggested that Trump's followers, and the post-truth populist rhetoric he so successfully weaponized, will not simply fade away or be solved by his ban from Twitter. The migration from Twitter to far-right alternative platforms could aggravate trends that pre-dated Trump and further fracture public discourse (Zudjik and Wagner 2021). These kinds of right-wing social cultures specifically target feminist goals and seek to dismantle social justice agendas which advocate for the rights of women, LGBTQI+ communities, people of colour, those with disabilities, immigrants, precarious and working-class communities, and refugees. This, of course, caused consternation and frustration for us as feminist scholars located in the supposed 'ivory towers' of academia, who have long been invested in the work of feminist knowledge-making and the political possibilities of education. We felt compelled to respond to these cynical, violent and destructive attacks on the kinds of knowledges that underpin the building of collectivity, care and social justice.

Writing in early 2021, we can see the continuing impact of damaging divisions, conflicts and the expressions of entrenched distrust and resentment. In such a context of atomized individuality and inequality, crisis appears to be the norm. As fatalities caused by the COVID-19 pandemic number in the millions globally, the narrativizations of the virus have widely shown their 'amenability' (Hemmings 2011) for political gain in authoritarian discourses of border closure as well as conspiracy groups that dispute the existence of the virus at all. In the UK, Wood and Skeggs (2020) observe the continued 'neglect by design' of disadvantaged populations already adversely affected by austerity measures – those with disabilities, the elderly – and healthcare workers on the frontline, of whom Black and Minority Ethnic (BME) workers are disproportionately at risk. Combined with reckless indifference is the exacerbation of xenophobia under COVID-19, with an inflation in hate crimes against those of Asian descent in different Western nations (Jeung, Yellow Horse and Cayanan 2021; Kassam and Hsu 2021). Such expressions of targeted xenophobia and a turning away from vulnerability in the context of neoliberal atomization mark much of the context of Anglo-American life under the pandemic.

It is difficult to take time to reflect in such a moment. This indeed is further exacerbated by rapid changes taking place in higher education, driven by narratives of the many financial 'crises' apparently caused by the COVID-19 pandemic and the related imposed imperative to refocus sharply on 'job-readiness', directly affecting the temporalities of intellectual work. The accelerated pace towards marketization and employability discourses is profoundly undermining the arts, humanities and social sciences, seriously threatening the sustainability, formation and development of critical knowledges broadly and feminist praxis more specifically. How might we (re)approach feminist knowledge-making under such conditions? Challenges to the legitimacy of feminist epistemologies have become increasingly apparent as wide-scale untruths gain ground in reinforcing forms of division, hostility and violence that have profound implications and effects for social justice in, through and beyond education. In these contexts, this collection has asserted the urgency of exploring what this means for feminist pedagogies and practices. How can feminists engage students with questions of truth, knowledge and power? If feminism has argued for knowledge that recognizes subjectivity, emotion and positionality, how might feminists grapple with a form of populism that relies on emotion and identity politics rather than reason and fact? How might feminist pedagogical strategies encourage consideration of the complex relationship across materiality, emotionality, objectivity, subjectivity and contextualization in a world where information is increasingly networked and decontextualized from its location? How do we locate the emergence of post-truth populism in the twenty-first century in relation to historical and global contestations over knowledge and truth, of which feminists have been actively engaged over this and the last century? What are the feminist pedagogical tools available and how might these be re/imagined, re/shaped and re/framed in the context of contemporary struggle over knowledge, knowing and truth?

We suggest this volume gives us some indication that we need to take stock of these shifting coordinates not as 'new' but continuing phenomena. In relation to the contested arena of 'truth', as Raewyn Connell pointed out in this collection, 'Big Lies' in the service of power have long been circulated as part of colonial strategies. For example, in the Australian settler–colonial context, from earlier days of colonization, blatantly false stories about First Nations people were circulated in the press, through education, and via popular memorabilia; and such lies continue in online culture regularly (Carlson 2020). Further, populism may not necessarily only be tethered to the premeditated incitation of doubt and confusion suggested by the term 'post-truth'. As Nguyen and McDonald (2021) argue in this volume, populism may be tied to varied political contexts, with differing strategies, scapegoats and economic histories. Kenway's chapter also connected the current mobilization of 'right wing fury' with overt attacks on feminist, social justice and environmental priorities through appeals to 'crises' (for example, 'the free speech crisis').

As such, in understanding populism as something that seeks to speak for 'the people' but frequently resurrects unequal gender, class and racial orders, we need to consider populism in relation to struggles over cultural terrains that shift according to context. There may be very different national settings for populism in terms of political history, as we have seen in this volume, with varying models of individualism, collectivism and market politics. However, it has been clear that many such struggles have occurred in connection with common shifts, albeit with differing effects. One such thread we can follow through many contributions to this volume is how populism arises in relation to neoliberal capitalism, whether in the highly neoliberalized, marketized academy and the shift to education as a consumer privilege, or in market reforms in a post-socialist context where certain gender orders are remade and reinforced. There is also a significant link across many chapters to the rise of online culture as an increasingly central and accessible means through which understandings of the social world are made. And of course, across many chapters in this volume is highlighted the aggrievement and sense of loss of those who feel that their worldviews should always remain *the* authoritative, normative worldviews. Isis Giraldo's chapter provided a detailed analysis of the ways gender and feminist pedagogies of care are currently caught in the 'ideological struggles' underpinned by colonial and capitalist mechanisms of power. Recent attacks on gender, Giraldo showed, are part of a broader and longstanding attempt to delegitimize all social justice projects. In this landscape, it is more important than ever for feminist scholars and activists to continue to challenge structural inequalities and advocate for social justice.

What has particularly stood out to us as feminist scholars is the imperative to acknowledge the forms of embodied and discursive knowledge-making that takes place both within and beyond 'the classroom'. Even as the classroom, as Nicola Rivers has argued, has become a highly surveilled space with an onslaught on feminist forms of knowledge-making from different sides, we note that the classroom is only one of the 'epistemic communities' (Ramazanoglu and Holland 2000) available in a highly networked world. As the chapter by Xumeng Xie, Idil Cambazoglu, Bárbara Berger-Correa and Jessica Ringrose demonstrated, there are particularly harmful implications associated with increased digital networked visibility for feminist scholars and activists who can become targets of online abuse through trolling and 'shitposting'.

Looking beyond the classroom, we are reminded by Susan Page that universities themselves have long been hierarchical spaces in which feminist, queer and Indigenous ways of knowing have only contingently been accepted into academic curricula. Now such areas have to account for themselves not only in terms of theoretical legitimacy but also in terms of institutional metrics: student numbers, employability and profit. Stephen Farrier, Alyson Campbell, Hannah McCann and Meta Cohen considered how queer theory can have different possibilities for 'queer feral pedagogies' beyond hierarchies of knowledge in formal university settings. Both Farrier et al. and Annisa Beta's chapters explored how feminist and queer activism and thought can become central in public digital pedagogies. Beta's chapter highlighted that the historical and political settings must be central in understanding how digital feminist public pedagogies and contemporary feminisms are enacted, looking beyond Western-centric narratives of feminism's arrival and incorporation.

Future Feminist Directions?

Where does this leave us as feminist educators and knowledge-makers? In taking these insights seriously, we suggest a need to strategically and selectively refuse debates that are predominantly constructed in terms of truths and falsehood. Enraging as it is to continually be faced with the knowing spread of lies in relation to the ravages of climate change, a global pandemic, or the vulnerability of particular identity groups, we need to analyse such assertions not only in relation to empirical realities but also in relation to the desires, investments and motivations that underpin them. Since these kinds of contestations, although appearing in different configurations, are not wholly new, we argue it is useful to return to the lessons learned from histories of debates in feminist theory. Feminists have long sought to question the authority of existing knowledge while advancing 'better' accounts of gender relations, and in doing so, often hold together multiple and frequently competing imperatives. As Ramazanoglu and Holland (2000) note:

> Feminists cannot claim authoritative knowledge of political and sexual identities unless they take these to be fixed or essential truths, but equally feminists cannot afford to abandon the investigation of specific power relations, their intersections and effects on the grounds that these are unknowable.
>
> (211)

Clare Hemmings, in *Why Stories Matter* (2011), offers an account of feminist stories about feminist theory's past, present and thus implicitly, feminism's future. In holding to the question of *how* we tell the stories, and *how* we acknowledge our own motivations and interests, Hemmings refuses the question of 'accurate' accounts of the past, even as she is questioned: 'what's so wrong with aspiring to find out *what has really happened* in academic feminism's recent past?' (emphasis added) (Torr 2007: 59). Hemmings notably responds that seeking a *singular* authoritative account must be understood as epistemic violence. Following Hemmings, this is not a question per se of *dispensing* with accuracy but rather, focusing on the underpinning investments and *effects* of such certain pronouncements. To echo Sara Ahmed's (2004) framework in which she engages with performativity: what does a certain speech act, truth claim or statement *do*?

In paying attention to the *effects* of our statements, and the statements of others, we need to also pay attention to the relationality that shapes the effects of claims. For example, the veracity of even highly privileged women has long been considered suspect, particularly in relation to accounts of harm, injury, pain and violence. It is no coincidence that the activism of #MeToo swelled in the US Women's March following Trump's presidential election. But we also need to pay attention to more nuanced differences and investments in our claims that may be more difficult to acknowledge. As feminist scholars have argued over decades, our attempts at knowledge are never innocent, nor neutral (Haraway 1988; Harding 1991; Mohanty 1984). In making claims, we note Nagar's (2002) suggestion that it is important to not simply narcissistically observe our 'positionality' – but to substantially reflect on our own desires, anxieties and blind spots which are in and of themselves racialized, classed, able-ist and geopolitically driven. As Hale pointed out in her chapter, it is imperative that feminist activism and scholarship responding to 'post-truth' does not unwittingly impede decolonizing and democratizing processes. In this landscape, critical pedagogical strategies are more important than ever.

In concluding, we think it important to acknowledge there is no single, simple or politically uncontentious way to proceed when it comes to the necessity and difficulty of feminist truth-telling because 'producing knowledge of gender relations remains both politically urgent and epistemologically problematic' (Ramazanoglu and Holland 2000: 217). Feminist endeavours to produce theory and knowledge have long and self-critically acknowledged such work as motivated, and partial, but also part of a collective epistemic community/communities. Although this task is urgent, reflection is critical; we cannot abandon the gains of feminist questioning, uncertainty and locatedness now.

References

Ahmed, Sara (2004), 'Declarations of whiteness: The non-performativity of anti-racism', *Borderlands* 3 (2). Available online: http://www.borderlands.net.au/vol3no2_2004/ahmed_declarations.htm

Carlson, Bronwyn (2020), 'Love and hate at the cultural interface: Indigenous Australians and dating apps', *Journal of Sociology*, 56 (2): 133–50.

Haraway, Donna (1988), 'Situated knowledges: The science question in feminism and the privilege of partial perspective', *Feminist studies*, 14 (3): 575–99.

Harding, Sandra (1991), *Whose Science? Whose Knowledge? Thinking from Women's Lives*, Milton Keynes: Open University Press.

Hemmings, Clare (2011), *Why Stories Matter: The Political Grammar of Feminist Theory*, Durham and London: Duke University Press.

Jeung, Russell, Aggie J. Yellow Horse, Charlene Cayanan (2021), *Stop AAPI Hate National Report 3/ 19/20– 3/31/21*, Stop AAPI Hate Reporting Centre. Available online: https://stopaapihate.org/national-report-through-march-2021/ (accessed 28 April 2021).

Kassam, Natasha and Jennifer Hsu (2021), *Being Chinese in Australia: Public Opinion in Chinese Communities*, Sydney: Lowy Institute. Available online: https://interactives.lowyinstitute.org/features/chinese-communities

Mohanty, Chandra Talpade (1984), 'Under Western eyes: Feminist scholarship and colonial discourses', *Boundary* 2 (12/13): 333–58.

Nagar, Richa (2002) Footloose Researchers, 'Traveling' Theories, and the Politics of Transnational Feminist Praxis, Gender, Place and Culture: A Journal of Feminist Geography, 9:2, 179–186.

Ramaznoglu, Caroline and Janet Holland (2000), 'Still telling it like it is? Problems of feminist truth claims', in S. Ahmed, J. Kilby, C. Lury, M. McNeil and B. Skeggs (eds), *Transformations: Thinking Through Feminism*, 207–20, Routledge: London and New York.

Tansel, Cemal Burak (2017), 'Authoritarian neoliberalism: Towards a new research agenda', in Cemal Burak Tansel (ed), *States of Discipline: Authoritarian Neoliberalism and the Contested Reproduction of Capitalist Order*, 1–28, London: Rowman and Littlefield.

Torr, Rachel (2007), 'What's wrong with aspiring to find out what has really happened in academic feminism's recent past? Response to Clare Hemmings' "Telling feminist stories"', *Feminist Theory*, 8 (1): 59–67.

Wood, Helen and Beverley Skeggs (2020), 'Clap for carers?', *European Journal of Cultural Studies*, 23 (4): 641–7.

Zuidijk, Daniel and Wagner, Kurt (2021) 'Trump's Twitter (TWTR) ban after capitol riots will have lasting impact', *Bloomberg Business*, 21 January 2021 https://www.bloomberg.com/news/articles/2021-01-14/trump-s-twitter-twtr-ban-after-capitol-riots-will-have-lasting-impact

Index

Abbott, Tony, *Quadrant* 33
Aboriginal and Torres Strait Islander people 11, 115–16, 123
Aboriginal deaths (associated with custody) 114, 123
accountability 2, 4, 87–8, 160
activism 3, 7, 16, 114, 196
   community 80, 115
   complaint 158–62, 167
   (digital) feminist 5–6, 12–13, 38, 71, 88, 134, 211, 235
   HIV 202
   left-wing 11, 102, 109
   men's rights 12, 27, 89, 145
   queer 72, 196, 201, 233
   students' feminist educational 12–13, 159
affective politics 5, 12, 28
Africa 67
Ahmed, Sara 12, 108, 167, 206, 234
   complaint activism 158–62, 167
   Feminist Killjoys research blog 158
   Living a Feminist Life 86
   on safe spaces 106
   willful subjects 106
alternative facts 2, 15, 79
alt-right 5, 21, 26–8, 35, 82
   alt-right gaze 151
   Nagle on 26
   playbook 148
   populism 90
American-Vietnam War 180
Amerindia, colonization of 46
anarcho-activists 87
andragogy 199
Anglo-American 45–7, 213, 219, 231
antagonism 2, 15
anthropology/anthropologists 9, 81, 88–90, 200
anti-bullying programmes 71–2
anti-colonial movement 44, 51–2, 185, 214, 225 n.1

anti-feminism/feminist 3, 27, 30, 36, 51, 71, 131–4, 137, 141, 148, 150, 213, 219
   meme 146
anti-gender campaign 49, 71
anti-immigration 3, 66
anti-parasitic medication 35–6
anti-racism/racist 11, 44, 75, 104, 120
Anzaldúa, Gloria 9
   Borderlands 86
AOC. *See* Ocasio-Cortez, Alexandria
Arendt, Hannah 9
   The Origins of Totalitarianism 79
Army of the Republic of Vietnam (South Vietnam) (ARVN) 180
Arndt, Bettina 7
   award/honor 30
   'Fake Rape Crisis' 31
   protest against (by students of University of Sydney) 31
Aronowitz, Stanley 90, 93 n.11
ASEAN (Association of South-East Asian Nations) 181
Asia/Asian 4, 103–4, 173, 184
   East Asia 176
   xenophobia (hate crimes against) 231
Atwood, Margaret 82
audits 30–1
Australia/Australians 4, 6, 11, 26, 30, 32–3, 66, 84, 113
   abandoned steelworks in Newcastle 65, 69
   Australian Higher Education 123
   Australian 'Safe Schools' programme 71–2
   First Nations people 3, 33
   gay marriage in 74
   Indigenous Australians 11, 26, 32–4, 113–15, 123
   non-Indigenous 115–16, 123
   Ramsay Centre 33
   universities in 114

IGA project 115, 117–19
Indigenous content in curriculum 114–15, 117–18, 121–2, 124
non-indigenous academics 118
authentic/authenticity 22, 24, 82, 89, 213
authoritarian/authoritarianism 1–2, 8, 13, 29, 65, 67, 70–2, 90, 173, 176, 181–2
nationalism 70, 72, 75
neoliberalism 177, 230
New Order authoritarian regime 214–15
populism 184
authority 2–3, 16, 22–3, 36–7, 54, 75, 84, 132, 176, 234

backlash narrative 48, 75
Badenoch, Kemi 56–7, 101–2, 107
bad truths 23, 28
Bakhtin, Mikhail 28
Banet-Weiser, Sarah
popular feminism 38
popular misogyny 99
Beierle, Scott, *The Rebirth of my Misogynism* and *The American Whore* (video) 27
Belenky, Mary, *Women's Ways of Knowing* 86
Berger-Correa, Bárbara 12, 233
Berlant, Lauren 201
Berlin, Germany 67
Beta, Annisa 15, 233
Big Lies contest 9, 67, 71, 232
Bindel, Julie 105
Black and Minority Ethnic (BME) workers 231
Black, Asian and Minority Ethnic students 103–4
Black History Month 5, 56
#BlackLivesMatter movement 5, 16 n.1, 101, 113, 230
Bloch, Ernst 92
Bolsonaro, Jair 2, 196
Brazil 28, 196
Brexit referendum 2–4, 66, 229
Brim, Matt 195, 197, 205
Gay and Lesbian Quarterly 206
Britain. *See* UK
British Empire 141
Brooks, David 80
Burke, Penny Jane 88, 91, 122, 197

Cambazoglu, Idil 12, 233
Campbell, Alyson 14, 233
Campus Trends survey 106
Canada 67, 114
cancel culture 29–30, 103
capitalism 8, 47, 52
capitalist exploitation 47, 56, 175, 182
global 100
platform 25
productive 59 n.2
state 177
Carolissen, Ronelle 88, 197
Carroll, Hamilton 104
Case, Mary Anne 59 n.3
censorship 101, 105
Centre for Independent Studies 31
change.org petition 104
China 70, 91, 141, 175
Chouliaraki, Lilie 56
Christian/Catholic 43, 45, 48–50, 52, 54–6. *See also* religion
Catholic Church 51–3
Catholicism 51–2, 54, 59 n.1
Catholic orthodoxy 44, 52–4, 57, 59 n.1
counter-reformation 51, 53, 59 n.1
Roman Catholic 53, 59 n.3
civilization 21, 141
European 49
Western 27, 33, 35
class 35, 37, 49, 71, 75, 81, 88, 177–80, 194, 213, 232
classical ideology 68
classroom 81–2, 85–7, 91, 115, 121, 233
feminism beyond 13–16, 36, 159, 233
feminist 99–109
pedagogy 88–90
Rivers on 233
safe space 106
student resistance behaviour 121
climate change 8, 25, 66, 179, 229, 234
Clinton, Hillary 12, 37, 157
CNN 229
Cohen, Meta 14, 233
Coley, Jonathan S. 55
collectivism 232
Collins, Patricia Hill 9, 87
Colombia/Colombian 8, 44–6, 50–2, 55
Kelly on 46

mass-murder by army of (2002–2010) 59 n.6
colonial-capitalist system 8
colonialism 44, 52, 67, 89, 200
  colonial violence 115
  settler 67, 232
coloniality 8, 47, 49, 55–7
  coloniality of power 8, 44, 46, 57–8
communism 44, 51, 59 n.2, 180
Communist Party of Vietnam (CPV) 174, 178–9, 181, 185 n.1
  Marxist-Leninist philosophy 177
community pedagogies 88–90
complaint activism 158–62, 167
Confucianism 176, 183, 185
Congregation of the Doctrine of Faith (CDF) 44
Connell, Raewyn 8–9, 72, 74, 90–91, 232
consciousness-raising strategy 13–14, 84–6, 217
Consejo Episcopal Latinoamericano (CELAM) 52
conservatism 71, 182, 215
  in Indonesia 225 n.1
consumer culture 176–7
contestation 4, 7, 10–11, 21, 74, 232, 234
context collapse 148
Conway, Kellyanne 79
counter-insurgency war 50
COVID-19 pandemic 107
  and domestic violence 6
  fatalities caused by 231
  new variants of 230
  pandemic pedagogy 135–9
  vaccination 4
  xenophobia 231
critical pedagogy 9, 81, 83, 85, 91–2, 235
critical race theory 3–5, 9–10, 101, 103, 107, 109
critical theory 51, 53–7
critical thinking 109, 143, 212
criticism/self-criticism 85, 91
Croatia 182
cultural Marxism 57
cultural symbolism 1
culture wars 26, 29, 74, 101–2, 196

D'Agata, John, *The Lifespan of a Fact* 79–80
Daniels, Jesse 15

Davis, Glyn 31
decolonial approach 9, 43–4, 46–7, 49
deconstruction approach 72, 80, 82
defamation 12, 131–2, 225 n.2
democracy 6–7, 15, 38, 47–9, 103, 109
  liberal 48, 103, 173–4, 176
Democratic Republic of Vietnam (North Vietnam), DRV 175, 180, 185 n.2
de-platforming 32
depletion 32, 34
Dharma Wanita organization 215
digital culture 14–15
digital feminist public pedagogy 15, 148, 150, 211–14, 216, 224, 233
digital pedagogy 90, 92, 233
disability 2, 106, 213, 230–1
discrimination 5, 14, 132–3, 185, 213. *See also* non-discrimination
diversity 10–11, 37, 55, 90, 102–4, 196
Đổi Mới (renovation) 13, 174–6, 181, 183
Dosekun, Simidele 213
Duelli Klein, Renate 84
Đường Trường Sơn (Ho Chi Minh Trail) 180

economy 8, 68
  economic inequality 70–1
  financial markets 69
  global 69, 174, 176
  grey/informal 70
  market 13, 175, 179, 184–5
  military spending 70
  neoliberal development strategy 69–70
  and patriarchal power 68–70
  political 178
  Vietnamese 175–9, 181
education 65, 87
  Australian higher education 123
  as commodity 99
  and feminism 9–13, 15, 72
  and gender 1, 3, 73–6
  higher 10–12, 99, 115–16, 122–3, 231
  Indigenous higher education 116–17, 122
  and Knowledge 116
  moral 56
  non-Indigenous academics 118
  and populism 195–7

sex (*see* sexuality, sex education)
tertiary 117, 123
e-learning 92
elite(s)/elitism 2, 4, 29, 37, 49, 140, 176, 194, 215
   corrupt elites 2, 177, 229
emotion/emotionality 6–7, 66, 73, 80, 114, 134, 232
   emojis 139, 143, 148
empowerment 12, 37, 135–6, 147, 220, 223–4, 225 n.1
   gender 213, 215, 219, 223–4
   sexual 136, 142, 145, 149
environmentalism 3, 173, 176
Episcopal Conference of Latin America. *See* Consejo Episcopal Latinoamericano (CELAM)
epistemology 2, 4, 6, 23, 58, 65, 71, 116, 173
   epistemic community 36, 233, 235
Equality and Human Rights Commission 109
ethnicity 101, 106, 213
ethnographic methods 88–90
ethno-nationalism 71
European Union 66
Europe/European 1, 4, 45–7, 49, 52, 57, 84, 173, 178, 213
   attack on feminist achievements 28
   European civilization 49
   Western 45, 84, 176
experience(s) 2, 5, 9, 11–14, 44–6, 52, 54, 65, 82, 200
   as Aboriginal academic 115
   queer 201–2
   of racism 116
   of sexual harassment/assault 160, 162–4, 215
   of trolling 134
Eyal, Gil 23

Facebook 25, 51, 212, 230
   Facebook-Cambridge Analytica data scandal 4
facilitator 81, 90, 93 n.3, 135
facts 57, 68, 79–81
fake news 15, 23, 25, 101, 109, 179, 196, 229
Farrier, Stephen 14, 233
Fascists 27–8, 103

Faulkner, N., creeping fascism 28
femininity 144, 179, 183, 213–14, 217, 221
feminism 3, 6–7, 11–12, 15–16, 21–2, 27–8, 30, 34–5, 37, 71–2, 89, 99–100, 133, 135, 142, 148, 176, 193, 211–12, 214, 216, 218–19, 224–5, 232
   beyond classroom 13–16, 36, 159, 233
   contemporary 105, 213, 233
   and education 9–13, 15, 72
   feminists (*see* feminists)
   and gender relations 29
   glass ceiling 37
   Global-North 68
   in Indonesia 214–16
   liberal/neoliberal 37–8, 55, 99
   popular/populist 38, 211–12
   radical 195, 202
   white 87, 221
Feminism for the 99% A Manifesto (Arruzza, Bhattacharya and Fraser) 38
feminists 2, 4–5, 7, 28, 44, 82, 84, 145, 149, 194
   classroom 99–109
   epistemologies 6, 231
   feminist pedagogies 2–3, 6–7, 9–10, 43, 91, 99, 103, 131, 143, 148, 150, 158–9, 163, 168, 232–3
   feminist process 82, 84–8
   Indigenous 87
   intersectional 158–9, 162, 165
   knowledge-making 9, 71–3, 75, 231, 233
   online feminist groups 16, 216–18, 222 (*see also* Instagram)
   research/researchers/educators 65, 68, 71, 74, 151
   strategies in education 73
   successes 9
   truth 28–9, 235
   workforce 73
   young feminists in Indonesia (*see* Indonesia, young feminists in)
ferality 193, 200, 203
feral pedagogies 193–5, 204–6
Feral Queer Camp (FQC) 194–8, 203–5
   alternative kinship/queer kinship 200–1
   Melbourne FQC 200–1

First World War 67
Fish, Stanley 109
  on free speech 107
  on students 108
  There's No Such Thing as Free Speech: And It's a Good Thing Too 106
Floyd, George, murder of 5–6, 113. *See also* race/racism/racist
France 180
Frankfurt School 51, 53–4
Fraser, Nancy, progressive neoliberalism 37
freedom of expression 107–8
Freeman, Elizabeth, chrononormative 203
free speech crisis 7, 10, 12, 29–31, 103, 107–9, 232
  in Australian universities 32
  types of 29
Freire, Paulo (Freirean pedagogical strategy) 9, 80, 84–6, 88–90, 92
French Model Code on university free speech 32
French, Robert 31
F Troop 113
Fuerzas Armadas Revolucionarias de Colombia (FARC) 44, 50

gay/gay marriage 72, 74, 204. *See also* lesbian
gender 7, 14, 21, 23, 28–9, 34–5, 48–9, 54–5, 57, 71, 103, 106, 135, 141, 195, 197, 216, 218, 224. *See also* sexuality
  and education 1, 3, 73–6
  equality 51, 59 n.4, 173, 180, 183, 186 n.6, 216, 220
  equity 1, 14, 30, 133
  gender critical 195–6
  gendered power 65, 68, 74, 133, 142, 212
  gendered violence 5–7, 14, 38, 151
  gender-trolling 12, 131–4, 139, 145, 150–1 (*see also* Twitter)
    as trap of unwanted visibility 147–50
  gender whisperers 72
  heteronormative 68, 141, 182, 215
  hierarchy 74–5, 141–2
  ideological struggle 7, 43, 48, 51, 57–8
  ideology of 8, 28, 43–4, 46, 48–51, 71, 196

  inequalities 150, 185, 218
  justice 8, 71–2, 75
  order 13, 28–9, 71, 174, 176
    in Vietnam 179–84
  politics 14, 134, 215
  studies (programmes) 10–11, 55, 99–101, 103, 109, 217
  weaponization of 43–4, 46–51, 54, 58
Gender and Education for All report, UNESCO 73
Gender and Far Right Politics in Europe (Köttig, Bitzan and Pető) 36
Gender Hate Online: Understanding the New Anti-Feminism (Ging and Siapera) 36
genealogy 8, 51, 59 n.3
genocidal/genocide 45, 67, 104, 115
Germans 67, 141
Gerwani (*Gerakan Wanita Indonesia*). *See* Indonesian Women's Movement
Gill, Rosalind 213
Giraldo, Isis 7–8, 233
Giroux, Henry 88, 90, 109
Giroux, Susan 102
globalization 173, 176–9
Global North 9, 66, 68–9, 75, 211, 220
Global South 1, 69, 75, 92, 211, 213, 225
Goebbels, Joseph 67
Google 25, 230
Greer, Germaine 105
grievance studies 57, 100, 104

Haidt, Jonathan, *Why Universities Must Choose One Telos: Truth or Social Justice* 55
Halberstam, Jack 92, 201
Hale, Sondra 9–10
Harding, Sandra 85
harm 3, 8, 10, 16, 24, 101, 149, 234
hegemonic/hegemony 1, 49, 56–8, 74–5, 81, 86, 88, 92, 119, 213
Hemmings, Clare, *Why Stories Matter* 234
Higher Education Restructuring Regime 107
Hofstadter, Richard 67
homophobia 3, 51, 70–1, 103, 194
homosexual 48, 71
homosocialization 133
hostility 6, 9, 11, 71, 86, 120, 140, 143, 148, 231

Howard, John 33
humanities 7, 11, 21, 30, 32–5, 57, 72, 99–100, 231
Hungary 100, 182
hyper-parasites 24, 28–9, 32

identity/identification 6–7, 10, 14, 21–2, 200
   identity politics 6, 32, 100, 104, 107, 143, 200, 213, 232
   national identity 21, 176
immigration/immigrants 2, 12, 173, 178, 230
imperialism 7, 38, 44, 52, 175
inclusion/inclusiveness 11, 92, 102–3, 119, 195–7
Independent Review of Freedom of Speech in Australian Higher Education Providers 31
India 2, 28, 81
   Kashmir 67
Indigenous Graduate Attribute (IGA) project 115, 117–19, 122, 124
   challenges (*see* patience; persistence; persuasion)
Indigenous people 3–4, 113–14
   higher education 116–17
   Indigenous Australians 11, 26, 32–4, 113–15, 123
   Indigenous Knowledge 11, 75, 114, 116, 119
   Indigenous studies 114–15, 118, 120, 124
   Indigenous truth 11, 114
   massacres of 115
   students/staffs 116–17, 119–21, 123
Indigenous Strategy 2017–2020 (Universities Australia) 117
individualism 2, 72, 176, 213, 221, 232
Indochinese Communist Party (ICP) 174–5, 185 n.1
Indonesian Communist Party (PKI) 214
Indonesian Electronic Information and Transactions Law (UU ITE) 216
Indonesian Women's Movement 214
Indonesia, young feminists in 15–16, 211–12
   Anti-Sexual Violence Bill (RUU PKS) 218, 222–3
   authoritarian regime 214–15
   conservatism in 225 n.1
   Criminal Code (RKUHP) 218, 223
   digital feminist public pedagogy 15, 148, 150, 211–14, 216
   Family Resilience Bill 218
   feminism and women's movements in 214–16
   National Commission on Violence Against Women (Komnas Perempuan) 222–3
   online feminist groups (*see* Instagram)
   post-authoritarian 215
   post-feminist media culture 212–13
   post-Suharto 215
   sexual violence 222–3
industrialization 68–9
inequalities 1, 4–6, 8, 10, 13, 35, 37, 44–5, 53, 56–7, 108, 150, 197, 217–18, 230, 233
Instagram 15, 212, 216
   Feminis Surabaya (@arekfeminis) 217
   Feminis Yogyakarta (@feminisyogya) 217
   Hollaback! Jakarta (@hollaback_jkt) 217
   Indonesia Feminist (@indonesiafeminis) 217
   Lawan Patriarki (LP) (@lawanpatriarki) 16, 212, 216–18, 224, 225 n.2
   autonomy and image of body 220–1
   call out posts 218–19
   confessional accounts 218–19
   explainer posts 218
   inspirational posts 218–20
   laws and protests 223–4
   posts of protests and demonstrations 218–19
   sexual violence 222–3
   Perempuan Tagar Tegar (@perempuantagartegar) 217
   Perkumpulan Lintas Feminis Jakarta (@jakartafeminist) 217
   post on teaching session 136
Institute of Public Affairs (IPA) 30–1
intellectualism 4
International Gender and Education Association conference (2018) 3
Iran 91

Islamophobia 70
ivory tower 201, 231

Jäger, Anton 47
Jiménez, Ileana 12–13, 230
job readiness 34, 231
Johnson, Boris 67
Johnson, Samuel 70
Jowett, Benjamin 140

Kakutani, Michiko, *The Death of Truth: Notes on Falsehood in the Age of Trump* 80
Keene, Andy 104
Keller, Jessalynn 106
Kelly, John F. 46
Kenway, Jane 7, 84–5, 88
kinship 193, 200–1
knowledge/knowledges 2, 5–7, 22, 65, 68, 89, 232, 234
  embodied 73, 194
  expert 4, 10
  feminist knowledge-making 9, 71–3, 75, 231, 233
  formal/institutionalized 13, 15
  forms of 83–4
  geopolitics of 46
  Indigenous Knowledge 11, 75, 114, 116, 119
  legitimate 14, 143, 151, 196
  minoritarian 197, 199
  politics of 10
  production 14, 50, 73, 81, 83, 92, 151, 185, 197, 235
  queer 14, 193
  renegade 24–5
  self-knowledge 86
  sharing 2, 14, 216
  social 86
  transmission of 83–4
  and truth 7, 10, 12
  Western 75
Koch brothers 8, 66
Kováts, Eszter 28

Laclau, Ernesto 1, 47
Lahad, Kinneret 100
Latin America/Latin American 4, 8, 43–6, 51–3, 55, 58, 87, 173, 229

Lefebvre, Marcel 58 n.1
left-wing 11, 30, 45, 50–1, 81, 102–3, 107, 230. *See also* right-wing
legitimation 10, 70, 132, 140
lesbian 48, 72, 74, 202. *See also* gay/gay marriage
Lê Thị Nhâm Tuyết 180
LGBT groups 55–6, 90
  LGBTQI+ 2, 36, 90, 194, 203, 230
  LGBTQIA+ 201
liberal democracy 48, 103, 173–4, 176
liberalism 36–7
liberation 43–4, 52–5, 57, 65, 82, 177, 180–1, 185
liberatory pedagogy 83, 85, 89
libertarianism/libertarians 28–9
lie(s)/liars 2, 7–8, 27, 67–8, 75, 79, 88, 179, 230, 232, 234
literacy 9, 73. *See also* education
Littler, Jo 106, 109
Love, Heather 201

Maher, Frances 84
mainstream media 35, 49, 81, 103, 106, 179
Mai Thị Tú 18
Makarrata Commission 34
Manne, Kate 27
manosphere 133
marginalization 5–6, 194
Marr, David 185
Marxist 47, 50
masculinity 1, 12, 27, 35, 72–4, 133, 141, 151
  baseline 144
  dominance of men 65
  fragile 145
  hegemonic 74
  homosocial 143
  hyper-masculinity 27
  masculinized professions 68–9
  politics 70
Massie, Alex 105–6
McCann, Hannah 14, 233
McCarthy, Joseph 67
McDonald, Matthew 13
McInnes, Gavin 26
McLaren, Peter 88
McRobbie, Angela 213

Medellín CELAM 53
Mendieta, Eduardo 51–2
Men's Rights Activist 12, 27, 145
#MenToo 31
#MeToo movement 5–6, 157–8, 160, 167, 211, 235
Mickey Mouse degrees 100
Midsumma Festival Melbourne (2020) 194, 203
Mikelionis, Lukas 100
misogyny/misogynist 2–3, 6, 12, 14, 27, 70, 131–4, 137, 145, 147–51, 167, 211, 220
modernity 46, 49–50
modernity-coloniality project 44, 46–7, 56, 58
Modi, Narendra 2, 67
Modra, Helen 84–5
Montford, Kelly Struthers 193
Moore, Suzanne 105
moral panics 12–13, 48, 132, 139, 148, 150, 182
Moran, Marie 109
Morrison, Scott 67, 113–14
multiculturalism 1, 36, 102
Muñoz, José Esteban 197, 199, 202
Mustafa, Bahar 103–4

Nagle, Angela 26–7
narrative antagonism 2
nation 49, 175, 178, 180, 182
    national identity 21, 176–8
National Aboriginal and Torres Strait Islander Higher Education Consortium 117
nationalism 131
    authoritarian 70
    ethno-nationalism 71
    white 141
National Liberation Front (Việt Cộng) 180
Native American tribe 113
Nazi/Nazism 8, 79
neoliberal/neoliberalism 1, 5, 37, 50–1, 81, 83, 85, 102, 109, 176, 182
    authoritarian 177, 230
    and economy 69–70
    feminism 37, 99
    policy regimes 70
    progressive 37

neo-Marxism 30, 54
neo-masculinist (rebel masculinity) 27
neo-Nazis 27
new mental models 119
News Corp 24–5
New Zealand 114
Nguyễn, Thanh-Nhã 13
Nguyễn Văn Linh 181
Niccolini, Alyssa 159
Nichols, Tom, *The Death of Expertise: The Campaign Against Established Knowledge and Why It Matters* 102
Nietzsche, Friedrich 28
Nixon, Richard 59 n.2
non-binary 82, 104, 195
non-discrimination 37, 55, 102. *See also* discrimination
non-government organizations (NGOs) 85, 215, 217, 223
non-Indigenous Australians 115–16, 123
non-truth 81. *See also* truth (Truth)
non-white 5, 12, 15, 45, 53, 56
no-platforming in the UK 32, 103, 105
North America 113, 176
North Vietnamese Army (NVA) 180

Ocasio-Cortez, Alexandria 157, 168
online culture 14–15, 233
    online feminist groups (*see* Instagram)
online sites, features of 27
online violence 131
    hate/harassment 12, 132, 134, 136
    Twitter pathways of 139–47 (*see also* Twitter)
    techno-politics of 133–5
oppression 5, 11, 13–14, 44, 52, 55, 115, 117, 133, 183, 196
Orban, Viktor 101
Orientalist 141
Other/Otherness 3, 56, 85, 91
Outburst Queer Arts Festival Belfast (2019) 194, 198
Out of the Ruins: The Emergence of Radical Informal Learning Spaces (Haworth, Elmore, and Kadoda) 87

Page, Susan 11–12, 233
pandemic pedagogy 135–9
parasitic ecology 24–5, 28–9

Paris Agreement 229
Paternotte, David 48–9
patience 11–12, 115, 119–22
patriarchy 49, 181, 216–18
   and body shaming 220–1
   digital 134
   familialism 182
   heteropatriarchy 133, 135
   patriarchal ideology 71–2, 74
   patriarchal power 68–71
   Puritan 165
patriotism 70
Patterns of Prejudice (Spierings, Zaslove, Mügge and De Lange) 36
Paul II, John 52, 59 n.1
pedagogies of care 43, 45, 58, 88, 233
pedagogies of cruelty 8, 44–7, 54–8
persistence 11–12, 115, 119–20, 123–4
persuasion 11–12, 24, 115, 119–21
Peterson, Jordan 56
phallogocentrism 132–3
Phipps, Alison 27
Piketty, Thomas, *Capital in the Twenty-First Century* 70
Pinker, Steven 55–6
platform capitalism 25
Play-Doh genital models 12, 131–2, 135–6, 140, 142, 144, 146, 150
Poland 182
Policy Institute at King's College London 106
politics/politicians 66, 83, 102–3, 107–9
   affective 5, 12, 28
   gender 14, 134, 215
   identity 6, 32, 100, 104, 107, 143, 200, 213, 232
   institutional 10
   of knowledge 10
   masculinity 70
   nativist 2
   paranoid style in the US 66–7
   partisan political views 101
   populist 1–2, 6, 13, 173–9, 184–5
   post-truth 3, 13, 36, 147, 151, 173–4, 179
   right-wing 1, 26, 28, 30, 35–6, 70–1, 230
   Western 1
popular culture 38, 74, 99, 196

populism 1, 6, 46–7, 49, 51, 54, 99, 182, 230, 232
   alt-right 90
   and education 195–7
   misogynist 2, 27, 52
   populist politics 1–2, 6, 13, 102, 174, 176–9, 184–5
   post-truth 1–5, 7–9, 11, 131, 173, 232
   right-wing/left-wing 15, 37, 81, 109, 173, 178
positivism 9, 82, 85–6
post-feminism 15, 38, 100–1, 212–13, 217, 224
postmodernism 30, 80, 82
post-truth 2, 6–9, 11, 14–15, 21, 23, 25, 36, 65–8, 79, 82–4, 91–2, 108–9, 114, 132, 134, 147, 149, 151, 159, 174, 230, 232, 235. *See also* untruth
   politics 3, 13, 36, 147, 151, 173–4, 179
   populism 1–5, 7–9, 11, 131, 173, 232
   in Vietnam 13, 173–4
   and truth 22–3
   Word of the Year (*Oxford English Dictionary*) 2, 66, 80
power 2–3, 5–6, 8–9, 16, 22, 47, 49–50, 79
   coloniality of 8, 44, 46, 57–8
   gendered 65, 68, 74, 133, 142, 212
   and knowledge 22
   speaking truth to power 9, 22, 82
professional truth parasites 24–5, 28–30. *See also* territorial truth parasites
progressive neoliberalism 37
Prynne, Hester 165–6
public pedagogy 212–14, 217, 224, 233

queer feral pedagogies 14, 203, 233
   alternative kinship/queer kinship 200–1
   queer enough 200
   queer performance 198, 201, 203–4
   queer theory 3, 14, 68, 72, 194, 196, 201–2, 233
   poor 205
   queer theorist 201–3, 205
Quilty, Aideen 202

race/racism/racist 2–3, 5–7, 10, 14, 21, 36, 38, 49, 70–1, 99, 101, 103–4, 106, 109, 113, 118–19, 124, 131,

134, 141, 194, 196. *See also* Floyd, George, murder of
Ramsay Centre, Australia 33
rape culture course 158–9, 162–5
Ratzinger, Joseph 44, 52–5, 59 n.1
The Ratzinger Report (Ratzinger and Messori) 45, 53, 55, 59 n.3
religion 7, 21, 29, 50, 106. *See also* Christian/Catholic
Republican voters 71
Republic of Vietnam (South Vietnam) 175, 180
resistance, forms of 2, 11
Retallack, Hanna 158, 162, 164
Revolutionary Armed Forces of Colombia – People's Army. *See* Fuerzas Armadas Revolucionarias de Colombia (FARC)
right-wing 2, 7, 22, 27–8, 35, 80, 100, 102, 131, 142, 173, 178, 230. *See also* left-wing
  border protection 66, 70
  fury 7, 21, 26–30, 232
  politics/politicians 1, 26, 28, 30, 35–6, 70–1, 230
  populism/populists 15, 37, 81, 109, 178
  subcultures 15
Ringrose, Jessica 12, 131–2, 135–6, 139–40, 143, 145–7, 149, 233. *See also* sexuality, sex education
Rivers, Nicola 10, 233
Rohrer, Judy 90–1, 206
Rosenfeld, Sophia 22
Rottenburg, Catherine, *The rise of neoliberal feminism* 37
Royal Commission into Aboriginal Deaths in Custody 123
Rudy, Susan 72

salaryman model, Japan 74
same-sex marriage 173
Schniedewind, Nancy 84–5
School of Sexuality Education (SSE) 135
Schumer, Amy 221
Second Vatican Council (Vatican II) 51–3, 58–9 n.1
secular academics 45, 56
Segato, Rita 47, 56
self-determination 177, 180, 220
self-reflexivity 91

sexuality 7–8, 14, 21–2, 28–9, 34–5, 38, 48–9, 55, 57, 99, 106, 147, 195–7, 215–16, 218, 224. *See also* gender
sex education 12, 71, 141, 143, 148, 215
  and China 141
  Twitter trolls on (*see* Twitter)
sexism 5, 103, 131, 134, 167
sexual assault/harassment (digital) 6, 13, 15, 30, 132–4, 145, 157–8, 168, 211, 215, 219, 224
  complaint activism 158–62
  embodied wilfulness 13, 158–60, 162–8
  LP's post on Instagram 222–3
  rape culture course 158–9, 162–5
  testimony 167
sexual empowerment 136, 139, 142, 145, 149
unwanted sexual attention 145
shitposting 12, 134, 138, 148, 150
  pathways of hate 139–47 (*see also* Twitter, pathways of hate)
Smith, Evan 32
snowflake millennials, students 103, 106–7, 196
Snyder, Timothy, *On Tyranny: Twenty Lessons from the Twentieth Century* 79
social change 51–2, 102, 202
social Darwinism 27
social inequalities 4, 56, 108, 213
social injustice 4, 44, 57, 182. *See also* social justice
socialism 44, 174, 185
social justice 1–2, 5, 8, 11, 43–5, 54–8, 59 n.6, 72, 119, 132, 135, 167, 178, 229, 231, 233. *See also* social injustice
social media 3–5, 8, 14–16, 26, 35, 66–7, 81, 84, 88, 91, 133–4, 148–51, 179, 211–12, 215–17, 222, 224, 230. *See also specific companies*
social order 7, 44, 48, 53, 56–8
social sciences 7, 11, 21, 32, 34–5, 55, 99–100, 231
socio-political movement 53–4, 212
South Africa 87
sovereignty 113, 179, 185
Soviet Union 175
Spenser, Richard 26
Stalin, Iosif 67

Stalinism/Stalinist 8, 13, 178
Stavrakakis, Yannis 47
Stewart, Kathleen 166
Stokes, Patrick 34
subjectivity 2, 6–7, 232
Sudan 9, 81, 88–90
Suharto 214
surveillance (and silencing) 70, 158, 168

Taylor, Chloe 193
Taylor, Yvette 100
Teaching in Higher Education (Burke and Carolissen) 3
Tea Party movement in the United States 66–7
technology-facilitated violence 133
tension (between truth and falsehood) 8–9, 36, 67
terra nullius 33, 67
territorial truth parasites 24, 26, 28–9, 32, 34. *See also* professional truth parasites
theology of liberation 43–4, 46, 52–5, 57
 Nixon on 59 n.2
Thomas, Dylan 83
TikTok 212
Torres, Carlos 88
totalitarian 79
transformations 14–15, 49, 178
transgression 28, 87
trans groups 71, 105
transphobia 131, 140, 194, 196
trigger warnings 103, 106
Trujillo, Alfonso López 52–3
Trump, Donald 2–3, 12–13, 23, 26, 37, 46, 66–7, 79, 101–2, 107, 157, 168, 196, 229–30, 235
trust 22–3, 36, 83, 85–6
truth parasites 7, 21, 23–5, 30, 32, 36, 38. *See also* professional truth parasites; territorial truth parasites
truth (Truth) 2, 4, 6–10, 15, 24, 65–6, 72, 79–80, 82–3, 89–90, 115, 232, 234. *See also* post-truth; untruth
 bad 23, 28
 diminishment of 21, 26–30
 dominant 22
 feminist 28–9, 235
 Indigenous 11, 114
 and post-truth 22–3
 received 81
 speaking truth to power 9, 22, 82
 truth-telling/tellers 22, 34, 235
 uncomfortable 36, 102
Twitter 4, 12, 25, 133, 148–50, 212, 222, 230. *See also* shitposting
 Artificial Intelligence (AI) hate speech detection 150
 pathways of hate 139–47
  feminist academia 140–1, 150
  feminist sex education (perverting innocent child) 146–7, 150
  heterosexist defensiveness 143–6
  from mocking to anti-feminist abuse 142–3
 #TrendTopic 134
 troll attack on sex education 131–9 (*see also* gender, gender-trolling)
  Andrew Old (@oldandrewuk) 136–7, 140
  Peter Lloyd (@suffragentleman) 137–9, 142
  snowman meme 144–5

UK 4–5, 10, 27, 66, 101
 Brexit campaign in 66
 no-platforming in (Smith) 32, 103, 105
 UK Students Union 103
ultra-nationalist movement 7, 27, 66
The Uluru Statement from the Heart (2017) 34
The United Nations, report on multinational corporations 69
The United States 1–2, 4–5, 23, 26, 28, 32, 37, 51, 55, 66–7, 84, 101, 113, 173, 175, 178–9, 181, 229
 paranoid style politics in 66–7
 Tea Party movement in 66–7
 US election campaign (2016) 12, 66
 white feminism in 221
Unity High School for Girls in Khartoum, Sudan 81, 93 n.4
universities 4, 7, 9–11, 14, 27, 30–5, 151, 196–7, 206
 in Australia (*see* Australia/Australians, universities in)
 free speech crisis 21
 messy 197
 right-wing attacks on 21

sexual assault/harassment on campuses 31
Unterhalter, Elaine 72
untruth 6, 8, 15, 22, 25, 83, 88. *See also* truth (Truth)
    self-interested 67
Urban Dictionary 143, 151 n.1

Vietnamese Communist Party 181
Vietnam, post-truth populism in 13, 173–4
    bar girls 186 n.5
    from Communist revolution to Đổi Mới 174–6
    cultured family (Gia đình văn hóa) 181, 185 n.3
    economy/economic system 175–9, 181
    education campaigns 183
    gender order in 179–84, 186 n.6
    globalization 176–7
    Law on Domestic Violence Prevention and Control (2007) 183
    Law on Marriage and the Family (1959) 185 n.2
    market-Leninism 174, 177–9
    North Vietnam 175
    one-party rule 13, 174, 179
    prostitution 181–2
    social evils campaign 181–2
Vietnam Women's Union (VWU) 184
violence 7, 14, 108, 183
    and Colombia 45–6
    colonial 115
    domestic 6, 27, 30, 183
    gendered 5–7, 14, 38, 151
    misogynist (*see* misogyny/misogynist)
    online (*see* online violence)
    physical 7, 22
    racialized 5–6, 113 (*see also* race/racism/racist)
    sexual assault/harassment (digital) 6, 13, 15, 30, 132–4, 145, 157–8, 219, 224
    social 223

symbolic 22
technology-facilitated 133

Warner, Michael 201
Weiler, Kathleen 87
Werner, Jayne 186 n.6
Western 1, 5, 13–14, 49, 55
    institutions of learning 81, 91
    Western civilization 27, 33, 35
    Western-European society 45
    Western knowledge 75
white fragility 120–1
White, Hayden 80
white privilege 5, 57, 117, 120–1
white supremacist/supremacy 7, 15, 27, 35, 157, 230
Wieringa, Saskia 214–15
Williams, Gavin 107
Winch, Alison 106
wokeism 57
women 37, 71
    attacks on 7, 15
    domestic violence 6, 27, 30, 183
    referendum against wearing burqa 59 n.4
    reproductive rights for 5, 48
    state control 13
    terrorist attacks on 27
    trolling of 12, 15, 27 (*see also* gender, gender-trolling)
    women's movements in Indonesia 214–16
working-class communities 5, 230
    white 71

xenophobia 231
Xie, Xumeng 12, 233

Yiannopoulos, Milo 7
    Dangerous 26
    Troll Academy tour 26
YouTube 81

www.ingramcontent.com/pod-product-compliance
Lightning Source LLC
Chambersburg PA
CBHW062129300426
44115CB00012BA/1861